The City That Became Safe

Recent Titles in
STUDIES IN CRIME AND PUBLIC POLICY
Michael Tonry and Norval Morris, General Editors

THE CITY THAT BECAME SAFE

New York's Lessons for
Urban Crime and its Control

FRANKLIN E. ZIMRING

OXFORD

UNIVERSITY PRESS

Oxford University Press is a department of the University of Oxford.
It furthers the University's objective of excellence in research, scholarship,
and education by publishing worldwide.

Oxford   New York
Auckland   Cape Town   Dar es Salaam   Hong Kong   Karachi
Kuala Lumpur   Madrid   Melbourne   Mexico City   Nairobi
New Delhi   Shanghai   Taipei   Toronto

With offices in
Argentina   Austria   Brazil   Chile   Czech Republic   France   Greece
Guatemala   Hungary   Italy   Japan   Poland   Portugal   Singapore
South Korea   Switzerland   Thailand   Turkey   Ukraine   Vietnam

Oxford is a registered trade mark of Oxford University Press
in the UK and certain other countries.

Published in the United States of America by
Oxford University Press
198 Madison Avenue, New York, NY 10016

Library of Congress Cataloging-in-Publication Data
Zimring, Franklin E.
The city that became safe : New York's lessons for urban crime and its control / Franklin E. Zimring.
    p.   cm.
Includes bibliographical references and index.
ISBN 978-0-19-984442-5 (cloth : alk. paper); 978-0-19-932416-3 (paperback : alk. paper)
1. Crime prevention—New York (State)—New York.
2. Crime—New York (State)—New York. 3. Police—New York (State)—New York. I. Title.
HV7433.N49Z56   2011
364.4097471—dc22   2011007691

9 8 7 6 5 4 3 2 1

Printed in the United States of America
on acid-free paper

For Maury and Norval
Authors of Long-Term Predictions

Contents

Preface

SUSTAINED CHANGES IN rates of violent crime happened twice in the half-century after 1960, in each case altering both the realities of urban life in the United States and public attitudes toward criminal justice. The first nationwide shift in crime and violence started in 1964 and ended a decade later, doubling rates of criminal homicide and more than doubling serious street crimes such as robbery, burglary, and rape. While there were some variations in the size and timing of the crime wave of the 1960s, most urban areas had rather similar track records of explosive increases (Barnett et al. 1975). After the expansion from 1964 to 1974, the next two decades experienced fluctuations around the new high rates of 1974, dropping back in the mid-1970s only to return to the 1974 homicide rate in 1980, dropping again in the early 1980s only to climb back close to the 1980 high by 1991.

The nine years after 1991 were a second nationwide tidal movement of rates of crime and violence, but this time the tide was receding. During the 1990s, rates of all seven "index" crimes fell in the United States, with decline for five of the seven clustered in a range between 37% for auto theft and 44% for robbery, with homicide (down 39%), rape (down 41%) and burglary (down 41%) in this narrow window around 40%. This national decline wasn't as large as the increase during the 1960s and 1970s, but it was the largest documented crime decline of the twentieth century. But since I have already written a book on this important national adventure (Zimring 2006), why this book? What is there about New York City that justifies yet another major statistical study of recent crime trends?

One prominent feature of the crime wave years after 1963 was that major urban areas had similar patterns of growth. A contemporary analysis concluded that "differences in recent murder growth among the cities can largely be explained as typical random fluctuations around a common trend" (Barnett et al. 1975 at p. 85). There were no exceptional stories during the great crime increase that ended in 1974, no singular case of a city that stayed unaffected or had a double dose of whatever was driving rates of crime and violence in the United States.

But the great American crime decline of the 1990s was different in that respect. New York, the nation's largest city, also experienced a crime decline different in kind from other metropolitan areas. The average city's crime rate decline hovered around 40% and stopped in 2000. The New York City decline has so far lasted twice as long, and the average rate drop is also twice as large. Rates of homicide, robbery, and burglary have dropped over 80% in 19 years. Auto theft has dropped 94%. Are these official statistics accurate? If so, it would be the largest crime drop ever documented during periods of social and governmental continuity. By 2009, the homicide rate in New York, which had been over 30 per 100,000 in 1990, had dropped to under 6 per 100,000, a rate lower than the city enjoyed in 1961.

Myth and Reality in the New York Story

The amazing facts of New York City's crime decline have been condensed into a sound bite in which a heroic mayor and aggressive police created a zero tolerance law enforcement regime that drove crime rates down in the 1990s.

Close scrutiny of the data reveals this popular fable to be almost equal parts truth and fantasy. The expansion of police and the radical changes in police strategy produced nearly half of the declines in robbery and burglary and smaller but significant proportions of the auto theft, rape, and homicide declines. But it wasn't zero tolerance and there was no consistent quality of life emphasis in the New York strategy.

Yet the biggest problem with the urban legend of the New York crime decline is the opposite of the usual hazards of exaggeration. Most of the fairy tales we hear about problem solving in the city claim too much importance for the event and its lessons for history. The simplified sound bite of New York City claims too little. The real lessons of New York are much more important than the myth, and more of a surprise.

The 20-year adventure in New York City was, to be sure, a demonstration project of effective policing, but it was much more than that. It was a demonstration that individual and aggregate crime rates can change substantially over time without either removing or incarcerating larger numbers of active offenders. There were no major changes in the population and ecology of New York but big changes in serious street crime. Active offenders stopped or sharply curtailed rates of predatory crime without major increases in incarceration. Drug-related violence fell by more than 90%, while levels of illegal drug use remained relatively stable. Persisting patterns of single-parent families, educational problems, limited economic opportunity, and gross economic inequality did not prevent the most dramatic crime reduction yet documented in any modern big city.

New York's experience challenges the major assumptions that have dominated American crime and drug policy for more than a generation. It shows that huge increases in incarceration are unnecessary and inefficient. It proves that targeted violence-prevention policies can reduce drug violence and reclaim public areas from drug anarchy without all-out drug wars.

But the most important lesson of the past two decades is that very high rates of violent crime are not hard-wired into the populations, cultures, and institutions of big cities in the United States. Life-threatening crime is not an essential feature of American urban life.

This volume is divided into three parts. Part I profiles the decline in crime over 1990–2009 and compares the current circumstances in New York City to a variety of other cities. Part II searches for an explanation not of the totality of the crime decline in the city but rather of the almost half of the decline that sets New York apart from other big cities in the era after 1990. Part III discusses the implications of New York's experience on what is known about the nature of crime and the promise and limits of crime control.

Acknowledgments

I HAVE BEEN ACTIVELY studying the 1990s crime decline in the United States since 2004, always with substantial support from my academic home base at the University of California and often with important help from other institutions.

The primary funding of the program came from the School of Law at the University of California, Berkeley, and the Werner and Mimi Wolfen endowment. Dean Christopher Edley at Berkeley Law understood the importance of the project and assisted its continuation at two or three critical junctures in the research and writing. The criminal justice research program at Berkeley enabled me to draw upon affiliated scholars in other institutions for data, conversation, and referrals. Anthony Doob of Toronto and James Jacobs of New York University played important roles in the progress of the research. Two other program fellows, David Johnson and Jeffrey Fagan, provided helpful critical readings.

The New York City research depended on a small army of research assistants performing an astonishing variety of tasks. Three of the researchers deserve special mention for the length and substantive depth of their involvement—Emmanuel Fua, Stephen Rushin, and Hannah Laqueur. The project also benefited from shorter and more specific tours of duty from Nicole Lindahl, Keramet Reiter, and Ginger Jackson-Gleich.

Much of the study depended on the generation or retrieval of nonpublic data. A wide variety of public and private institutions helped us collect and analyze data. The New York Police Department provided crime statistics, data on manpower levels and assignments, and detailed statistics on arrests. Philip McGuire, Michael Farrell, and Dante Scarazzini also provided ongoing help in resolving issues of measurement and interpretation. The New York City Department of Public Health provided data and guidance on vital statistics, drug use indicators, and available emergency room drug treatment data. Dahlia Heller of the Department of Public Health was a cheerful and knowledgeable guide to a complicated array of drug indicators. The Institute of Social Research at the University of Michigan provided access to annual totals and drug specific patterns in the ADAM data set discussed in Chapter 4. Andrew Golub of the University of Vermont helped put this testing data in context. Richard Rosenfeld provided helpful readings of the book as well as guidance to work on victim survey in the Metropolitan area.

My analysis of the police data benefited greatly from a series of discussions with Herman Goldstein of the University of Wisconsin, the dean of scholarly experts on operational policing. I was lucky enough to spend the final months of this study in New York City. The opportunity to become a Fellow at NYU Law School's Straus Institute for the Advanced Study of Law and Justice provided exposure to the city and the chance to test and refine the analysis in this book with scholars and administrators in the city. I thank Joseph Weiler, James Jacobs, and David Garland for making my visit possible and for providing a powerful assortment of criminal justice fellows as colleagues and critics. My New York readers and consultants included Herbert Sturz, Michael Jacobson, James Jacobs, and Michele Sviridoff.

Toni Mendicino of Berkeley's Institute for Legal Research presided over the preparation of the book for publication with her customary skill and creativity. Putting a book together with an absentee author presented some logistical complications that she mastered with good cheer. Earlier versions of five chapters were word processed by Christopher Felker. James Cook at Oxford advised on both the book and a short article from it.

It is no accident that this study comes at the beginning of my fifth decade of work on crime and crime policy in the United States. The perspectives of my earlier work and training have had pervasive influence on the design and analysis of this volume. The dedication identifies two of my most important teachers who would not be surprised by the timing and content of this effort.

PART ONE

Anatomy of a Crime Decline

The first section of this book presents a detailed profile of New York City crime over the period 1990 to 2009. Chapter 1 provides the vital statistics of the crime drop by type of crime, by borough, and by year. There are two reasons that such exhaustive detail is required as a beginning to the study. First, the size and the length of the decline are without precedent in the recorded history of American urban crime. Are these declines real? The second reason that the details of the crime decline are needed is as a road map for explaining what changes in the city and its government might have caused this epic decline. The more we know about the specific character of the decline—when it happened, where it happened, which offenses—the better our capacity for sorting through different theories of what caused the drop.

Chapter 2 shifts the focus from the two decades of the decline to an assessment of current conditions in the city. How safe is New York City now? Has the record-breaking decline simply shifted New York City's statistical ranking, or has there been a substantive transformation in this city from dangerous to safe? If so, how can the threshold between danger and safety be defined and when was it crossed? If New York City is not yet safe, what will it take to achieve a transformation?

Chapter 1

The Crime Decline: Some Vital Statistics

THE MISSION OF this chapter is to provide a statistical profile of the substantial crime decline that started in New York City in the early 1990s and has continued well past the turn of a new century. The first section of my analysis will concentrate on three important features of the official statistical portrait of declining crime in the largest city in the United States—the magnitude of declining crime rates, the breadth of the drop, and the length of the decline. Each of these determinations sets New York apart from other big cities in the United States and elsewhere. For example, New York would be special because the size of its drop is so substantial even if the breadth and length of the drop were unremarkable. The length of the city's decline also sets it apart from shorter cyclical variation of crime rates in metropolitan areas in the developed world; and the breadth of the decline across a wide band of different types of crime is not common in most eras. But it is the combination of these three dimensions that makes New York City a very special case and provoked this study.

A. How Big a Drop?

There are two important benchmarks for the size of the crime drop in the city: one measures recent crime levels against the high point for crime in the city, and the other compares current crime with more typical crime years. Figure 1.1 compares crime rates per 100,000 in New York for 2009 with the peak rate for the offense in the period after 1985.

The magnitude of crime declines from peak rates ranges from 63% to 94% with four of the seven "index" felonies showing a rate drop greater than 80%, and five of the seven over 75%. The most modest declines—theft and aggravated assault—drop by about two-thirds, while the rates of the other crimes decline to less than 20% of the city's highest recent rates.

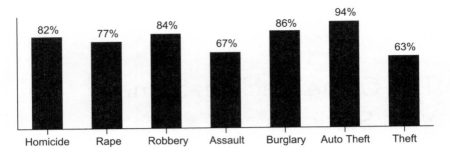

FIGURE 1.1 Percentage Decline from Peak Rate in Seven Crimes, New York City, 2009.
Source: Federal Bureau of Investigation, New York Police Department.

The average drop in the crime rate is well beyond the target magnitude that any serious students of crime would have believed possible before it happened. The proof of this is imagining the reaction from analysts and experts if a mayor or police chief had proposed an 80% decline in robbery or homicides as the objective in a crime reduction program. Yet the only significant exceptions to this magnitude of decline come from the two residual categories of index crime—larceny theft and aggravated assault—where a large mix of behaviors are aggregated into an essentially miscellaneous category. The homicide rate in New York City is 18% of its 1990 total in 2009. The auto theft rate is 6% of the 1990 level. If these readings are accurate, they are astonishing.

But expressing the size of a crime drop from its highest historic level may exaggerate the shift in long-term trends by adding all reductions from unrepresentative peak periods in crime cycles into the equation. How much more modest would the crime drop appear if the baseline for comparison was a less extreme year in New York crime or an average of several periods? Figure 1.2 takes a less extreme crime period in the city's history as the baseline for comparing current crime levels; 1985 was the year just after a reduction in crime trend in the early 1980s that was national in scope and of substantial size (Zimring 2006 at Figure 1.1, p. 5).

The use of a non-peak year to measure the size of the crime decline has a more than minor effect on only two offenses—homicide, where the drop slips from 81% to 69% and assault, where the reduction is just over half instead of two-thirds. The median decline from a 1985 base is the 76% drop in robbery, with rape, burglary, and auto theft having

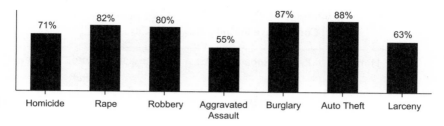

FIGURE I.2 Percentage Decline in Index Crime Rates, New York, 1985–2009. *Source*: Federal Bureau of Investigation.

larger drops, and larceny, assault, and homicide showing less of a drop. Five of seven crimes are lower by more than two-thirds from 1985 and four of seven have dropped by more than 75%. The clear message of Figure 1,2 is that cyclical fluctuations of the kind that separate typical years like 1985 from peak years like 1990 play only a small role in the size of the city's crime drop. In 2009, the chances of becoming a robbery victim were about a fifth of the risk run during 1985; the risk of homicide was down by over two-thirds. Burglary and auto theft were reported at a population risk less than one-sixth the rate of two decades earlier. The spike in homicide in the late 1980s was one reason that the total drop in killings exceeded 80% by 2009, but the most important explanation for the steep statistical drop was not any unusual increases in the late 1980s—it was the unrelenting decline of the 1990s and after.

How Long a Decline?

The second aspect of New York City's statistical profile that stands out is the length of time that crime has persisted in a downward trend. The broad national crime decline of the 1990s ended almost exactly in 2000, and even that eight-year run was the longest consistent downward trend in postwar crime (Zimring 2006, Chap. 1). If it is appropriate to view the entire period from 1991 through the end of 2009 in New York as one of continuous decline, then the recent decline in the city is twice the length of the national downward trend and the longest big-city decline that has yet been documented with reliable crime statistics.

Table 1.1 begins the analysis of the crime decline by separating the two time periods lumped together in the two previous figures to compare the

Table 1.1 Movement in Crime Rates for Seven "Index" Offenses in Two Consecutive Periods, New York City.

	Homicide	Rape	Robbery	Assault	Burglary	Auto Theft	Larceny
1990–2000	-73%	-52%	-70%	-46%	-72%	-73%	-53%
2000–2009	-33%	-51%	-46%	-38%	-52%	-72%	-23%

Source: Federal Bureau of Investigation.

1990s decline with the post-2000 pattern for the seven index offenses in the city.

The rate of each of the seven offenses falls in each of the two separate periods, but the magnitude of the decline is smaller in the later period for homicide, robbery, and theft. Further, the larger percentage drop in the first period also represents a much larger volume of crimes. The 73% drop in homicides from 1990 to 2000 represented an annual drop of more than 1,500 homicides between the two years, while the 29% drop after 2000 represented 177 fewer homicide victims, a much smaller number because of the lower volume already achieved by 2000.

While the magnitude of the pre-2000 declines is much more substantial, the two periods are much closer in the consistency of their declines. In the 49 year-to-year comparisons after 2000 (seven crimes over seven years), all but six year-to-year transitions are rate drops, a rate of 88%. If the mass of September 11 killings is counted as a single case, then none of six post-2000 crime rate increases exceeds 5%. The declines were even more uniform prior to 2000, with 97 of 100 year-to-year transitions showing a rate drop.

Figure 1.3 operates on the graphic equivalent of "seven pictures are worth a thousand words" and shows line graphs of annual rates per hundred thousand of the index crimes. There are differences in the slopes of curves for various index offenses, depending on both the rate of decline and its timing, and there are minor interruptions in the downward slope for a few offenses both before and after 2000. But the visual impression in the simple line diagrams is of a single downward tendency operating without counter-trend or significant interruption over the post-1990 years. The slope of decline slows for several offenses, in part a function of

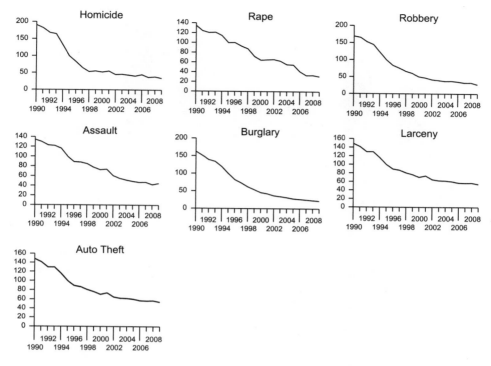

FIGURE 1.3 Trends in Rates of Index Crime (1995 rate = 100), New York City, 1990–2009.
Source: Federal Bureau of Investigation.

movements away from the cyclical peaks in 1990. But the working hypothesis of the study is that the trend that must be comprehended is a single trend—almost two decades in length, and twice as long as any other recorded and studied. This both sets the New York City experience apart from other recent urban histories and complicates the task of understanding and explaining these long effect shifts in the urban dynamic of New York after 1990.

The magnitude of the crime decline in New York was so great during the 19 years after 1990 that a new method of accounting may be required to appreciate its size and to compare the patterns for different crime. Figure 1.4 restates the data presented in Figure 1.1, this time estimating what percentages of the crime risk that was reported in 1990 is left in 2009.

The focus on what's left of index crime in New York City shows very clearly the large difference between the remaining levels of assault and theft and those of other offenses. It also provides a good visual portrait of the singularity of the auto theft trends—the 6% residual of the 1990 rate

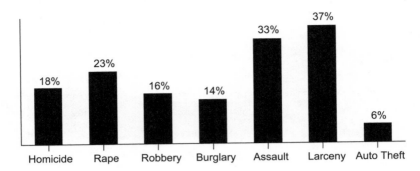

FIGURE I.4 New York Crime in 2009 as a Percentage of 1990 Level.
Source: Federal Bureau of Investigation.

is less than half the remaining level of burglary and robbery. And the emphasis on residual risk also shows the singularity in the serious offense trends (homicide, rape, robbery, and burglary).

How Broad a Crime Decline?

The third aspect of New York City's decline worth special emphasis is what I shall call the breadth of the drop, the spread of a similar decline across a wide variety of crimes and of places. These two dimensions of breadth—crime type and geography—each deserve detailed attention.

For reporting purposes, crimes and arrest are divided into two categories: index and non-index. The crime index consisted for many decades of the seven offenses featured in the figures and the table in this chapter: homicide, rape, robbery, aggravated assault, burglary, auto theft, and larceny theft. An eighth category—arson—was added to the index but has not gained much credibility as a police statistic because the reporting and detection of arson are chancy, and fully half the arrests for arson in the United States are for persons under 18 (Zimring 2004 at p. 42). Many but not all of index offenses are serious crimes, with homicides, rapes, and robberies serving as obvious examples. But the larceny theft category (which alone dominates the volume of index crime in many places) includes all thefts of goods of all value—a reform intended to end police downgrading by underestimating the value of goods when only those losses over $50 entered the index. But avoiding the undercount that the old system invited flooded the crime index with many minor events that are not the source of public fear. For example, the total index crime rate reported by San Diego in 2007 was 7,015 per 100,000 (OJP, usdoj.gov), but 66% of that total were larceny events with no minimum value or other indicator of seriousness.

If the index includes all theft of any value, what sorts of criminal behavior fall into the non-index category? One major category is crimes without victims inclined to report to authorities—including public order offenses like drunkenness, D.W.I., prostitution, curfew offenses, and the entire range of narcotics possession and sale, which currently result in the imprisonment of hundreds of thousands of persons. A further group of offenses are excluded from the index as non-serious. One significant example here is assaults that are not classified as aggravated because they are thought to lack the harm, the intent, or the weapon used or threatened to produce an "aggravated" assault.

The seven so-called index crimes involve a wide variety of different types of harm, motives, settings, and victims. How much similarity is there between a homicide and a car theft in setting and motive? What other than penal treatment and some harm to victims do larceny and forcible rape have in common? And yet *all* these crimes dropped together in New York for the same extended period and in a pattern that showed many other similarities. Homicide dropped 82% during 19 years when auto theft dropped 94% and burglary declined 86%. Even the year-to-year pattern of decline exhibited uncanny similarities across a wide variety of crimes. Between 1990 and 2007, a total of 119 different year-to-year changes for the seven index crimes were reported, and 110 of those year-to-year transitions were downward. Except for the 2001 surge in September 11 homicides, the eight other year-to-year upticks in crime rate were minor and temporary. Each of the seven index offenses reported declining crime in at least 14 of the 17 transitions during the period. So rates of widely different types of criminal behavior drop at the same times, and in pretty similar patterns. This breadth of the drop across crime categories is both worthy of special note and a theoretical puzzle. Why the similarities in drop timing and what are the common influences that produce close to parallel movement?

In other developed nations, theft and life-threatening violence have different trends, with theft increasing but serious violence tending toward stability and decline (Zimring and Hawkins 1997, Chap. 2).

There are good theoretical reasons that these different kinds of conduct should show different trends. What might be the theoretical explanation for a common pattern across widely different behaviors? Might the counter-measures used to prevent or suppress offenses have similar impacts on different crimes? On street crimes such as auto theft and street robbery, perhaps? But on inside location rape and larceny as well? Why?

Yet whether or not we understand the causes of this across-category decline, the categorical breadth of the decline noted is one major feature that both underscores the importance of the New York story and demands explanation.

Geographic Breadth

A second type of breadth that demands attention is the geographical diversity of New York City and of the city's crime decline. New York City is not only the largest city in the United States, but its geographically separate boroughs actually contain four separate urban masses, *each* of which would rank in the top 10 cities of the United States. Table 1.2 provides the demographic detail.

When measured against the current list of the largest cities in the United States (including New York City), the four large counties each would be one of the seven largest cities in the country in 2007, and three of the four would rank in the top five. Even the Bronx is larger than San Antonio, San Diego, Dallas, and Detroit, and the two largest counties

Table 1.2 Population and City Rank of the Four Large Counties in
New York City, 2009.

	2009 Population	Rank against Major American Cities
Brooklyn (Kings County)	2,556,598	4th
Queens	2,293,007	4th
Manhattan (New York County)	1,634,795	5th
Bronx	1,391,903	7th

Source: U.S. Bureau of the Census.

rank just below Chicago and above Houston. With such large and discrete urban units, one further test of the breadth of the citywide crime decline is the extent to which it is spread evenly across these separate urban enclaves.

Figure 1.5 shows the trends in the seven index felonies for each of the four major boroughs of the city. The figure emphasizes time trend by expressing each borough's rate as a proportion of its 1995 crime rate. What we thus see is the similarities and differences over time.

For robbery, burglary, assault, and auto theft, the time trends are indistinguishably similar over the period, while homicide trends become closely similar after 1994. For larceny, there is a modest tendency for Brooklyn and Queens to stop declining after 2002 and this creates some contrast with Manhattan and the Bronx. For rape, there is no clear downward trend in Queens after 2002.

So the pattern described by Figure 1.5 is not quite one of universal uniformity, but it comes pretty close. For at least five index crimes, the magnitude and duration of the downward trends are quite close in these four very different segments of the city.

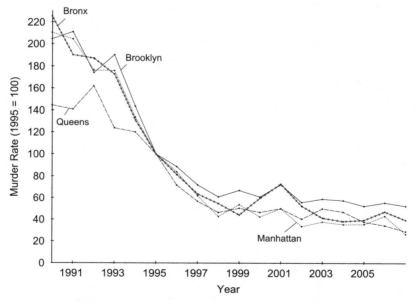

FIGURE 1.5 Trends in Seven Index Crimes in Four Boroughs (1995 rate = 100), New York City, 1990–2007.
Source: New York City Police Department (see Appendix D).

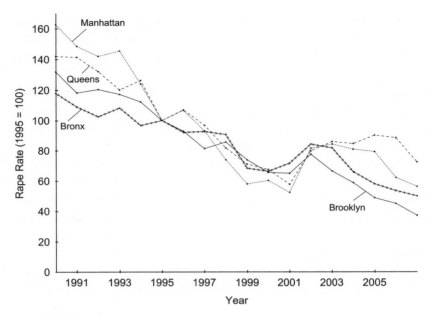

FIGURE I.5 (Continued)

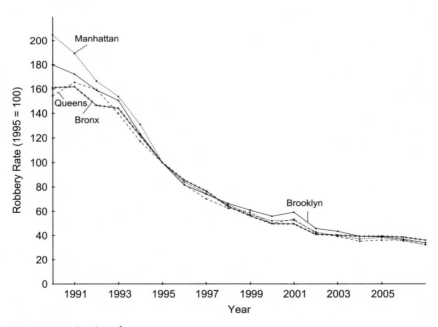

FIGURE I.5 (Continued)

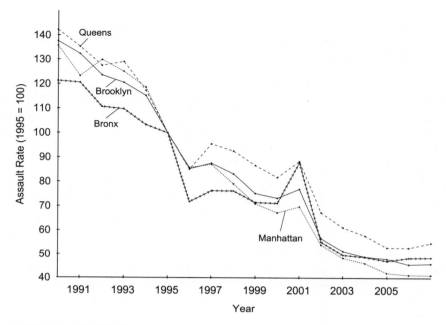

FIGURE I.5 (Continued)

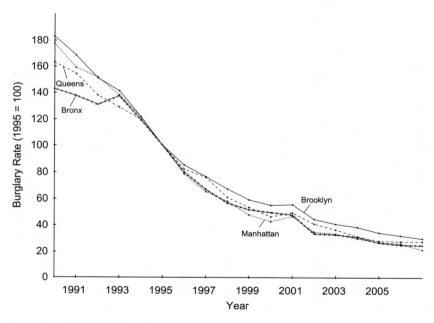

FIGURE I.5 (Continued)

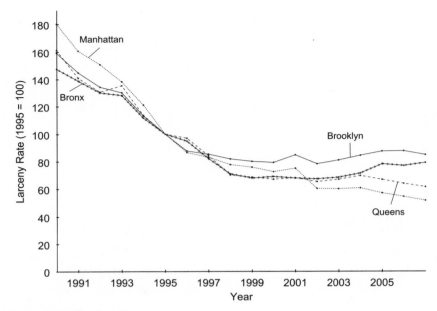

FIGURE I.5 (Continued)

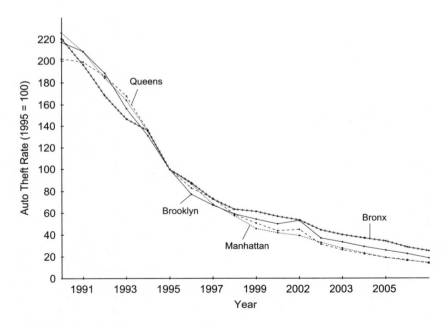

FIGURE I.5 (Continued)

B. The Pattern in Other American Cities

This section examines the recent crime trends in other large U.S. cities for two reasons. First, the changing patterns of crime in major cities is interesting in its own right: What has been the longer term effect of the crime decline of the 1990s on crime? What happened in the post-decline history of big cities? Second, the history and current status of other major cities is an important comparative template for New York City. To what extent was it different in the scale of its changes or in its timing?

To obtain a broad reading of trends in the cities, this section will focus on the largest cities of the United States. To further assess the singularity of New York, I will compare the city to other places identified earlier as experiencing major crime declines the 1990s, an overlap with the major cities but also including Boston.

Table 1.3 profiles the aggregate crime patterns over 1990–2009 for the ten largest cities other than New York. The first lesson of Table 1.3 is that big-city crime is still down, in most cases substantially down, from 1990 levels. Crime rates are lower in 2009 than in 1990 in at least six out of the seven categories for eight of the ten cities, with Philadelphia and San Antonio the exceptions. And the decline is spread across most crime categories—homicide, robbery, burglary, and larceny remain lower than 1990 rates in at least nine out of the ten cities, and rape drops in seven of the nine cities with available data. Further, the magnitude of the drops in many cities is substantial. Los Angeles, Chicago, San Diego, Dallas, and Houston report about half or less the crime risks in 2009 when compared with 1990. By this measure, the great American crime decline of the 1990s has had a continued and positive impact on urban crime.

It is equally clear, however, that the period since the turn of the new century has not generated a continuation of major declines in most cities. Table 1.4 isolates the period from 2000 to 2009 and shows crime trends for the same cities as Table 1.3.

Three of the ten cities show clear, large, and general declines over the post-2000 period—Los Angeles, Chicago, and Dallas—while the other seven cities show a mixture of increasing, steady, and decreasing rates. San Jose shows increases in several crime categories as does San Antonio for robbery and rape. Many cities show small increases or decreases for homicide and burglary, with increases in the first years of the decade being countered by declines after 2007.

Table 1.3 Crime Rate Trends in the 10 Largest Non-New York Cities, 1990–2009.

	Homicide	Rape	Robbery	Assault	Burglary	Auto Theft	Larceny
Los Angeles	-71%	-59%	-69%	-78%	-68%	-68%	-58%
Chicago	-47%		-58%	-63%	-48%	-69%	-41%
Houston	-64%	-56%	-37%	20%	-51%	-74%	-30%
Philadelphia	-38%	25%	-28%	25%	-53%	-72%	-9%
Dallas	-71%	-72%	-59%	-74%	-54%	-67%	-56%
Phoenix	-42%	-39%	-32%	-60%	-59%	-66%	-54%
San Diego	-75%	-39%	-63%	-57%	-66%	-74%	-69%
San Jose	-36%	-49%	-19%	-46%	-47%	5%	-52%
Detroit	-29%	-77%	-49%	2%	-18%	-52%	-49%
San Antonio	-68%	0%	-36%	36%	-52%	-73%	-34%

Source: Federal Bureau of Investigation.

Table 1.4 Crime Rate Trends in 10 Largest Non-New York Cities, 2000–2009.

	Homicide	Rape	Robbery	Assault	Burglary	Auto Theft	Larceny
Los Angeles	-46%	-41%	-24%	-69%	-28%	-40%	-28%
Chicago	-26%		-17%	-40%	-5%	-47%	-25%
Houston	7%	-13%	18%	-8%	8%	-37%	-1%
Philadelphia	-7%	-14%	-15%	-21%	-11%	-58%	-21%
Dallas	-34%	-29%	-28%	-54%	-12%	-46%	-25%
Phoenix	-34%	3%	-17%	-34%	-15%	-59%	-37%
San Diego	-30%	-15%	0%	-31%	-7%	-26%	-27%
San Jose	38%	-28%	42%	-49%	31%	93%	2%
Detroit	-3%	-57%	-21%	-10%	-76%	-47%	-39%
San Antonio	-3%	15%	32%	-35%	-30%	-18%	-7%

Source: Federal Bureau of Investigation.

There seems to be something close to a regression phenomenon operating for both crime categories and for cities. Homicide, robbery, and burglary were three of the four biggest crime drops in the decade prior to 2000 (see Zimring 2006 at Figure 1–2, p. 6) while larceny and assault dropped far less than the other five index offenses during the 1990s (ibid.). Three of the biggest drop offenses during the 1990s trend upward in 2000–2009, while the two relative laggards categories during the 1990s—assault and larceny—recorded declines in most cities in the seven years after 2000. The exception to this pattern is rape—with a high 41% decline during the 1990s but with further declines also recorded in seven of ten cities after 2000.

A similar regression or bounce-back effect seems to take place at the city level after 2000. San Diego, San Jose, and Houston were the three cities reported in Table 1.4 (other than New York) that were singled out as high crime-decline jurisdictions in the 1990s (Zimring 2006 at Appendix A). All three cities show a mixture of flat trends and increases after 2000. There thus appears to be some tendency for the law of averages to catch up with the high fliers among urban areas with crime declines in the 1990s when post-2000 statistics are added in.

Except in New York City—as Table 1.1 showed, the same big city that had the nation's most substantial crime drop between 1990 and 2000 did it again in 2000–2009. The magnitude of the 2000–2009 decline was almost double that of the next largest drop city (New York median decline of 45% versus Los Angeles median decline of 24%). New York City has the largest decline of all eleven cities for three of the four "safety crimes" (rape, robbery, and burglary) and a homicide drop equal to Dallas and Phoenix and below only Los Angeles. The best way to approach the meaning of this persistence is to revisit the cities singled out in my earlier study as "high decline" during the 1990s, but also to add Los Angeles—the city with the largest and most consistent decline during the period after 2000. Table 1.5 compares New York City with the four other high-decline candidates from the earlier study and Los Angeles, repeating data already presented on the 1990–2009 period.

The first effect of adding nine more years to the comparison of New York and the previous high-decline cities is that the difference between the New York decline and the other four 1990s high-decline cities has grown substantially. The second impact of this longer time period is that Los Angeles has overtaken the previous high-decline cities and now is second

Table 1.5 Crime Rate Trends in Six Cities, 1990–2009.

	Homicide	Rape	Robbery	Assault	Burglary	Auto Theft	Larceny
New York	-82%	-77%	-84%	-67%	-86%	-94%	-63%
Los Angeles	-71%	-59%	-69%	-78%	-68%	-68%	-58%
Houston	-64%	-56%	-37%	20%	-51%	-74%	-30%
San Diego	-75%	-39%	-63%	-57%	-66%	-67%	-56%
San Jose	-36%	-49%	-19%	-46%	-47%	-66%	-54%
Boston	-68%	-54%	-65%	-52%	-73%	-89%	-52%

Source: Federal Bureau of Investigation.

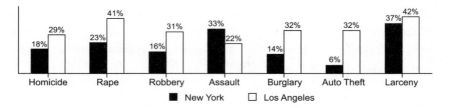

FIGURE 1.6 2009 Crime Rates as a Percentage of 1990 Levels, New York and Los Angeles.
Source: Federal Bureau of Investigation.

only to New York in its aggregate 17-year decline. The median L.A. decline is 66%, much larger than the other non-New York cities, and Los Angeles has a decline second only to New York in homicide, burglary, and auto theft, and first among all cities in assault. So if there is a candidate for similarity in long-term crime trends to New York City, among big U.S. cities, it would be Los Angeles. The fact that the two largest cities in the nation are also first and second in crime declines is unexpected. But how close are these two high-decline metropoles?

My method of approaching this question might be criticized by skeptics as an optical illusion. Figure 1.6 repeats the percentage decline information for Los Angeles and New York City but presents the profile of New York and Los Angeles crime rates as the percentage of the total crime rate in 1990, the technique used in Figure 1.4. So New York's 82% homicide decline is expressed instead as 18% of its 1990 rate. The visual emphasis shifts from the size of the drop to the size of the residual crime rate.

The shift in Figure 1.6 to emphasis on the size of the current crime rate relative to its prior level does have some dramatic visual impact. The Los Angeles decline in auto theft is 67%, which is 73% as large as the New York City reduction of 92%. But Figure 1.6 produces a more dramatic contrast—Los Angeles currently has 33% of its prior auto theft rate, while New York City has only 6%, which is a five to one difference. And auto theft is only the most striking of the five offense categories where the percentage of previous crime levels is significantly lower for New York City—homicide, rape, robbery, and burglary. The current crime rates in New York are more than twice as far removed from their 1990 levels for rape, burglary, and auto theft.

There are two qualifications that seem appropriate to using current crime levels compared to base rate as a measure of a crime decline. The first is that this method is rather sensitive to the particular base rate selected for comparison, so some use of multiple bases might be an appropriate test of how consistently the New York decline looks singular in its relative magnitude. The second qualification is that the different *levels* of crime decline do not necessarily indicate different *causes of decline*. When making comparisons over different times and among different cities, one natural question is how the timing and magnitude of a particular city's decline match up against different theories of the causes of crime declines.

With these qualifications, the case can be made that the size of a remaining crime risk relative to previous level is the way that citizens feel and define the risk environments of their current existence. John Smith isn't interested in how much the auto theft rate dropped from 1990 as a question of a percentage so much as he is interested in what his chances are of losing a car this year compared to earlier times. His critical statistic is the 6%, the fact that he is only one-sixteenth as likely to lose his car this year, and less than a fifth as likely to be killed.

Using Independent Measures to Test Official Statistical Trends in New York

One institutional weakness of the official crime statistical system in the United States is that the official scorekeepers for crime numbers are the same law enforcement agencies who frequently get evaluated by whether crime is up or down. Because of their incentives to influence crime rates, police agencies were regarded as unreliable official crime statisticians for most of the twentieth century, and not without reason. The perverse incentives and history of statistical problems with official statistics led to two separate reform efforts in the last third of the twentieth century. One effort was to create quality controls in the FBI systems for police reporting, at least for the seven "index" crimes. These efforts in the uniform crime reporting system have without doubt improved the quality and city-to-city comparability of official crime statistics over the last 35 years, but there is still uncertainty about the size of remaining problems and the margin of error in many city level crime statistics in the Uniform Crime Reporting system.

The second effort to improve the measurement of crime was the creation or use of independently collected data to measure levels of crime and to check against the trends reported in official statistics. The most prominent effort of this kind was the creation and routine use of a national research instrument administered by phone to compile crime rate estimates by surveys of crime victims. During the national crime decline of the 1990s, observers tested the trends established by police statistics, and in almost all cases the victim survey drops were equivalent to the police estimates or in two cases greater (for assault and larceny, see Zimring 2006 at p. 87).

There are no routine high-sample victim survey programs at the city level for New York or any other large city, so this useful independent measure of trends in crime is not available to test the magnitude and timing of the police reported drops for the entire period. But there are estimates of two crimes generated by non-police sources that can be used to create independent estimates of trends over time and of the magnitude of changes noted in police statistics. For a third crime, robbery, we can use the volume of robbery killings from monthly supplemental homicide reports to index expected trends in non-fatal robberies. And one set of victim survey findings provides a check on household burglary as well for much of the period after 1990.

Homicide in Vital Statistics and Police Statistics

The criminal homicide numbers in the earlier sections of this chapter come from cases referred to the police and classified by the police as killings that were either intended to cause death or great bodily harm. This data comes from city-level police agencies. A separate count of deaths caused by violent assaults comes from county-level offices that must be notified of all deaths and are responsible for a tightly regulated classification of all deaths by cause. Figure 1.7 compares the police and vital statistics homicide reports for New York City by year for 1990 through 2008. There are only tiny differences between the two homicide rates and a perfect fit over time in reporting trends. The zero order correlation of the two measures exceeds .99.

Insurance Losses and Police Reports of Auto Theft

Auto insurance firms universally offer what is usually called "comprehensive" coverage to drivers who own cars, and theft is one of the perils insured against. While drivers are not required by law to insure against theft loss, the purchase of comprehensive coverage is quite common. Insurance companies have no incentive to understate their loss experience. Instead, insurance companies need accurate data to calculate their costs and to justify their rates in reports to regulatory agencies. So the incentives in insurance reporting are for full disclosure and these records should be a very good independent check on the timing of trends and their magnitude. Most of the large auto insurers in New York City belong to a National Bureau and report theft loss claims to the Bureau's central repository. Figure 1.8 compares trends in reported insurance claims and police auto theft incidents by year, starting each theft series with its 1990 rate equal to 100 so that trends are represented on the same scale.

Overall, the trends over time and magnitude of decline are very close for these two independently documented theft measures. The 18-year drop in the police statistics is 93% and the insurance bureau aggregate drop to 2008 is 88%. The official rate of auto theft decreased 73% from 1990 to 2000, while the insurance claim level decreased 71.5%. In the eight years

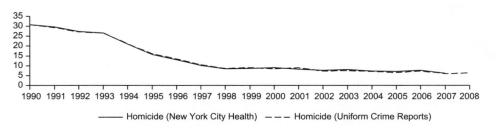

FIGURE 1.7 New York City Homicides per 100,000, 1985–2008.
Source: New York City Police Department and New York City, Department of Health.

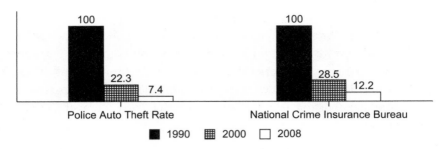

FIGURE 1.8 Time Trends in Police Reports of Auto Theft and Reported Auto Theft Insurance Claims.
Notes: Police, 1990 = 2009 per 100,000; NCIB 1990 = 13,000 claims reported.
Source: Police, Federal Bureau of Investigation; Insurance claims, National Crime Insurance Bureau.

after 2000, the insurance rate dropped another 57% while the police reported decline in rate was about 70%. The claim data from insurance haven't adjusted to reflect the city's population increase, or the two sets of estimates would be even closer. But this is close enough. Given the different counting methods and information sources, Figure 1.8 is a robust confirmation of the size and timing of the largest drop in any major crime rate ever recorded in this or any other major city over an 18-year period. And since the insurance numbers had never been compiled or published before, the police data could not have been influenced by them.

In theory, insurance claims for losses from burglary could also have been consulted to test burglary trends. But the New York State Department of Insurance denied having loss data for the City, and two insurance carriers refused access to their experience rates.

Robbery Killings and Robberies

For the offense of robbery, there is no completely independent count of events to parallel the insurance data for auto theft or the public health registry of killings. But the high risk of death associated with robbery provides an important opportunity to use trends in killings during robbery as an indicator of trends in the volume of robbery events. Only a small percentage of all robberies result in victim death. If that rate doesn't change much over time, the trend in robbery killings should mirror the trend in robbery rate. This provides one measure of the accuracy of police statistics on robbery, explored in Figure 1.9.

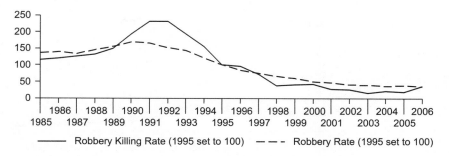

FIGURE 1.9 Robberies and Robbery Killings, New York City Base 100 = 1995.
Source: New York City Police Department (robbery rates); FBI, Criminal Justice Information Services Division, *Supplemental Homicide Reports* (robbery killings).

The figure uses 1995 robbery and robbery killing rates normed to 100
to trace time trends for each over two decades. The correlation over time
between robbery killings and robberies is high (.94) with the only large
discrepancy in the two trends happening in 1991–1993, when the killings
go up more than the reported robberies. This divergence could be a sign
that the average robbery was more dangerous in these years (higher gun
use is one possibility), or it might suggest that there was less reporting of
non-fatal robberies during those years. But whatever the cause of this gap,
it means that the official robbery rate decline is a good minimum estimate. The drop in robbery killings from 1990 to 2006 is actually larger
than the drop in reported total robberies.

Whatever the final verdict on the early 1990s divergence, the net effect
of the robbery killing comparison is to support the official data on robbery
as an accurate minimum estimate of actual decline.

A final opportunity to test the size and timing of the officially reported
crime decline involves comparing police reports of offenses with victim
surveys taken in the New York metropolitan area from 1980-2003.
Figure 1.10 shows annual rates of robbery and burglary for the National
Crime Victimization Survey (NCVS) and for police statistics from
1980-2003. The dotted lines show the victim survey trends and the solid
lines show police reports.

The victim survey data is not a perfect match for the official statistics—
the metropolitan area is somewhat larger than the city and the burglary
category excludes commercial settings—but the time trends for robbery
and burglary in the survey data area very close fit with the time trends in

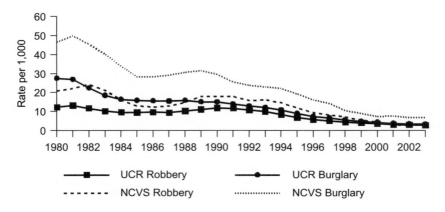

FIGURE I.IO Victim Survey and Police Rates of Burglary and Robbery, 1980–2003. *Source*: Janet L. Lauritsen, Brian E. Oliver, Robin J. Schaum, and Richard Rosenfeld. 2008. *Crime and Victimization in the New York Metropolitan Area, 1980–2003: Comparing Victims' Reports of Crime to Police Estimates.* Available at www.crimetrends.com.

the police crime statistics. Indeed, the big drop in survey rates of burglary in the years after 1989 is somewhat larger than in the official burglary rate. But the clear message in the time data from victim surveys is again to confirm both the relative magnitude and the timing of the crime decline portrayed in police statistics.

All four efforts to audit the accuracy of official statistical reports on Part I crime in New York City have validated the official statistics on trends.

C. Seeking the Lessons of Recent History

The statistical focus of the introductory materials presented in this chapter is not on the current status of New York City—its crime profile and risks when compared to other modern urban environments—but rather on the 19-year crime decline as the process that produced current conditions. The reason for this emphasis on the dynamics of New York's crime decline is the unprecedented nature of the downward shift in offense levels. As will soon be apparent, New York City is by no means unique in its level of street safety in the second decade of the twenty-first century. There are a few other cities in the United States with safer streets than New York, and Chapter 2 will show that most principal cities of other developed nations have much lower rates of life-threatening violence than New York, even after its sharp decline.

What separates New York City from all other urban settings is the extent of its documented changes over a short period of time in crime and criminal violence. The physical, economic, and social structure of New York City changed only modestly from 1990 to 2010, but the changes in crime rates were quite substantial.

This kind of high magnitude change provides a special opportunity to investigate both the causes of urban crime levels and the effects of crime on an urban environment. It is one thing to compare cities with high rates of crime and violence to cities with much lower rates and to speculate on what features of population, culture, or environment are associated with the different levels of crime. But places with sharp and long-standing differences in crime are also different in many other ways—and no amount of statistical sophistication can convince a careful observer that one or a few elements in the manifold differences between such cities are the cause of differences in crime and violence. Choosing what strands of difference to emphasize in cross-sectional comparison is a necessarily speculative enterprise.

But following the fortunes of the same city over a discrete time period seems a much more promising method of isolating changes that might have caused shifts in crime and violence. This is particularly true when big changes in crime take place because the number of significant changes that are plausible candidates to explain major crime changes should be limited. Thus, following the same city over time seems a better method of hunting for the causes of crime shifts than comparing urban apples and oranges. But the problem is that most cities don't have huge changes to study. This is what makes New York's post-1990 experience a particular opportunity to try to isolate the causes of its crime decline.

There is a second respect in which big changes in crime in a city presents an important research opportunity—in this case as a window into the effects of change in crime rates and risks on other aspects of city life. Comparing the social and economic conditions of high-crime and low-crime cities is just as speculative as trying to use cross-sectional variations of very different cities to sort out the causes of crime. But when crime levels increase or decrease in the same city, the opportunity to study the timing and magnitude of other social and economic shifts provides a more promising way of studying the effects of crime risk on altered conditions of city life.

The ideal setting for this type of analysis would be a place where very few large changes in populations, institutions, and opportunities took place but crime levels varied substantially. What difference does this make in the life experiences and perceptions of different age, class, and racial groups? If there is less crime victimization and offending, how does that alter the lives of those who would be most likely to be the victims and offenders in a higher crime environment? Do the poor enjoy the benefits of safer neighborhoods or are they priced out of previously available housing? What happens to high-risk young men in bad neighborhoods who are not arrested for the crimes they don't commit in a lower crime environment? The careful study of the effects of lower crime on urban life is at least as important as the study of the causes.

One further value of a careful study of changes in crime levels is as a natural laboratory for testing many theories of crime causation and prevention that are the current foundation of academic theory or government crime policy. Here is a new context to consider a wide range of theories about the social and cultural determinants of crime as well as the risks and protective factors that influence the rate of crime and its distribution. Do the long-held theories about drug use, educational failure, loss of economic opportunity, and family structure as influences on rates of crime get reinforced or questioned by the way in which crime changed in New York City? Are different factors important to explain the general level of crime in a community and the distribution of crime rates among a population, so that even increases in circumstances that might predict a relatively high individual risk of offending do not necessarily mean that the general rate of offending will increase over time? I will revisit this question when comparing social risk factors and youth crime trends in chapter 4.

Some Implications of the Patterns of Decline

There are two distinct values to the detailed information on the character and timing of the crime decline provided in this chapter. The first and most obvious is to document the size and singularity of this city's crime drop. The data on length, breadth, size, number of offenses, and borough-to-borough constancy is impressive cumulative evidence of a crime drop that sets this single city apart from others in the recent past.

The second use of the particular characteristics of the city's crime decline is as a pattern requiring explanation when searching for causes. The more specific the characteristics that set this New York City decline apart from others, the better our criteria for sorting through plausible explanations of causes. We are now looking for a set of phenomena that have a depressive effect on at least seven different types of crime over a period of 18 years in a pattern of closely similar impact in all four populous boroughs of the city. These features of the decline become a pattern that should match the characteristics of plausible causes. The details of the crime decline become the fingerprints of its causes, the pattern that plausible explanations of the origins of the decline must explain.

Chapter 2

A Safe City Now?

THE LESSON OF Chapter 1 is that New York City has experienced a decline in rates of serious crime that is unprecedented in modern American history. The focus of this chapter is on the current circumstances of this largest American city. Is the city safe? Compared to what?

The statistical profile of current conditions in New York City is subject to many different interpretations. Chapter 1 showed that the risk of becoming a homicide victim in New York City was 18% of its 1990 rate during 2009, a drop of more than four-fifths in less than 20 years. But murder is still literally an everyday occurrence in the city with a rate per 100,000 citizens that is just below six per year, and with homicide risks many times as high for the young minority males who are everywhere at the highest risk of serious violence. The city is safer, but is it safe? How should observers approach this question?

Is New York now a safe and relatively crime-free city? One cannot come to meaningful conclusions about safety and risk without standards, and the way that standards are constructed on issues like urban crime and violence is by invidious comparisons with other places, usually other cities. The method of my analysis here is to present three different layers of comparison for the current circumstances of New York City. The first analysis is to look at crime rates and risks in New York in 2009 in comparison with its 1990 circumstances—to compare the city with its former conditions and to repeat this comparison for the four major boroughs of the city. Past experience is one basis for expectations and for satisfaction with current circumstances.

A second series of comparisons will involve the current circumstances of the other major cities in the United States, not simply as a matter of statistical ranking but of the relative risk run by individuals for "fear crimes." At what point do statistical differences in risk translate into qualitative differences in emotion—feelings of security rather than fright. And in this comparative study of American cities, we will also disaggregate the city into its four major components and see how they compare to urban settings of a similar size.

A third layer of comparison will measure New York's current circumstances against other major cities in the developed world. How does New York City in its current condition measure up against London, Paris, Tokyo, and Sydney?

Why so many different comparisons? Our extended tour of urban crime is not the search for the single best comparison that can provide definitive indications of where New York City should be classified in the annals of urban safety. There is no such litmus comparison. Instead, a series of careful comparisons can help inform the judgments that lead to appropriate standards of urban safety and crime security. Do we worry more about homicide, or robbery, or the security of property from theft? How much street robbery is too much? Is a robbery twice as much of a threat as a housebreaking? The best way to consider such questions is to compare cities. Rather than lobby for my own conclusion to this chapter's central question, I hope to provide a foundation for informed judgments by readers. So this is an effort at a consumer's guide, an attempt to establish criteria for safety and crime security in a modern city.

A. New York City, Then and Now

Figure 2.1 provides the first and most important comparison that most long time New Yorkers make when evaluating the current conditions in that city, a contrast with the bad old days at the beginning of the 1990s. The focus of the figure is on annual rates of individual crimes, which provides a less abstract profile of crime risks than percentage declines. The relative height of each bar measures relative risk (but the homicide and rape bars are ten times the size their numbers should produce to show

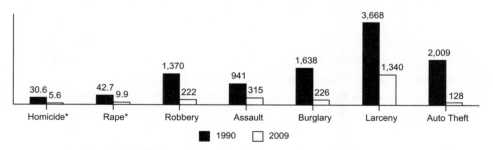

FIGURE 2.1 Annual Rates per 100,000 for Seven Index Crimes, New York City, 1990 and 2009.
* scale expanded 10x
Source: Federal Bureau of Investigation.

shifts over time more clearly). This emphasis on aggregate rates shows that even in the dangerous dawn of the 1990s, fully three-quarters of all New York City crimes were clustered in the three "index" property offenses of larceny, auto theft, and burglary. We have to multiply the scale of rape and homicides by 10 to make these rates clearly visible on the chart. But this is more an argument against unweighted aggregation of crime numbers than a suggestion that citizens should worry equally about homicide and larceny. They don't.

Just as the average New Yorker would be drawn to compare current conditions with previous rates in the city, the primary crimes of concern— the well-titled "fear crimes" are homicide, rape, robbery, and home burglary. A focus on these crimes in Figure 2.1 shows the same large drops that characterize the total index crime profile. The homicide rate falls from over 30 per 100,000 to 5.6. That is an abundantly clear demonstration that New York is a much *safer* city these days, but is it a *safe* one? Robbery is a particularly frightening crime because it occurs at a very high rate in many cities, usually involves an assault by a stranger in a public area, involves the use or imminent threat of force, and kills victims more often than other crimes where the victim and offender are usually strangers. The robbery rate in New York City in 1990 is 1,370 crimes per 100,000 citizens, and dropped by 84% by 2009.

By almost any standard, a rate of 1,370 robberies per 100,000 persons per year is quite high—that is a citywide total of over 100,000 robberies for New York in 1990. What is less clear, however, is how we should regard the current robbery rate of 222 per 100,000 per year. If robbery is a dominant concern, is that level a sign of major accomplishment, or of a safety problem, or of both?

The statistics on rape invite the same type of subjective accounting issue. As long as the 2009 rate of 9.9 is considered in a comparison with a 1990 risk that was over 40, the current crime level is a reassuring statistic. But the odds that a young woman might be raped in a few years' time are close to one in a thousand. That is a non-trivial risk.

Any change in the basis of comparison provides an opportunity to revert to the question of the safety of current conditions. But as long as the emphasis for comparison is past risk, the present looks very safe. Here is one important question: How long will the public memory of previous high crime levels provide the dominant comparative standard for evaluating current crime rates in New York City? What is the half-life of public gratitude as the frame for evaluating the city's current crime circumstances?

The further removed in time the city becomes from its high crime era, the more likely public expectations and values are likely to move from past rates of serious crime as the standard against which current conditions will be judged. In this sense, the continuous success of the city may work to its disadvantage over time as expectations change.

There is one other respect in which the data in Figure 2.1 may signal important features of what factors influence public perceptions of risk and safety. The statistical dominance of property offenses in city crime also creates a possibility that experience with rates of property crime may influence the perceptions of citizens about their risk for violent offenses. Both auto theft and burglary are offenses where personal victimization is higher than the most serious offenses of violence. It may be that experience with these crimes influences perceptions of risk. But both of these rates dropped as much as for violent crimes over the period since 1990, so that even if expectations about fear crimes such as robbery and homicide were generated by less-violent offenses, the recent outcomes would have been the same except for larceny. But any divergence in trend between property crime trends and violent crime trends might lead to different results.

B. Crime and Risk in Four Boroughs

The previous chapter showed that the timing and the relative magnitude of the crime decline were quite similar in New York's four large boroughs. Appendix A provides parallel data for the much smaller borough of Staten Island. This similarity in decline was all the more remarkable because rates of crime and violence in these discrete sub-cities vary substantially. Crime fell by similar proportions at similar times, but crime rates were very different through the city's modern history and remain so currently.

Table 2.1 compares the four large boroughs for index crimes of violence reported in 2009. Appendix A presents parallel data for Staten Island, the city's smallest and least "citified" borough.

The widest rate variations among boroughs for violent crime are found at the top of the seriousness scale, for murder. The highest homicide rate is three times the lowest in 2009, with Queens and Manhattan showing homicide rates half or less as great as Brooklyn and the Bronx. For robbery, by contrast, there is only a difference of 41% between the top rate (the Bronx) and the bottom rate (Queens), and the three boroughs other than

Table 2.1 Violent Crime in Four Boroughs, New York City, 2009; Rates per 100,000.

	Homicide	Rape	Robbery	Assault
Brooklyn	7.9	13.1	246	275
Queens	4.2	13.0	174	136
Manhattan	3.6	15.0	230	190
Bronx	8.1	19.3	296	309

Source: New York Police Department.

Queens are clustered quite closely. The cluster in robbery is for three boroughs at the high end and one divergent unit 40% lower. For rape, three of the four boroughs are closely clustered near the bottom of the distribution, between 13.0 and 15, while the Bronx is distinctly higher (rates in all boroughs for rape in Table 2.1 are higher than the 2009 citywide level of 9.9 because the borough statistics are based on a broader definition of the crime than the FBI definition used at the city level). The assault rates of the four boroughs follow the same rank order as for murder (as they should), but the Manhattan rate is closer to that of Brooklyn and further up from Queens than the homicide rates predict. This may indicate greater willingness to consider assaults serious in Manhattan. That might explain why a borough with half the killings per 100,000 only reports 32% fewer non-fatal "aggravated" assaults.

The distribution of property crime rates among the four populous boroughs is, with two mild exceptions, quite even, as shown in Table 2.2. Reported rates of burglary in 2009 vary much less than violent crime from borough to borough. The highest reported rate (260 per 100,000), is only 23% above the lowest reported rate (210). These four rather different city segments are indistinguishable in current burglary rate. And a very similar rate profile for other property offenses is found for Brooklyn, the Bronx, and Queens with only an 18% difference from highest to lowest for larceny and 28% for auto theft. Manhattan breaks this pattern with a larceny rate more than double the next highest borough and an auto theft rate about half that of the other three boroughs. In each case, the difference reflects distinctive ecological features of Manhattan, a dense and compact urban zone with fewer cars and a much larger concentration of retail businesses and merchandise than the rest of the city.

Table 2.2 Property Crime Rates in Four Boroughs, New York City, 2009;
Rates per 100,000.

	Burglary	Larceny	Auto Theft
Brooklyn	231	390	135
Queens	210	330	145
Manhattan	231	979	66
Bronx	260	346	173

Source: New York Police Department.

The two important lessons of the property crime distribution are first that there is very substantial similarity across the four boroughs in reported property crime, and that this flat distribution is in contrast to the substantial differences in homicide rates and some other reported violent offenses.

The data in Tables 2.1 and 2.2 are not evidence that all New Yorkers face similar risks of crime and violence. The smallest unit of analysis in Tables 2.1 and 2.2 is a heterogeneous collection of vastly different types of neighborhoods and populations into aggregations of more than a million. More detailed profiles of New York City's thousands of neighborhoods would produce very large differences in risks for most types of crime. But the four major subdivisions of the city have similar levels of most crimes other than homicide.

Demography and Crime in Four Boroughs

When comparing rates of crime and violence in the city's four metropolitan boroughs, it is appropriate to consider not only the racial and ethnic composition of the city as a whole but also the extent to which different boroughs have different racial and ethnic compositions. Table 2.3 provides census estimates of the percentage of four population groups in each of the four boroughs for 2006.

While the city as a whole and each of its major boroughs are a mixture of racial and ethnic groups, there are important contrasts in racial and ethnic composition. Almost half of Manhattan's population is white non-Hispanic, compared to about one-third of the population in Brooklyn and Queens and one-eighth the population in the Bronx. Brooklyn and the

Table 2.3 Population Distribution by Race and Ethnicity, Four Boroughs, 2007.

	White Non-Hispanic	Black	Hispanic	Asian
Manhattan	49%	16%	25%	11%
Bronx	13%	33%	51%	4%
Brooklyn	36%	35%	20%	9%
Queens	31%	19%	27%	21%

Source: U.S. Bureau of the Census.

Bronx have 35% and 33% Black population, more than double the percentage of Blacks in Manhattan and almost double the percentage in Queens. If we divide the demographic distribution into groups with very high homicide victimization in 1990 in New York (Black and Hispanic) and relatively low homicide vicitimization (Asian and white non-Hispanic), there is a very big difference in the four major boroughs. The Bronx and Manhattan are the extremes—84% of Bronx residents fall in high-victimization Black or Hispanic categories, more than twice the 41% concentration found by 2007 in Manhattan. Brooklyn is a distant second to the Bronx, with 55% Black and Hispanic concentration, and Queens has a 46% share for these two groups.

The demographic differences track the noted differences in homicide rates for 2007 pretty clearly. The highest rates of homicide in the United States are reported for Blacks, about seven times the white non-Hispanic victimization rate (Zimring and Hawkins 1997, Chap. 5; National Center for Health Statistics 2007). There is less precision in estimating rates of homicide among Hispanic populations, but the rate is usually higher than for non-Hispanic white population groups living in similar settings. And Chapter 3 will show very high homicide rates (close to African American) in 1990 in New York City. Most East Asian ethnic groups in the United States have quite low homicide victimization rates. But the demographic differences in present-day New York produce very large geographic differences in homicide only, not in other crimes.

The two high homicide boroughs have about twice the proportion of Black population as the two low-rate boroughs, and the Bronx reports more than eight out of ten of its residents are either Black or Hispanic. Queens and Manhattan report the highest concentrations of lower rate homicide populations—59% of Manhattan is white non-Hispanic or Asian and 52% in Queens.

What is both surprising and important in the borough-specific crime statistics is the relatively even spread of most crime rates over areas with different population mixes. The more than two-to-one difference in homicide rates between the top two boroughs and the bottom two is a singular phenomenon. For the other violent crimes, Queens has a much lower assault rate and a robbery rate that is about one-third lower than the other three boroughs, but Brooklyn and Manhattan have robbery and rape crime rates that are nearly equal and the Brooklyn assault rate is only 15% higher than Manhattan. For property crime, the highest burglary rate reported in 2009 is only 23% above the lowest, and all the non-Manhattan boroughs are clustered with auto theft rates between 135 and 173 and larceny rates that range only from 330 to 390 per 100,000. While the Bronx has a homicide rate three times that of Queens, its burglary rate is only 23% higher than Queens and its larceny rate is 5% higher. There is little evidence in these statistics that demography is criminological fate.

The closer links of homicide to demographic variations in the major boroughs is evidence that rates of homicide are more closely linked to patterns of social interaction than most other criminal acts. The relatively even distribution of offenses such as burglary and larceny in the city's major urban areas may reflect the mobility of offenders to some extent, but most common crimes are usually committed pretty close to the offender's place of residence or usual social environments. Since most of New York City's property crime is committed close to home, the evenness of the crime distribution across the four major boroughs is remarkable. Both the drop in all crime rates and the current distribution of most crime rates in New York City by borough are among the most important of this city's lessons for criminological scholarship.

C. The Relative Safety of America's Biggest Cities

The second obvious method of comparing crime and violence in New York City is to measure current New York conditions against rates in other major U.S. cities. Figure 2.2 provides rates of homicide for the 11 largest cities in the United States. Homicide is both the single most serious and feared crime and a good measure of other forms of life-threatening violence.

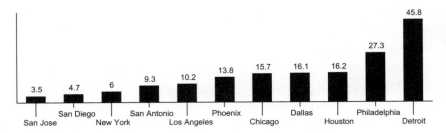

FIGURE 2.2 Homicide Rates in the 11 Largest U.S. Cities, 2007.
Source: Federal Bureau of Investigation.

The range of homicide rates is quite wide in U.S. big cities, from 3.5 per 100,000 in San Jose to over 45 per 100,000 in Detroit. The 2007 New York City rate is the third lowest of the major cities, at 6 per 100,000. But this rank ordering is not as important in judging safety and danger as is the size of the homicide risk. The 2007 New York City rate is within 2.5 killings per 100,000 of the lowest big-city rate in the country. By contrast, New York in 2007 is 39 per 100,000 lower in homicide than Detroit, and less than half the median rate (Chicago's 15.7) for the nine non-New York top ten cities. From the standpoint of death risk, New York in 2007 is much closer to the lowest-rate big cities, than to the cluster of cities in the middle range of current homicide experience—Phoenix, Chicago, Dallas, and Houston.

One clear illustration of the different implications of relative rank versus actual death rate is the contrast between New York's position in 1990 as a matter of ranking. Figure 2.3 shows the homicide rates of the same ten cities profiled in the 2007 homicide analyses.

In 1990, the homicide rate in New York City put it right in the middle of the biggest cities, all but indistinguishable from Los Angeles, Chicago, Philadelphia, and Houston. If New York's homicide rate that year had been 28.1 instead of 30.7, its rank among the top 10 cities would have been fourth lowest, compared to its number three position in 2007. But New York's homicide rate in 1990 was just over 98% of the mean rate that year for Los Angeles, Chicago, Houston, and Philadelphia. Even with general declines in homicide over the 1990s, the four cities closest to New York in 1990 have a mean homicide rate of 17.35 per 100,000 in 2007, about three times the 6 per 100,000 in New York City. So the homicide rate in New York in 2007 is just over one-third the median for major cities in the United States.

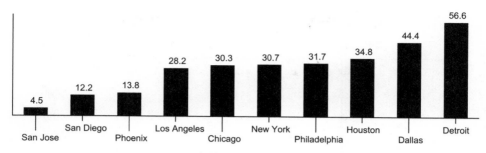

FIGURE 2.3 Homicide Rates in the Ten Largest U.S. Cities, 1990.
Source: Federal Bureau of Investigation.

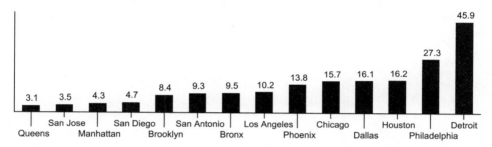

FIGURE 2.4 Homicide Rates for Four Largest Boroughs of New York and Ten Major U.S. Cities, 2007.
Source: Federal Bureau of Investigation.

Another significant comparison involves the major boroughs of New York City, so Figure 2.4 reports the same 11 city homicide rates seen for 2007 in Figure 2.3 but adds the four major boroughs as independent entries, since each of them is big enough to qualify as a major population area, and the previous section documented very different homicide rates in the different boroughs.

Dividing the major segments of the city into separate reporting areas intensifies the concentration of New York at the lower end of the big-city homicide distribution, Queens and Manhattan, the two lowest homicide boroughs, report what would be the lowest and third-lowest major city homicide rates in the United States. Brooklyn and the Bronx have victimization rates under Los Angeles and close to San Antonio.

Table 2.4 reports 2007 rates of the six index felonies other than homicide for New York and the other cities found in the top population categories in either 1990 or 2007. This analysis does not break out the major boroughs of the city because of the lack of big differences reported in the previous section.

Table 2.4 Crime Rates in Major U.S. Cities, 2007.

	Robbery	Rape	Assault	Burglary	Auto Theft	Larceny
New York	265	11	332	254	161	1,403
Los Angeles	348	26	334	507	608	1,506
Chicago	546	NA	617	876	659	2,937
Houston	529	32	555	1,339	897	3,449
Phoenix	321	33	356	1,246	1,353	3,227
Philadelphia	715	67	667	803	774	2,728
Dallas	583	41	429	1,814	1,113	3,850
San Diego	166	24	309	609	1,049	1,845
San Jose	114	23	261	476	686	1,412
San Antonio	186	48	313	1,272	511	4,607
Detroit	764	40	1,440	2,064	2,279	2,430

Source: FBI, Uniform Crime Reports.

For violent crimes, the reported New York City rates are on the lower end of the distribution, usually in the company of smaller big cities. Rape in New York is half or less the rate of other reporting top ten cities, but robbery in New York is significantly higher than in San Jose, San Antonio, and San Diego. But only Los Angeles and Phoenix came close to New York in robbery among the much bigger cities. New York reports half the rate or less of robbery in Houston, Chicago, Dallas, Philadelphia, and Detroit!

Assault rates are bi-modally distributed across the major cities, with no clear pattern by population. New York and Los Angeles are clustered with lower violence cities like San Diego and San Jose as well as San Antonio. Then cities like Chicago, Houston, and Philadelphia have about double the low assault city rate and Dallas falls in between that and the highest rate cities. For robbery and assault, New York City has lower than average reported rates, but it is not clearly separate from the rest of the cities in aggregate risk.

The gap is much wider for property crimes not usually associated with life-threatening violence. To some extent, this reflects lower rates of car ownership and better mass transit. Auto theft in New York City is only one-third the level in the next lowest rate in any big city and less than a quarter of the median rate in the major cities. But the New York burglary rate is also just over half of the next-lowest rate (San Jose) and less than one-third the median rate for all major cities. There is no ecological feature of the city that generates low burglary expectations. Larceny is lowest in New York by a narrow margin and about half of the median rate for other cities in the table, although larceny is not an offense with a reputation for precision in reporting.

Why should New York City in 2007 have half or less the burglary of any other major city but still report robbery rates higher than three major cities and not far removed from other cities like Los Angeles and Phoenix? The answer to this puzzle is *not* to be found in any difference in the pattern of decline from historic levels for robbery and burglary. Chapter 1 showed that robbery rates dropped 84% over the years after 1990, quite close to the burglary rate drop of 86%. Evidently, New York City's historic rate of robbery was much higher relative to rates of burglary. The current robbery rate in New York City is almost level with the burglary rate, while the median ratio of burglaries to robberies in the 11 cities in Table 2.4 is about three burglaries for every robbery.

The current robbery rate in New York City is more than a statistical detail—it is the single most important exception to the profile of the city as quite safe by American urban standards. While assault rates also remain high in New York relative to other crime indicators, robberies more often involve strangers and therefore generate more public anxiety.

There are two further simple measures that provide information on the relative scale of New York crime. One is the 2007 rank of New York against the other ten big cities. New York has the lowest 2007 rate for four of the six offenses, with assault and robbery being the two exceptions. But the better measure of the magnitude of difference is to compare the New York City rate to the median rate for the 11 big cities profiled in Table 2.4.

Figure 2.5 shows the percentage of New York City's rate for each of the six offenses compared to the median for the largest 11 cities including New York.

For two crimes, assault and robbery, the New York rate is not greatly different from the rate reported in other big cities. For three other crimes—rape, burglary, and auto theft—the volume of the offense in New York is a third or less of the median big-city rate. For these crimes (and for homicide as well), the recent crime rate in New York is not merely lower than other larger cities but very much lower. Larceny, a residual crime classification, is something of a contrast. New York's rate is the lowest of

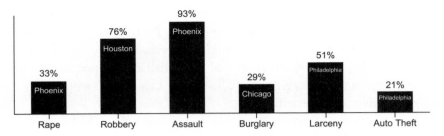

FIGURE 2.5 New York Crime Rate as a Percentage of Median Rate for 11 Largest U.S. Cities, Six Offenses, 2007.
Source: FBI, Uniform Crime Reports.

the big cities but is only half the median rate, the term "only" being justified by the much greater difference between New York and its peers for rape, burglary, and auto theft.

When compared to other large U.S. cities, New York's credentials as a low property crime city are more consistent than its safety profile. Rates of auto theft and burglary are at levels very substantially below normal for major cities. If there is a low crime major metropolis in the United States, the twenty-first-century edition of New York City would seem to qualify. For violent crime, two of the four offenses (homicide and rape) are much lower than average, and only rape is the lowest of all big cities. On the issue of its vulnerability to violent crime, New York is one of the three major cities with violent crime rates that are consistent with credible claims of safety.

The Comparative Demography of Low Violence Cities

It has long been known that rates of lethal violence in the United States are concentrated among disadvantaged minority populations and most starkly among African Americans living in high-risk areas (Zimring and Hawkins 1997, Chap. 5). When comparing rates of homicide in U.S. cities, it may be useful to make such comparisons with due regard to population differences.

Figure 2.6 provides demographic detail for 2007 for New York City and the only two big cities with lower homicide rates that year, San Diego and San Jose. The demographic profile in San Jose and San Diego both have concentrations of two groups with low crime victimization—white

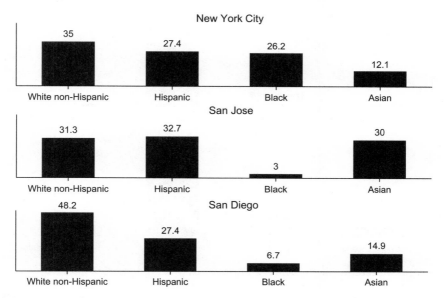

FIGURE 2.6 Population by Race and Ethnicity, Three Low Crime Cities, 2007.
Source: Census Bureau American Community Survey (2007).

non-Hispanics and Asians are over 60%. Each city has about the same concentration of Hispanics as New York, but far smaller percentages of Black residents: 3% and 6.7% compared to 26.2%.

Figure 2.7 shows the substantial differences in homicide risk for different population groups in the same city, by constructing rates per 100,000 residents in the city for the four main population groups found in the supplemental homicide reports for New York City in 2007, and provides parallel data for San Diego in the same year. (San Jose is excluded from this comparison with a total Black population under 30,000.)

In each city, there is a similar hierarchy of homicide risk, with Black victimization the highest and Hispanic rates the second highest. White non-Hispanic and Asian/Pacific Islander rates are together at the low end of the distribution and very close to each other.

There are two ways in which this kind of specific homicide rate data can inform an arithmetic of intercity comparison. The first is simply to compare the victimization rates for each group in San Diego and New York. For all four groups, the risks of homicide are lower in New York than in San Diego, with margin exceeding two to one for the two low risk groups and just under a 40% advantage for the Black and Hispanic populations.

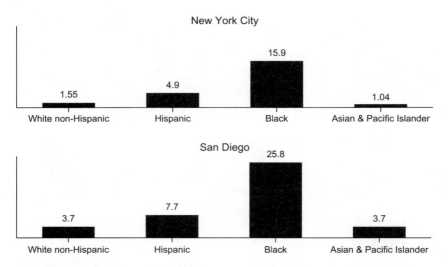

FIGURE 2.7 Homicide Rates per 100,000 for New York Ethnic Groups, 2007.
Source: Federal Bureau of Investigation, Criminal Justice Information Services Division, *Supplementary Homicide Report* (2007).

The second method uses a more complicated arithmetic to estimate the aggregate intercity gap. If one were to project the San Diego specific homicide risks during 2007 on the New York City population distribution, the use of San Diego's specific risks on New York City's population would produce an increase from 480 to 821 total deaths, or a homicide volume that is 73% greater than New York's actual rate that year. In that sense, New York's actual rate is much lower than San Diego's when population composition is taken into account. While the consistency of New York's advantage seems reliable, the margin of error in projecting a specific difference in homicide is not small. Table 2.5 shows the arithmetic.

The largest percentage increases in victimization happen in the low-risk Asian and white non-Hispanic populations, with the white non-Hispanic rate more than doubling from 44 actual killings to 107 projected killings. But the biggest increase in homicide volume is for the higher risk Black and Hispanic populations.

What this adds to the comparison with other U.S. cities is the fact that New York's very low rates have happened in a setting of populations that usually have higher victimizations. This makes a remarkable statistical achievement even more remarkable when considered in demographic perspective.

Table 2.5 **Crime Volumes and Rates Compared, San Diego and New York City, 2007.**

	New York City Homicides	New York City Homicides with San Diego Group Specific Rate	Increase/Decrease
White non-Hispanic	44	107	63
Hispanic	111	175	64
Black	315	503	188
Asian/Pacific Islander	10	36	26
Total	480	821	341

Source: U.S. Bureau of the Census (population); Federal Bureau of Investigation (reported crime).

D. Major Cities in other Nations

One other obvious strategy of comparison for New York City is with the crime experiences of major cities located in other nations, but differences in crime definition and reportage often complicate the task of international crime statistical comparisons and limit the value of the enterprise.

Table 2.6 begins the comparison by contrasting 2007 data for New York City with information from Statistics Canada for that nation's two largest cities, Toronto and Montréal. The Canadian data is collected for areas in each locale somewhat larger than the city limits reported for New York and other city police jurisdictions. If these boundary issues have any impact on rate comparisons, they would tend to lower the Canadian crime rates by including larger sections of less citified areas.

Comparative data were available for only four of what we call "index" offenses. Homicide, robbery, and auto theft were comparable as reported. For burglary, the Canadian data involves three different categories of breaking and entering (residence, business, and other) that I aggregated into a single burglary category. Canada doesn't report its sex crimes under the rape heading but instead has two aggravated forms of sexual assault and one general sex assault category broader than the Uniform Crime Report rape (see Zimring 2006 at pp. 110–111). The Canadian

Table 2.6 Crime Patterns in New York City, Toronto, and Montréal, 2007; Rate per 100,000.

	Homicide	Robbery	Burglary	Auto Theft
New York	6.0	265	254	161
Toronto	2.01	113	362 ·	279
Montréal	1.58	133	755	601

Source: Federal Bureau of Investigation (New York); Statistics Canada (Toronto and Montréal).

system also divides larceny and assault in ways that U.S. crime statistics do not (Zimring 2006 at pp. 112–113; id. at pp. 115–116).

The contrast between New York City and its two Canadian cousins is quite striking. For auto theft and burglary, the rate of reported offenses in New York City is substantially lower than Toronto and Montréal. For auto theft, the New York rate is slightly more than one-fourth that of Montréal and just over half the rate in Toronto. Toronto has a burglary rate 40% higher than does New York City, while burglary in Montréal is three times higher than New York. But the robbery rate in New York City is twice that in Toronto and two and one-half times that found in Montréal. For homicide, New York reports three times the rate of Toronto and four times the level reported in Montréal.

The big distinction here is between crime and violence. For non-violent property crimes like auto theft and burglary, New York City has much lower rates of offending. For the one property crime infused with the threat of bodily harm—robbery—the rate in New York is substantially higher than north of the border, and the difference in homicide rate is a factor of three or more.

Because property crimes are far more frequent than serious violence, the data in Table 2.6 indicate that crime of all kinds in New York City is probably much lower than in Toronto and Montréal.

Table 2.7 extends the geographic foundation of the comparison beyond North America, adding London, Sydney, and Tokyo to the pattern.

The comparison between New York and London and Sydney is quite close to the pattern found with Montréal and Toronto, with New York displaying much lower rates of burglary, rape, and auto theft and much higher rates of homicide. But both London and Sydney report rates of rape and burglary three to five times higher than New York City. London also reports higher rates of robbery than New York in 2007, while Sydney's robbery is 40% lower than New York. Still, the dominant contrast with

Table 2.7 Crime Patterns in New York City, London, Sydney, and Tokyo, 2007; Rate per 100,000.

	Homicide	Rape	Robbery	Burglary	Auto Theft
New York	6.0	10.6	265	254	161
London	2.2	30.7	610	1,290	501
Sydney*	1.5	51.4	159	1,008	461
Tokyo	1.0	1.8	4.7	137	12

*2006

Source: http://maps.met.police.uk/tables.htm (London); http://www.bocsar.nsw.gov.au/lawlink/bocsar/ll_bocsar.nsf/pages/bocsar_lga_region (Sydney); http://www.npa.go.jp/english/seisaku5/20081008.pdf (Tokyo; Table 5, p. 68); U.S. Department of Justice, FBI (New York).

London and Sydney is one where New York's recent crime rates are lower but its rate of lethal violence is much higher.

The contrast with Tokyo is more dramatic, because rates of both lethal violence and most common crime are so much lower in Tokyo. Homicide in Tokyo is one-sixth the current New York rate on this report but even lower on some other accounts (see Johnson 2006), but Tokyo rates of rape, robbery, and auto theft are vastly lower than the other cities. Just as rape in New York is only one-fifth the rate estimated for Sydney, rape in Tokyo is only one-fifth of the New York level. Robbery is one-fiftieth the New York rate, and even auto theft in Tokyo is less than one-tenth the tiny remaining New York rate. Only burglary, where the Tokyo rate is half the New York City rate, produces any indication of similarity of scale with Western cities. In most respects, Tokyo is almost an order of magnitude lower in rates of crime and violence than current New York City conditions. This difference in scale between Tokyo and the other cities is a powerful reminder that different cultural conditions do produce major impacts on crime and violence, and other Asian cities also report very low rates of lethal violence (Zimring, Fagan, and Johnson 2010).

The Lessons of Three-Way Comparison

When the current conditions in New York City are compared to the earlier crime profile of the city, a dramatic reduction in all forms of major crime is evident, with serious violence declining just as fast as property crime, and with non-homicide crime rates that are rather similar in boroughs of the city with very different demographic profiles.

When New York's current conditions are compared to other large U.S. cities, the city's level of property crime is much lower than major city averages—burglary, auto theft, and larceny are as low or lower in New York City as in any major American metropolis. Homicide and robbery rates are quite low when compared to the biggest cities in the United States, and homicide rates are probably the lowest of all major cities when the demographic profile of New York's population is taken into account.

When the current conditions in New York City are compared to major cities in the Western developed world, the important contrast is between crime rates generally and life-threatening violence. Rates of burglary and auto theft are much lower in New York than in London or Toronto or Sydney. For homicide, however, even with its huge declines the city of New York has much higher rates than other big Western cities.

And a statistical comparison with Tokyo shows that while levels of crime and violence in New York are low by American standards, they still tower over Japan's largest city.

New York has become a safe city by American standards and a very low crime city when compared with other leading cities in Western nations. The amount of lethal violence that remains even after the huge New York declines still places it well above metropolitan norms for the rest of the Western world. And Tokyo remains as far removed on the low side from New York's current rates of crime and violence as New York now is separated from its bad old days.

As long as the dominant standard of comparison in New York City's crime profile is the early 1990s, the city will seem quite safe whether the topic is property crime or lethal violence. But the passage of time changes expectations, and the further removed New York becomes from its high crime history, the less important will be the major declines of the 1990s. As of 2011, there are no signs of real public anxiety or discontent with levels of public safety, but the novelty of the relatively low crime environment has passed. New Yorkers take their low crime environment for granted.

When the focus shifts from historical patterns to New York's standing in comparison with other major cities in the United States, there is little statistical basis to disturb the civic complacency of New Yorkers. The current rates of both property crime and lethal violence are at the low end of the distribution of crime rates in major American cities. The only exception to the pattern of consistent New York superiority is for rates of reported robbery, where even the 84% decline of the past two decades had not erased a long-standing concentration of robbery in New York crime.

The shift from domestic to foreign cities as the basis for comparison produces a more complicated pattern. New York City remains a very low crime setting when compared to major cities in the West, but lethal violence is much lower in major cities throughout the developed world. And the crime profile in Tokyo is so much lower than for major Western cities that it requires a different statistical scale.

PART TWO

In Search of the New York Difference

The goal of the analysis in the next three chapters is one important step short of what most observers would want to know about the causes of New York City's crime decline. Ideally, when crime drops by four-fifths in a major city, the goal would be to find what caused the entire drop. But the timing of the crime decline in New York City makes a comprehensive explanation of the city's total crime decline intractably difficult. The first ten years of New York's decline happened during a dramatic nationwide drop in crime, a drop that is only partly explained by factors such as the changing age structure of the population, general prosperity, and increases in incarceration. This national trend—which lasted until 2000 and was slightly less than half the magnitude of New York City's decline—is largely unexplained in its size and timing, which makes it highly unlikely that the same level of decline during the same years would be easier to explain in New York City.

The strategy that I adopt here is an attempt to explain the difference between New York and the general trend, to focus on the larger drops during the 1990s and the longer decline period in the city, and to link this distinctive New York drop to other facets of social and governmental life in the city that also were not common to the rest of the country. The search is for distinctive changes in the city that fit the timing and magnitude of the exceptional New York crime decline. Even the best result from this type of analysis will explain a 40% crime drop rather than the 80% entirety that was charted in Chapters 1 and 2. But this half-a-loaf approach will not bog down in attempting, yet again, to find causes for trends that have eluded explanations when national-level data were examined. How might observations in one city resolve these national level uncertainties? If that sort of breakthrough is implausible, the prudent course is to put the national pattern to one side and explore the distinctive 18-year city level decline and the factors that might explain this New York difference.

The three chapters in this part of the book are organized as an increasingly specific process of elimination of potential explanations of New York

City's special success in crime reduction. Chapter 3 is a wide-ranging survey of population, social, and economic factors thought to influence crime trends, which shows that most of the usual predictors of crime risk didn't change in New York in ways that would help to explain the additional crime decline. Chapter 4 then examines the two predominant theories of crime risk in the 1990s: the expansion of high-risk youth and the high rates of drug sales and use. These pessimistic indicators didn't change much but also didn't produce the criminogenic future that was expected. Chapter 5 examines the major changes in police force levels, organization, and tactics, which are the only plausible changes in New York City available to help explain the length and the extra size of the city's crime decline.

Chapter 3

Continuity and Change in New York City

A. A Tale of Two Precincts

THE BASIC QUESTION addressed in this chapter is whether there have been distinctive and visible changes in New York City that are likely explanations for the city's record-setting crime decline. This introductory section provides a context for thinking about the statistical materials that follow by contrasting two police districts in Manhattan where crime dropped over the 19 years after 1990. For reasons that will soon be apparent, sorting out the causes in one of the precincts is almost impossible.

The first precinct that illustrates the issues involved in determining the causes of declining crime is the 14th Precinct in Manhattan, "Midtown South," the site of the most famous urban renewal effort of the era in New York City or anywhere else.

The "before" and "after" for this major surgery is in the area surrounding Times Square on 42nd Street. The redevelopment was, as usual, a two-part process, removing high-risk and undesirable facilities and replacing them with upscale entertainment and office facilities.

A 1997 description in a Dallas newspaper provides a not-untypical set of contrasting nouns and adjectives:

> In all, nearly $2 billion worth of investment on what was until recently one of the sleaziest and most violent streets in Manhattan. No more peep shows, mud wrestling or three-card monte. Triple X has given way to Triple G in the form of family musicals such as *King David* and *The Lion King*. (Dillion 1997)

Two years later, a local observer emphasized the changing populations generated by the Times Square transformation:

> Just a short while ago, it was sleazy, blighted and crime-ridden; today it is all but crime free, it has driven out the prostitutes and

pornographers who made it seedy, it bustles with tourists day and night, and world-spanning corporations such as AMC, Disney and Viacom prosper within it. (Stern 1999)

While Mr. Stern's 1999 description of 42nd Street as "all but crime free" may have stretched matters a bit, there is no doubt that crime rates around 42nd Street did decline.

The Midtown South 14th Precinct reported eight homicides in 1990 and only two in 2009, a 75% drop. The robbery story was even more impressive—there were 4,227 robberies in 1990 and 220 in 2009, a 95% drop in robbery volume on stable population numbers. There is some complexity involved in deciding the right population base to use in transforming these crime volumes into crime rates because so many more people spent time on 42nd Street than resided there. Using the census numbers for resident population, the robbery rate in 1990 would be 24,838 per 100,000 residents, a one in four robbery rate for a prosperous population that was 62% white non-Hispanic. As bad as crime was in 1990, that risk estimate is not a plausible one. The police department generated a rate based on the area's population during business hours, and the robbery rate based on that estimate was 7,404 per 100,000 in 1990, a rate less than 30% of the one in four resident-based rate, but still very high by the big-city standard of the era. The rate drop using business hour population from 1990 to 2009 is still a 95% drop, but the rate estimated for 2009 is 395.1 per 100,000, higher than the Manhattan and citywide averages posted for 2009 and discussed in Part I. The 14th Precinct's homicide rates dropped much less than the robbery rate, but that rate was lower to begin with. The 74% homicide drop based on residents was from 47 to 12.1 per 100,000 and based on business hours population it dropped from 14 to 3.6 per 100,000. So the business hours rate was lower than the citywide average (which had more risk exposure than simply business hours) but the homicide decline was also less than the city average.

What were the causes of this cascade of happy crime news on 42nd Street? Too many to mention and far too many to sort through with any hope of estimating the specific contribution of particular changes without all the others. Driving "out the prostitutes and pornographers" who made 42nd Street sleazy drove out their customers as well, a major influence on the supply of very attractive robbery targets and therefore also probably the number of predatory robbers looking for easy marks. "No more peep shows, mud wrestling or three-card monte" makes this small part of the city much less a magnet for the thirsty and thrill-seeking populations always at highest risk as both crime victims and offenders. When "Triple X has given way to Triple G in the form of family musicals," the population and character of the area has been altered profoundly.

If one were looking for a place to test the effect of specific new tactics in policing or an experimental drug court program on urban crime, trying to use crime data from before and after the 42nd Street makeover to measure the program's effect would be a sure path to disaster. Of course, 42nd Street had much less crime in 2009; it is a fundamentally different place. There were so many different changes in 42nd Street that passing out credit for crime prevention to any one of the multitude of physical, economic and human usage changes is impossible.

From 42nd Street to Canal Street

Canal Street in lower Manhattan never had either the fame or the notoriety of 42nd Street, but is not without a unique urban character and some fame. Canal Street is the longtime home of Manhattan's Chinatown district and its Little Italy. Canal Street is probably the Western world's capital of shops and street vendors selling $5 watches, cut-rate ladies' purses, and electronic equipment with impressive labels but dubious provenance.

No urban area stands still as the decades pass, but Canal Street has not changed dramatically since 1990 in its physical dimensions, buildings, commerce, demography, or the economic fortunes of its residents. It was never a rich neighborhood and isn't getting richer. A year 2000 estimate has 40% of its children under the poverty line and inflation-adjusted household income went down slightly during the 1990s (Asian American Federation 2004). Always an Asian majority district, the percentage Asian in the area crept up from 65% in 1990 to 74% in 2000, with the majority of the non-Asian decline in non-Hispanic whites. As the area's Chinatown increased incrementally, the area and population of the adjacent Little Italy neighborhood receded.

While the physical and demographic changes along Canal Street were modest, the changes in the area's reported crime were more than substantial. Homicide rates per 100,000 residents in the 5th Precinct area, which covers Canal Street, was 29 per 100,000 in 1990, equal to the citywide rate that year. In 2009, there was one homicide reported by the police in the 5th Precinct, a 95% reduction to a rate of 1.5 per 100,000 residents. Robbery volume went from 983 incidents to 125, the resident population robbery rate dropped from 1,501 per 100,000 to 181 per 100,000, a slightly bigger drop than the citywide average and a robbery rate in 2009 lower than the city's most recent average. What the Canal Street story represents is a contrast between consistency and stability in most social and demographic indicators and huge changes in crime levels. With that much consistency in structural characteristics, any large changes that can be identified in social or law enforcement or population features will stand as much more plausible candidates as causes of the big crime decline.

The fundamental issue that this chapter's statistical profiles address is whether and to what extent New York City has experienced substantial structural and economic changes—a 42nd Street story that complicates and obscures our ability to identify the particular causes of New York's larger than usual crime drop. How much of the city has been transformed from "Triple X" to "Triple G" and by what means? The bulk of the chapter will march through various data sets to test continuity or structural change in the city over two decades. A concluding section will summarize my view of the meaning of this empirical montage. My bottom line is a mixed verdict. One of New York's four biggest boroughs—Manhattan—showed big social changes in the period after 1990 that could help explain a major crime drop. The other three major boroughs—Queens, Brooklyn, and the Bronx—were not transformed in similar fashion.

Population Trends

During the 18 years of New York's crime decline, the nation's largest city grew modestly, from 7.3 million in 1990 to 8.4 million in 2009. This expansion of just over a million continued New York's status as more than twice as large as any other U.S. city. Table 3.1 compares population trends in the five largest U.S. cities from 1990 to 2009.

The 15% growth in New York is quite close to the pattern of Los Angeles, and these two are well under the expansion of Sun Belt metropolis Houston. But the expansion in New York is a sharp contrast to the 6.3% decline in its regional neighbor, Philadelphia.

Table 3.2 mixes race and ethnicity to provide a breakdown of the major population groups in the city in 1990. There is some overlap between one of the "race" groups (Black) and the Hispanic ethnic category, which pushes the percentages just over 100%. From the standpoint of homicide risk, the 1990 population of the city is divided between two groups with lower than average risks (Asian and non-Hispanic whites) and two groups

Table 3.1 Population Trends in the Five Largest U.S. Cities, 1990–2009.

	1990 (in millions)	2009 (in millions)	Difference	Percentage Change
New York	7.3	8.4	1.1	15.1%
Los Angeles	3.5	3.8	0.3	8.6%
Chicago	2.8	2.8	0	0.0%
Houston	1.6	2.3	0.7	43.8%
Philadelphia	1.6	1.5	-0.1	-6.3%

* Population numbers are rounded to the nearest hundred thousand.
Source: U.S. Bureau of the Census.

Table 3.2 Major Population Groups in New York City, 1990.

	Percentage
Non-Hispanic White	43.2%
Black	28.7%
Hispanic	24.4%
Asian	7.0%

Source: U.S. Bureau of the Census.

with higher risks (Black and Hispanic), with the Black rates higher than any other group in homicide risk.

Table 3.3 shows the changes in numbers and percentage for the same groups profiled in the previous table. The aggregate racial/ethnic redistribution of the city's population should not play a major role in explaining the crime decline. There is a decline in both the number and population percentage of lower risk non-Hispanic whites and a sharp increase in the lower risk Asian population. The population of Blacks is stable at 2.1 million, but their proportion of the city's population drops from 28% to 24% of the city, while the new population of the city is evenly divided between Asians and Hispanics. While the percentage of higher victimization groups goes up slightly, the mix of minorities has a larger proportion of the somewhat lower victimization group. Ethnic and racial population redistribution looks like a break-even proposition for the vulnerability of groups to crime and violence.

Table 3.3 Changes in Population in New York City, 1990 and 2007, by Race and Ethnicity.

	1990 Population (millions)	Percentage (1990)	2007 Population (millions)	Percentage (2007)
Non-Hispanic White	3.2	42.1%	2.9	33.0%
Black	2.1	27.6%	2.1	23.9%
Hispanic	1.8	23.7%	2.3	27.0%
Asian	0.5	6.6%	0.97	11.8%

Source: U.S. Bureau of the Census.

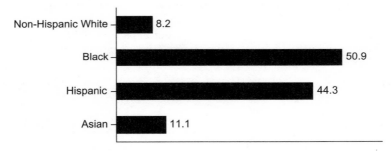

FIGURE 3.1 Reported Homicide Victimization by Race and Ethnic Groups, New York City, 1990 (per 100,000).
Source: New York City Department of Health; 42 other and unclassified cases omitted.

Figure 3.1 provides data from the homicide section of the 1990 vital statistics for New York City to show the justification for division of the major population groups into "high" and "low" risk categories. The gap between high-risk and low-risk groups in 1990 is unambiguous, with the reported Hispanic rate four times the level reported for the next highest victim group.

If we take the 1990 homicide distribution and assume the same rate for each group with its 2007 population, we project a total of *2,411*, an increase from the homicide volume of 1990, but a homicide rate per 100,000 almost exactly equal to the 30 per 100,000 of the earlier year.

Figure 3.2 compares the projected and actual homicide volumes for the city in 2007. Using this method of estimation, the population changes in the city account for none of its homicide decline.

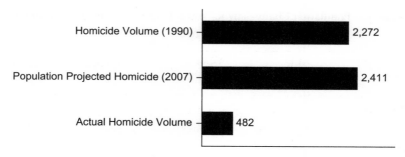

FIGURE 3.2 Projected and Actual Homicide Volume Using Population Changes from 1990 to 2007.
Source: Bureau of Census (population); Vital Statistics (Homicide by Race and Ethnicity, 1990).

There is a second way of testing the impact of population redistribution on crime rates in New York, and that is to examine the different population changes by borough and the impact if any on crime trends. Table 3.4 shows the different patterns by race and ethnicity of Manhattan, the Bronx, Brooklyn, and Queens for the period 1990–2007. The most direct way to test the impact of population changes on crime trends in the 17 years is to see whether those boroughs with the biggest reduction in risk also had the largest crime declines over the period since 1990. A population at risk change analysis would predict that Manhattan would have the best record over time followed by Brooklyn, Queens and, in last place, the Bronx. Figure 3.3 compares 19-year crime trends from the city police for the four major boroughs.

The one clear victory for demographic projection is that crime drops in Manhattan are larger than those in the other major boroughs for six of the seven crime categories. But only in the homicide assault and larceny data is there substantial difference between the four boroughs in the extent of 19-year decline. For burglaries, the range of decline is from 84% to 89%, with the highest drop 6% above the lowest, and for robbery the range is from 80% to 87%. The range of decline for auto theft varies only from 91% to 95%. These three crimes show so much similarity in decline that any interborough differences must play a tiny role in explanation. For homicide, the demographic prediction of a poor showing for the Bronx is the reverse of the actual pattern—the Bronx and Manhattan are very close in their declines and far ahead of the drops in Brooklyn and Queens.

Table 3.4 Population Changes by Race and Ethnicity, Four Major Boroughs, 1990–2007.

	1990	2007	Difference	Percentage Change
Manhattan				
Non-Hispanic White	727,000	791,000	64,000	8.1%
Black	327,000	252,000	-75,000	-29.8%
Hispanic	387,000	401,000	14,000	3.5%
Asian	111,000	175,000	64,000	36.6%
High Risk (%)	48	40	-8	
Queens				
Non-Hispanic White	938,000	696,000	-242,000	-34.7%
Black	423,000	438,000	15,000	3.4%
Hispanic	381,000	601,000	220,000	36%
Asian	238,000	487,000	249,000	51.1%
High Risk (%)	41	45	4	
Brooklyn				
Non-Hispanic White	923,000	919,000	-4,000	-0.4%
Black	872,000	864,000	8,000	-1.0%
Hispanic	462,000	494,000	32,000	6.5%
Asian	111,000	227,000	116,000	51.1%
High Risk (%)	58	55	-3	
Bronx				
Non-Hispanic White	273,000	175,000	-98,000	-56.9%
Black	449,000	459,000	10,000	2.2%
Hispanic	523,000	702,000	179,000	25.5%
Asian	36,000	48,000	12,000	25.0%
High Risk (%)	80	85	5	

Source: U.S. Bureau of the Census.

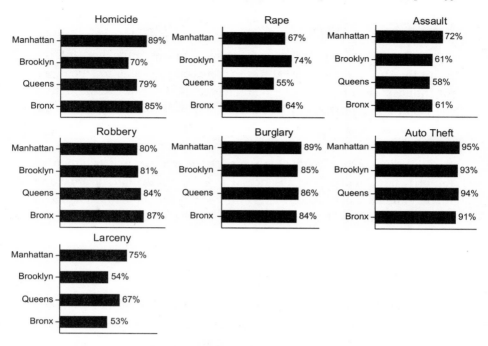

FIGURE 3.3 Crime Rate Declines by Borough, 1990–2009.
Source: New York City Police Department.

The four major boroughs show a wide variety of different population patterns, and the size and consistency of the decline in crime suggests that a redistribution of the city's population is not a major reason for the size of the crime decline. The failure of changes in borough populations to predict the relative positions of three of the four boroughs even in homicide is one more indication that population redistribution has played a minor role in New York City's recent adventures. The population changes in the city might support a projection of some increase in city homicide because of the historically high rate of homicide for non–Puerto Rican Hispanics, but these projections are just as weak as other exercises in assuming fixed rates of either offenses or victimization for minorities in dynamic social situations. By the mid-1990s, observers were noticing that some first-generation Hispanic immigrants had low rates of violence and criminal activity (Sampson 1996) so that the same social changes that were producing large increases in the city's Hispanic population may have been undermining the assumptions of fixed high victimization and criminal propensities.

The most prudent conclusion on present evidence is that changes in population composition played no important role in the citywide crime decline and certainly had no impact in the crime decline in three of the four major boroughs. Crime went down quite dramatically in places where high-risk minority populations were stable (Queens, Brooklyn, and the Bronx for African Americans) and even increasing (Queens and the Bronx for Latinos). The Bronx is close to Manhattan in homicide decline, and all the major boroughs have similar drops for robbery and burglary. So the detailed analysis of the borough-to-borough differences proves its value as a test of the predictive power of relocation of minorities in explaining the crime decline. Only Manhattan experienced a clear redistribution of minority populations. The absence of a wider Manhattan advantage in robbery and burglary suggests a very limited role for population change in the dynamics of the New York City decline.

Immigration and Crime Risk

One aspect of population composition that may modify the rates of crime associated with ethnic and racial groups is how recently the members of the group have arrived in the United States. The first generation of an immigration into a developed nation is a self-selected group with the capacity and ambition to make a transition to a new country, and typically this first generation has lower rates of arrest and other measures of criminal activity than other generations of the same group (see Bucerius 2010). The arrival of a significant number of new immigrants was one feature of New York City in the mid-1990s that was suggested as a reason for New York City's encouraging crime trends (Sampson 1996). Might this be an important feature of the New York City difference?

The best measure of the impact of a phenomenon associated with first-generation immigrants is the percentage of a city population that is listed by the census as "foreign born." Figure 3.4 provides this data for New York City for census years after 1980 and for 2006–2008 from the American Community Survey. For the estimates in the figure, persons who report being from Puerto Rico are not counted as "foreign born."

The percentage of the city's population classified as foreign born was high throughout the period but grew from a quarter to over a third of the city total. The period of the city's crime decline had an uneven pattern of foreign-born population expansion. The 1990s showed the largest growth of foreign born, up 8% compared to a 4% growth rate in the 1980s. But the most recent years of the crime decline era had the smallest increase, 1%

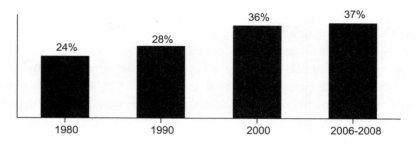

FIGURE 3.4 Percentage of New York City Residents Classified as "Foreign Born." *Source:* U.S. Census; American Community Survey.

spread over seven years. Both the growth and the current share of foreign born in New York City are far higher than the national average (around 10.4% in 2000) but typical of the bigger gateway cities such as Los Angeles, Boston, and Miami. And the rate of growth in Los Angeles during the 1980s (from 27% to 38%) was substantially higher than New York City in the 1990s.

The direct impact of increases in a first-generation population on crime rates should be to reduce the volume of crime associated with foreign-born persons, but by how much? Much of this depends on the age structure of the population and also on the crime rate that would be expected from persons resembling the immigrants who were not foreign born. The two ethnic groups most prominently found in New York City immigrants are Asian and Latino. The rates of criminal offending and victimization associated with New York's Asian population is quite low, as Chapter 1 showed. While an increase in the proportion of the city's population that is Asian would be expected to reduce crime levels, the added reduction associated with a foreign-born cohort of Asians would be rather small, because the expected offense rate for the group as a whole is so low.

For the Hispanic population, their traditional status as a relatively high-risk group for victimization and offending means that the marginal difference between foreign-born and native-born city residents in crime and violence may be greater. If immigrant status cuts crime expectancy in half, that will have a much larger citywide impact for populations at higher general risk. The larger protective effect would also extend to groups that count in the population surveys as Black, such as Jamaican and Haitian immigrants.

The same kind of ironic leverage exists when considering the age structure of an immigrant population when projecting its impact on crime. Very old and very young populations are low risk of crime involvement, so any net reduction if their age-specific rate is lower will have modest impact on aggregate crime volume. But a concentration of lower risk immigrants in high-risk age groups (18–24, 25–29) will produce much more crime avoided.

Table 3.5 disaggregates the growth in New York City's foreign born by dividing the foreign-born populations into Hispanic and non-Hispanic segments for all age groups and then also reports Hispanic and non-Hispanic foreign born in the high arrest 18–24 age group.

The first surprise reported in the table is that virtually all of the growth in New York City's foreign-born population during the years after 1990 was in non-Hispanic populations, despite the fact that the Hispanic origin share of the general population did increase during the period after 1990. So whatever protective impact first-generation immigration status confers on a foreign-born group is concentrated in populations that were already very low risk even when native born. So the expected crime rates from Asian populations are so low that the marginal savings that accrue because of even smaller first-generation criminality are modest. And the savings are further minimized by the age structure of the foreign born populations. Only 7% of the non-Hispanic foreign born are in the high arrest 18–24 age group. The percentage of foreign-born Hispanics in the 18–24 category is larger in 2006–2008, 10.6%, but the volume of foreign-born young Hispanics is actually slightly smaller in 2008 than it was in 1990.

Table 3.6 completes the disaggregation of trends in foreign-born populations by dividing the non-Hispanic foreign-born populations by race into

Table 3.5 Foreign Born New York Residents by Age and Hispanic Origin.

	1990	2000	Percentage Change	2006–2008	Percentage Change	18 Year Percentage Change
All Ages Non-Hispanic	1,416,987	2,019,799	+42.5	2,143,445	+6.1	+22.3
All Ages Hispanic	976,607	900,878	-7.8%	961,815	+6.8	-1.5
18–24 Non-Hispanic	124,022	179,117	+44.2	151,673	-15.3	+22.3
18–24 Hispanic	101,702	116,470	+14.5	102,196	-12.3	-.5

Source: U.S. Bureau of the Census.

Table 3.6 Trends in New York Population of Non-Hispanic Foreign Born.

All Ages

	1990	2000	2006–2008*	1990–2000 Percentage Change	2000–2008 Percentage Change	1990–2008 Percentage Change
Black	452,781	563,961	636,610	25%	13%	41%
Non-Black	1,046,914	1,455,832	1,506,835	39%	4%	44%
Total	1,499,695	2,019,793	2,143,445	35%	6%	43%

Non-Hispanic Foreign Born, Ages 15–24

	1990	2000	2006–2008*	1990–2000 Percentage Change	2000–2008 Percentage Change	1990–2008 Percentage Change
Black	51,029	54,446	52,089	7%	-4%	2%
Non-Black	81,146	124,671	99,584	54%	-20%	23%
Total	132,175	179,117	151,673	36%	-15%	15%

Source: Info Share: Public Use Micro-Sample: Bureau of the Census, U.S. Department of Commerce and American Community Survey, Census Bureau, U.S. Commerce Department.

* American Community Survey 2006–2008 Average

** Foreign-born does NOT include Puerto Rico and outlying U.S. areas or the 1990 "not specified" category.

Black and all other categories, to fit the earlier analysis that separated high-risk populations by color and Hispanic origin.

While the Black proportion of all ages foreign born are less than one-third of the total group in both 1990 and 2008, there is still a substantial 18-year increase in the population of 184,000. In the highest risk age group of 18–24, however, there was never significant growth over the period. The number of foreign-born young adults 18–24 in New York City expands by 2%—less than 1,000 of the 184,000 foreign-born Black residents added to the city's population are in this most significant group.

The direct effects of foreign-born populations having lower arrest propensities are reduced by both the age structure of New York's immigrants and by the concentration of the foreign born in ethnic groups with low crime rates whether or not they are recent arrivals. There was little or no direct impact on the City's concentrations of high-risk young persons as a result of the 1990s increase in immigration.

So the immigration data doesn't create any major shifts in the risk profile of the city's changing populations. The increase in low-risk Asian populations is good crime news, but their foreign-born status doesn't make a big dent in city crime because native-born Asian populations aren't high crime risks either. If there had been a substantial expansion of foreign-born Black and Hispanic young adults in the crime decline era, then the foreign-born cohort would be a larger part of the explanation for why this historically high-rate population expanded but its crime rate fell. But the absence of any sustained net growth in foreign-born Black and Hispanic young adults leaves this mystery unresolved. At best, the protective effect of foreign birth helps explain why the expansion in higher risk ethnic groups didn't increase the volume of New York crime. But the particular demography of New York City's post-1990 immigration isn't a clear explanation of a major crime drop.

All of the previous analysis deals with the direct effects of new immigrant populations on crime commission and arrest rates. It is still possible that the neighborhoods settled by a critical mass of foreign-born urban citizens generate environments that produce fewer crimes by their neighbors or passersby. Certainly immigrants in the 1990s could have saturated some neighborhoods. How this creates less crime-friendly environments—greater precautions, higher levels of observation, or less public presence—has not yet been specified. It would be good to have statistical and ethnographic studies of the more subtle ways that foreign-born arrivals affect urban micro-environments.

But the direct impact of even the large immigrations of the 1990s on expected levels of crime are far from obvious.

Economic Indicators

New York City is a very large, complex, and heterogeneous place where any sort of economic analysis based on aggregate statistics is hazardous. The city is the financial capital of the developed world and probably houses the largest collection of wealth on the planet. It also contains the largest concentration of poor persons of any geographic area its size in the United States. In such circumstances, the averaging of extreme values is singularly unhelpful in predicting the welfare and opportunities of working class and marginal populations.

This section examines economic trends in New York City with a special focus on the opportunities and environments that might plausibly influence the rates of offenses usually called street crime. For these purposes, the survey of trends in incomes, employment, and opportunities will pay special attention to lower rungs on the economic ladder, where most of the offenders and victims of common crimes reside. After the introduction of general data on income, the focus will turn to measures of economic activity at entry level, to unemployment rates and income trends at the lower end of the income distribution. I will also again disaggregate the city to see if the different economic trends in the four major boroughs might help test the impact of different economic conditions on crime trends in the city.

Figure 3.5 provides statistics on the trend in per capita income in New York City from 1989 to 2005–2007. The income levels have been adjusted

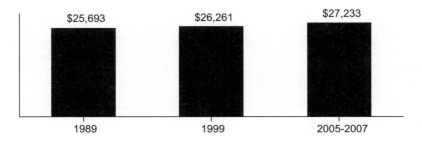

FIGURE 3.5 Inflation Adjusted Per Capita Income of New York Residents, 1989, 1999, and 2005–2007.
Source: U.S. Department of Labor, Bureau of Labor.

so that all earlier income levels have been adjusted upward in "constant 2005 dollars" to control for changes due to inflation.

The trend over the 18 years is modest but encouraging, with per capita income controlling for inflation up 6.2%, and with 60% of that growth coming in the years after 1999. In the aggregate, this expansion is much better than national averages. But it is also an object lesson in the dangers of New York City aggregations. Table 3.7 provides a breakdown of trends in per capita income in the four major boroughs—each big enough to be one of the seven largest cities in the United States.

The data in Table 3.7 show that Manhattan was always an extremely prosperous part of the complex and has also had sharply different trends from its urban neighbors. Manhattan starts with a per capita income well over twice the average of the other boroughs and then jumps 21% in inflation-adjusted dollars over the 18 years covered in the analysis. Brooklyn is the only other part of the four major clusters with any growth at all—a 4.6% increase, almost 90% of which came after 1999. For the first 10 years of the period (and 8 years of the crime decline), Brooklyn incomes were flat. But that was a better outcome than per capita income in Queens and the Bronx, both of which experienced substantial declines during the 1989–2007 period in inflation-adjusted incomes in the 6% to 7% range. If these were different cities, they would appear to have had very different economic trends from Manhattan over this period.

Should they be treated, criminologically, as different cities to study the impact of economic conditions on crime rates? The answer is probably no, and the reason is that the economies of the city are integrated in functionally important ways. Persons who live in the Bronx are a subway ride from

Table 3.7 Per Capita Income in Four Boroughs of New York City, in Constant Dollars.

	1989	1999	2005–2007	Percentage Change
Manhattan	$46,530	$53,223	$56,310	21.0%
Queens	$25,631	$23,835	$23,841	-7%
Brooklyn	$20,688	$20,801	$21,631	4.6%
Bronx	$17,593	$17,303	$16,496	-6.2%

Source: U.S. Bureau of Labor Statistics.

jobs in Manhattan, and the same is true for Queens and Brooklyn. So the city is a single common market.

But Table 3.7 is also a warning about assumptions based on economic aggregation. Queens and the Bronx may be part of the same common market as Manhattan, but the trickle-down effects of surges in Manhattan per capita income were pretty modest during the period after 1989, and even these borough-level statistics are still huge aggregations of different populations and economic classes. There are mega-millionaires in the Bronx and plenty of poor people in Manhattan. How then to explore the crime-relevant economic trends within this heterogeneous common market?

The three classes of citywide economic activity that best fit the entry level focus are: job opportunities, poverty and the economic prospects of low wage workers, and growth opportunities. Figure 3.6 compares unemployment rates in New York City with national rates for 1980 to 2009.

Over three decades, the city's unemployment rate follows the same cycles of growth and contraction as the national economy but is more volatile and also takes more time to recover from recessions in the early 1980s and 1990s. The New York level of unemployment stays higher than the national rate during recessions and recoveries, then comes near parity with national rates in times of prosperity.

The pattern of the city's unemployment rate over time is another cautionary tale about the relationship of employment opportunity and crime trends. The unemployment increases in the recession of the early 1980s came during a decline in the city's (and the nation's) crime, while unemployment dropped after 1985 when crime turned up in the city. During the 1990s—the period of the city's biggest crime drop—when

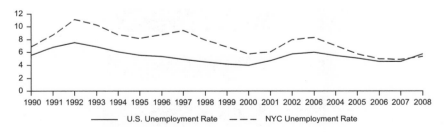

FIGURE 3.6 Unemployment Rate for Persons 16 and Over, New York City and United States, 1990–2008.
Source: Bureau of Labor Statistics at ftp://ftp.bls.gov/pub/special.requests/lf/aat1.txt (U.S.); http://www.labor.ny.gov/stats/laus.asp (NYC).

U.S. unemployment fell from around 6% to a low for the period of 4.2% in 1999 and 4.0% in 2000, the New York City unemployment rate lagged behind both in trend over time and in rate. During the 1990s crime drop, city unemployment was 9.7% as late as 1997. During the first six years of the new decade, the city first lagged and then equaled the national level.

In absolute terms, unemployment statistics in New York City look more like Queens and Brooklyn than like Manhattan per capita income trends. Relative to the national trends over time, there is no sustained period in the time series where the city's unemployment significantly outperformed national trends. So if we are looking for the causes of the New York difference in crime declines, unemployment levels are not a promising candidate. Growth in job opportunities may explain some crime decline in the late 1990s and since 2000 for both the city and the nation, but there is no sustained period when the job market was much better in New York.

A second method of measuring the economic status of the less well off in the city is to examine trends in per capita income for persons at the 20th percentile of the city's distribution. This strategy is an effort to see how low-wage and entry-level employed persons fare in the city's economic changes. Figure 3.7 provides this data from the Department of Labor Statistics in constant 2005 dollars.

Income at the 20th percentile increases at an inflation-adjusted rate of 6.2%, equaling the citywide growth rate at the 50th percentile. The progress is consistently spread over a decade and a half, and shows much more participation in the city's economic growth at the lower end of the economic distribution than one might fear from the flat unemployment totals in Figure 3.6. What mix of increasing participation in

FIGURE 3.7 Per Capita Income in 2005 Dollars in New York City, 1987–1989, 1998–2000, and 2004–2006.
Source: Fiscalpolicy.org.

the labor market and increasing real wages produce this happier picture is beyond the scope of this chapter. One counterweight to the good news of increasing per capita income is the extent to which housing costs in New York City have also outpaced inflation during the 1990s and since. Payments for rent in constant 2005 dollars still expanded 16.4% in the 17 years after 1989 at the median and about 10% in the rent-paying 25th percentile.

Another set of important lower end economic indicators deals with officially measured levels of poverty. Figure 3.8 compares trends over time for the United States and the city in percentage of households in poverty.

Figure 3.8 is taken from the 2006 report of the mayor. Rates of poverty in the city exceed the national average throughout the period after 1980, occasionally by more than 30%. In the years after 1990, poverty rates rise until 1995, stay level until 1998, then drop back to the level of the late 1980s by 2000. The committee reports that the 2005 rate of poverty in New York City was the ninth highest of the 20 largest cities of the United States. On this measure of economic disadvantage, there was no time during the years after 1990 when relative success in alleviating poverty could be a basis for singling out New York as a positive outlier.

A final measure of economic activity that should be linked to trends in crime growth is young adult levels of unemployment. The percentages in Figure 3.9 are annual averages of unemployment for ages 16–19, the entry-level age group for full-time work and a peak age for serious crime arrest. There are three things worth special attention in this 29-year comparison of the city and national patterns. First, youth unemployment rates

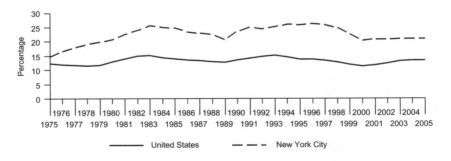

FIGURE 3.8 Poverty Rates, United States and New York City, 1975–2005.
* Based on two-year moving averages.
Source: Current Population Survey (CPS), U.S. Census Bureau. New York City CPS tabulations performed by Community Service Society of New York.

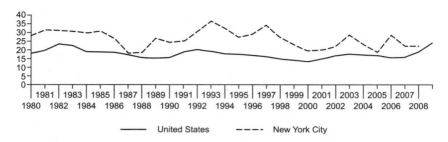

FIGURE 3.9 Average Annual Unemployment Rates for 16–19 Year Olds, New York City and United States, 1980–2008.
Source: U.S. Department of Commerce, Bureau of Labor Statistics, Unemployment (monthly 1980–2008).

are much higher than rates for older workers in New York and nationally. The national level varies from a low of 13.1% in 2000 to its 29-year high of 24.3% in 2009, between two and three times the general rate. For New York, the rate varies from 17.9% to a 1993 and 2009 high of 36%—often more than three times the general rates reported in Figure 3.6. The second significant feature of the youth unemployment story is that recession year 2009 is the peak rate for youth unemployment for both New York City (tied with 1993) and the national aggregate, in each case overtaking a previous high point during the recession of the early 1980s. But that means that the high point for youth unemployment in New York is at the low point for crime rates in 2009.

The third message from Figure 3.9 is that New York's youth unemployment is higher than the national rate in all the years covered. When the gap is widest (in the 1990s) the city's rate is just under twice the national rate, while the gap narrows to under 2% in 2005, but there is no clear trend over time—2009 and 2006 have very large differences, while 2007 and 2008 have much smaller gaps. Since young persons in the labor market are never better off in New York City, the comparison tells us that better job opportunities than in other settings for a young person are not the "New York difference" that explains the city's larger than average crime drop.

Social Indicators

As will be described in Chapter 4, a number of social indicators played a role in pessimistic projections about future crime levels during the mid-1990s, but then discourse about social indicators of crime risk fell off when crime rates dropped in the late 1990s. This section examines three different social indicators mentioned in the earlier discussions to examine what New York City's recent experience might suggest about the value of this kind of data as a leading indicator on crime.

Table 3.8 provides census data on the percentage of children with single parents for three census years beginning in 1980 and for 2005. New York City trends and national data are compared. The proportion of children living in single-parent households increases substantially in the city and in the United States over the 25 years, by 11.9 percent in the United States and by 11.3 percent in New York City. This should be bad news for crime trends if single-parent custody were a good leading indicator in both the city and the nation, but New York City should be at a particular disadvantage because the proportion of children in single-parent settings exceeds the national total by a wide margin, both at the beginning of the time series in 1980 and at its end in 2005. To the extent that single-parent custody is at all relevant to crime rates, New York is at a disadvantage. But the increases in the total nationally and in the city do not appear to be a good prediction of crime when combined with 5- or 10-year lags.

A second risk factor for future crime involvement is failure to complete high school. Figure 3.10 shows completion rates seven years after high school entrance, combining all methods of high school completion. This is the official rate of success, so non-completion is for each year in the figure the difference between completion and 100%.

The eventual completion rate fluctuates between 65.9 and 70.7 for the first 18 years after 1985, then ends at a new high of 72.2. There is no clear trend over time between 1988 and 2002. The failure to complete rate therefore hovers around 30% in the city, with no clear time trend over the big decline years. The seven-year completion standard differs from shorter

Table 3.8. Percentage of Children Living with Single Parents, New York City and United States, 1980, 1990, 2000 and 2005.

	1980	1990	2000	2005
New York City	32.8%	32.7%	37.9%	41.1%
United States	17.1%	21.5%	27.7%	31%

Sources: U.S. Census and U.S. Census, American Community Survey.

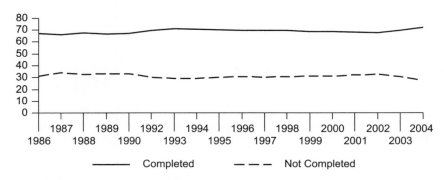

FIGURE 3.10 Percentage of High School Graduation within Seven Years.
Source: New York City Department of Education, final reports of classes of 2000, 2001, 2002, 2003 and 2004.

time frames, and this makes direct comparison with school systems using other measures difficult. Yet as a measure of aggregate risk it seems superior to use eventual graduation rather than after the normative four years. A non-completion rate of 30% combined with a modestly higher youth population to generate a high school non-completion cohort that didn't vary much in the 1990s and early years of the next decade.

Changes in Standard Crime Causation Indicators

In this section, attention turns to the three issues that my earlier book on the U.S. crime decline called "the usual suspects" in discussion of what caused the nationwide crime decline in the 1990s—the declining proportion of youth in the population, increasing incarceration, and economic prosperity. The question of the moment is whether New York's performance in any of these standard measures related to crime causation might help explain the larger than usual crime declines in the city. So the question considered here is not whether demography or incarceration or economic expansion may have helped reduce crime in New York City but rather whether extraordinary developments in any of these areas might help explain the New York City difference. But, without exception, the city's performance on these standard explanations for declining crime don't help explain the singular performance of this city. The pattern of economic conditions and changes in the city was covered in the opening section of the chapter. Here I will explore the changes in incarceration and age structure in New York City.

Incarceration

Incarceration is not only a frequent consequence of crime but it is also a hundred billion dollar effort to prevent crime. Over 1.5 million persons are in prison in the United States, up fourfold in the years after 1972, and a total exceeding 2.3 million are confined in either prison or jail. The massive expansion of imprisonment was designed and has been justified as a crime control effort through deterrence of potential offenders who wish to avoid imprisonment (Zimring and Hawkins 1972) and by removing active offenders from the community into settings where they are incapacitated for the duration of their confinement. Incapacitation is both the single comparative advantage of confinement over other punishments and by far the dominant motive for prison expansion (Zimring and Hawkins 1995).

All of the states in the United States expanded their use of incarceration over the 30 years after 1972, and prisons and jails were a major part of the crime-control effort in New York City and New York State. By 1990, where my analysis in this chapter will start, a total of 56,100 persons from New York City were incarcerated in the state's penitentiaries or in the city's jails, a rate per 100,000 population of about 768. Figure 3.11 charts the total number of city residents incarcerated over the years after 1990, showing a volume of prisoners rather than a rate per population to focus on the capacity for incapacitation. Because population levels expanded, the trends in raw numbers overstate the growth per 100,000 population, and any declines in Figure 3.11 are less than the decline in rate.

The number of New Yorkers behind bars increases from 56,100 in 1990 to a high of 66,765 in 1997, an extra 10,000 persons who could not

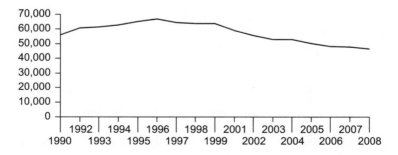

FIGURE 3.11 New York City Residents Incarcerated, 1990–2008.
Source: State of New York Department of Correctional Services.

be committing crimes in the street while locked up—an increase of 19%. But then total prison and jail numbers from the city start to decline. By 2002, a smaller number of persons were confined than in the 1990 base year, and by 2008 there were 10,000 fewer criminals being incapacitated from New York City than in 1990. In the ten years after 1996, about 20,000 more criminal offenders were released from prisons and jails in the city than were locked up.

Figure 3.12 transforms New York City's total confinement numbers into rates per 100,000 and compares the trends in New York City with national trends. To isolate trends each rate in 1990 is translated to a base rate of 100 and future variations are expressed as rations of the 1990 rates.

During the first seven years of the 1990s, total incarceration rates increase both in the United States and in New York City, but at very different rates. Per capita incarceration grew 15% in New York City and 41% nationally. Then the two trends head in different directions. By 2001, the national incarceration rate had increased almost exactly by half in 11 years, while it had declined by 4% over the same period in the country's largest city. By 2008, the national rate of incarceration had increased by 65% in 18 years, while the New York City rate had declined by 28%.

There are many factors that may have contributed to this sharp difference in incarceration trends, not the least of which is the extra crime decline in the city. But crime declines do not inevitably produce decreasing rates of imprisonment; the proof of this is the 49% expansion in the United States during the 1990s, a decade that witnessed the biggest and longest crime decline of the postwar years (Zimring 2006). Whatever its causes, the question of the moment is whether the contrast between U.S.

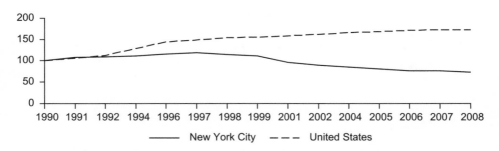

FIGURE 3.12 Trends in Incarceration in Adults, New York City and the United States.
Source: State of New York Department of Correctional Services., 1990–2008; New York State Archives; Bureau of Justice Statistics.

increases and New York's decarceration might help explain New York's higher than average crime drop. And in terms of the standard theories of incarceration as crime control, the obvious answer is no. Indeed, to say that the gap in incarceration trends documented in Figure 3.11 is the opposite of a plausible explanation of the New York City prevention advantage is literally true. If we were to *reverse* the trends shown in Figure 3.11 so that national incarceration decreased by 28% while New York City's rate increased 65%, this large gap in additional incapacitation would seem a plausible reason that New York's crime numbers were much better than the national norm.

The remarkable capacity of the country's largest city to make huge strides in crime reduction without increasing investment in confinement has yet to become an important issue in crime control policy discourse but perhaps it should. The last section of this book will address that aspect of the New York experience. For present purposes, however, it is sufficient to note that the standard theories of imprisonment as crime control would not regard the much smaller reliance on incarceration in New York as an explanation for its double dose of crime reduction.

Youth and Young Adults

An emphasis on changes in the age structure of the population in explaining and predicting changes in crime rates is a legacy of the 1960s, when the huge cohort of postwar baby boom births became adolescents just as crime rates started to increase. Because arrest rates for the young are much higher than for older age groups, a population with a greater proportion of youth would be expected to produce higher numbers of arrests and presumably of crimes. There was also speculation that a greater proportion of young persons could put stress on the institutions and adult authority figures that educate and socialize the young, perhaps increasing crime beyond the direct impact of increasing numbers (Wilson 1975).

If an increasing proportion of young persons in the population increases crime rates, then a decreasing youth share of total population would be expected to produce declines in crime, and the period after 1975 produced declines in the youth share of the population as the baby boom bulge moved into its twenties, thirties, and forties. But the declining youth and young adult share of the U.S. population after 1980 was associated with a mixed pattern of crime trends—down in the early 1980s, way up between 1985 and 1991, then down in the 1990s. Obviously, much more than the age structure of the population was driving crime trends because the youth share of total population decreased steadily in the decades after 1980. But might an older population be an important part of explaining the crime decline of the 1990s? My answer is yes. And might a different pattern of age structure in New York City help to explain its larger and longer decline? The clear answer to this question is no.

The case for attributing some of the 1990s crime decline to an aging population is modestly strong, but there is no evidence that shifting age structure in its population is an important part of the New York difference that is the focus of this chapter.

Table 3.9 shows the proportion of total population ages 15–29 for the United States and for New York City for the two census years after 1980 and for 2007. The 15–29 category is selected as the age group at maximum current risk of arrest for serious crime. This group is not a leading indicator of crime risk but rather a measure of current risk so that increases or decreases should be associated with contemporary changes in crime. A younger group—say 10 to 17—would function as a leading indicator of crime trends, so that increases in the proportion in this young group would predict high crime rates five or ten years later.

The young share of U.S. population drops significantly from 1980 to 2000, then evens out in the first years of the new century. New York City starts with a slightly smaller youth share than the national pattern, which continues to decline throughout the period. During the 1990s, when the national 15–29 percentage goes down 2.5%, New York City's young population share declines only 1.5%, the reverse of a population dynamic that would predict a higher crime decline in the city. But the city ages more after 2000, dropping its 15–29 share by 1.7% when the U.S. youth share stays flat. Might that advantage after 2000 help explain the city's continued decline in the post-2000 period?

Table 3.9 Persons 15–29 as Proportion of Total Population, United States and New York City, 1980–2007.

	1980	1990	2000	2007
United States	27.3	23.2	20.7	21.0
New York City	25.4	23.4	21.9	20.2

Source: U.S. Bureau of the Census.

While some demographic dividend for the city in the most recent years is possible, an analysis of the age structure by racial and ethnic group provides some reason to doubt its extent. Table 3.10 shows the percentage of 15-to-29-year-olds in each racial and ethnic group profiled earlier in the chapter for 1990, 2000, and 2007 (1980 detail wasn't available).

The two groups previously characterized as "low risk" for offense and victimization, white non-Hispanics and Asians, account for all of the aging in New York City's population after 2000, with a 4.2% drop for non-Hispanic whites and Asians dropping 5% in the 15–29 population share. The 15–29 proportion for both Blacks and Hispanics remains stable. There is no decline in the most arrest-prone youth population and no prospect then of a significant decline in arrests and presumably of crimes from population trends. As was the case with the incarceration difference discussed in the previous sub-section, if the declines noted for Asian and white non-Hispanic 15-to-29-year-olds had occurred instead in the age distributions of Hispanic and Black populations, then a plausible case could be made that the demographic shifts after 2000 contributed to New York City's crime decline in the period after the turn of the century. As it is, the greater the detail that is examined in population trends, the smaller the chance that a plausible explanation for extra crime decline can come from population changes.

Conclusion: The Same City?

The focus in each of the previous sections has been on changes in the population, the social and educational systems, the economy, and the incarceration systems associated with New York City. There have been other

Table 3.10 Persons 15–29 as a Proportion of Total Population, New York City by Race and Ethnic Group, 1990, 2000, and 2007.

	1990 (Proportion)	2000 (Proportion)	2007 (Proportion)
Non-Hispanic White	20.8	18.5	14.3
Black	25.2	22.0	22.0
Hispanic	26.9	25.5	25.8
Asian	25.9	24.2	19.2

Source: U.S. Bureau of the Census.

changes in the city over two decades, including many changes in the physical structures and the institutions that govern and serve the population. Not mentioned in the summary statistics of this chapter was the destruction of the twin towers of the World Trade Center and the thousands of lives lost there in September of 2001. Changes in the composition, organization, and strategies of municipal police will be discussed in a later chapter, as will trends in illicit drug traffic and consumption.

The organizing concepts of this chapter were the contrasting themes of continuity and change in the city. With respect to most of the topics covered, there seems to be more continuity than change in the city's population, in its economic and social institutions, and in its social and economic problems. The New York City of 2010 is in most respects the same city as in 1990, and that is one reason that the big differences in common crime and violence rates are both astonishing and difficult to explain. The social and economic changes that have been documented in the city are modest over time and very much in line with trends in the rest of the nation.

A Mixed Verdict

Yet two aspects of the pattern observed in Manhattan create potential explanations of its crime decline that require close attention. The substantial decline in African American population and the extraordinary growth in income for this borough both set Manhattan apart from other cities in the United States and from the other boroughs in the city of New York. These are exactly the kind of differential features that might help to explain a larger-than-average crime decline.

But the "Manhattan difference" is not a "New York difference." The population shifts in the Bronx, in Brooklyn, and in Queens would not produce predictions of lower rates of crime and violence, and the economic fortunes of these boroughs were sharply different from the Manhattan pattern. This contrast provides two opportunities for analysis. In the first place, the much larger than average crime declines in these very large urban areas present a way to estimate how much of Manhattan's crime decline can be attribute to its special recent history and how much was probably produced by citywide influences. Second, the stability of the social and economic features of the other three boroughs gives a promising measure of how much of the entire city's decline wasn't produced by demographic change or spectacular income growth.

There are of course neighborhoods that have been socially transformed not only in Manhattan—Park Slope in Brooklyn is a paradigm case. But most of the city is much closer to the pattern of Canal Street rather than 42nd Street—the very large changes in crime risks and rates are not the product of physical, demographic or economic transformation. And that is very encouraging news for urban residents everywhere.

Table 3.11 summarizes the pattern of continuity and change reported across the four major boroughs of the city. Three of the four big boroughs which together are 80% of New York City's population show very little change that might explain the city's much larger than normal crime decline, yet all three exhibit crime declines far removed from those found in most cities during the 1990s and all three also experience declines after the turn of the century. Manhattan shows much greater population shifts and economic change, but even there, very few 42nd Street–style transformations occurred for this borough, with less than one-fifth of the total city population.

The essential contrast in New York City is between a change in serious street crime of about 80% and a change in urban conditions and populations

Table 3.11 Change in Population and Social Factors in Four Major Boroughs of New York City.

	Queens, Brooklyn, the Bronx	Manhattan
Population Trends for Traditional Risk Groups	Stable to Slightly Higher	Substantial Decline
Economic Progress Compared to National Trends	Stable	Much Higher
Social Risk Factors (School Graduation and Single Parent)	Stable	Stable
Age Structure	Same as National	Same as National
Incarceration Trends	Much Lower than National	Much Lower than National

that is very much more modest. One can't with any precision sum up all the factors surveyed in this chapter into a single index number—a percentage to compare with the crime drop. But it seems likely that any attempt to quantify the extent to which the population structures and institutions of the city had changed might be closer to 10% than the huge variations in crime. And that contrast between the modest changes in the city as a whole and the huge changes in crime is the central empirical surprise of New York after 1990.

This lack of dramatic shifts in institutions, population or policy to explain the large citywide crime drops is a very hopeful sign for other cities in the developed world. If New York City can alter its crime profile without making fundamental alterations in its character, why can't most other cities?

The next two chapters discuss topics that have been closely associated with analysis of crime and crime control and not extensively profiled in this initial survey. Chapter 4 concerns patterns and trends among high-risk youth populations and in illegal drugs in New York City. Chapter 5 addresses the one element of New York's crime control apparatus where major changes were apparent in the 1990s—the city's police.

Chapter 4

Of Demography and Drugs:

TESTING TWO 1990S THEORIES OF CRIME CAUSATION

THIS CHAPTER WILL focus on what the last 20 years in New York City can tell us about two sets of social and behavioral trends that were central concerns for persons worried about crime rates in the early 1990s. The years after 1985 were a puzzling and frightening era for many students of crime policy. Crime rates fell in the early 1980s as the rate of imprisonment increased and the proportion of the population aged 15–29 fell. After 1985, however, with both the demographic and prison trends still favorable to lower crime, rates of life-threatening violence in the United States turned up again, led by very substantial increases in homicide by persons 15–29, primarily minority young persons in the nation's biggest cities. This upturn had not been expected and produced concern and pessimism about the future, even during the first years of crime decline in the 1990s. All these trends were in evidence in New York City.

There were two widely held theories to explain the unexpected increase in urban violence, and each was associated with a series of proposals for shifts in crime control policy. The first theory to explain the late 1980s crime expansion was the growing number of disadvantaged and under-socialized youth in big cities who were starting long and violent criminal careers—the term coined for this group by John DiIulio, then of Princeton, was "juvenile super-predators," and the number of these dangerous offenders was supposed to expand at least as fast as the youth population in the 20 years after 1990. In 1995, James Q. Wilson used the following arithmetic about the years from 1995–2000: "By the end of this decade there will be a million more people between the ages of fourteen and seventeen than there are now . . . This extra million will be half male. Six percent of them will become high rate, repeat offenders—30,000 more young muggers, killers and thieves than we have now. Get ready" (Wilson 1995, at p. 507).

One year after Wilson's 30,000 estimate, John DiIulio (1996 at p. 1) pushed the horizon back 10 years and produced much larger frightening numbers: "By the year 2010, there will be approximately 270,000 more juvenile super-predators on the streets than there were in 1990. . . ." All of the research indicates that Americans are sitting atop a demographic crime bomb" (*Weekly Standard*, v. 1, n. 11 at p. 22).

The central policy that this certain expansion of dangerous offenders demanded, according to the Wilson/DiIulio school of public administration, was that "the government and the justice system give the American people what they have been demanding for years—incarceration for violent and repeat criminals . . ." (Bennett, DiIulio, and Walters 1996 at p. 136). So the policy implication of expecting a new wave of super-predators was building yet more prisons.

The second set of explanations for the unexpected increase in crime and violence after 1985 was the widespread use of a new crystallized form of cocaine called "crack." As the introduction to the National Drug Control Strategy of 1989 tells the story, crack is "an inexpensive, extremely potent, fast-acting derivative of cocaine with a limited-duration 'high' that encourages compulsive use. It is, in fact, the most dangerous and quickly addictive drug known to man" (National Drug Control Strategy 1989 at p. 3). The widespread use of crack in inner-city settings was believed to be criminogenic in several ways. Conflict over turf in crack markets and drug rip-offs both provoke lethal violence and also increase the number of persons in drug-impacted areas who carry and use deadly weapons. Available crack may also increase the rate of offending or its severity by persons seeking money to buy and use it. And once drug commerce increases the number of guns in circulation, younger persons and others who might usually go without guns obtain them and use them in many conflicts not apparently tied to drugs. But fine distinctions among these theories were not usually important to the strong belief in a fundamental link between illegal drugs and violent and property offending—"If one wants to know immediate causes of much of America's moral poverty, the destruction of large parts of our inner cities, and its record crime rate, it is impossible to overlook drug use" (Bennett, DiIulio, and Walters 1996 at p. 137).

This belief in a close drug/crime linkage apparently applied both to the historical explanation of crime increases in the late 1980s and also predicted that any real progress against street crime required reducing the availability and use of illicit drugs. In the early 1990s, drug policy in the United States was a central concern of those worried about street crime.

My intention in this chapter is to use New York City experience after 1990 as a case study, an urban laboratory for testing these two long-held theories about what causes street crime in the United States and how best to reduce crime. This chapter will use New York data to test the impact of social risk demographics and drug use on crime in the city. The last section of the book will then discuss what New York's experience teaches about the causes and control of serious crime.

A. Population, Social Risk, and Crime Rates in New York City

Both the population statistics and the social indicators in New York City after 1990 make it a good test of the predictions made about expanding youth population and indicators of social risk in the 20 years from 1990 to 2010.

The youth population 15–19, those at the beginning of the high-risk years for crime and criminal justice involvement expanded in the city after 1990, as shown in Figure 4.1. After shrinking almost 100,000 during the 1980s, the city's total population between 15 and 19 added 50,000 between 1990 and 2000, and an additional 30,000 in the age group from 2000 to 2008. On numbers alone, this additional 80,000 cohort members in the logic of James Q. Wilson should have been an additional "2,400 high-rate repeat offenders—muggers, killers and thieves" than the city had in 1990. And that is without any correction for demographic indications of special risk in the youth population. When race and ethnicity are taken into account, the prospects for youth crime look a bit worse, because the 15-to-19-year-old population in the low risk categories discussed

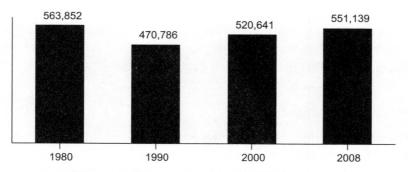

FIGURE 4.1. Youth Population (Ages 15–19), New York City, 1990–2008.
Source: U.S. Census Bureau.

in Chapter 3 actually declined. There was substantial growth in one high-risk category. The non-Hispanic Black population remained fairly stable (declining 4.8%), while the Hispanic youth cohort 15–19 grew by 38%.

Some social and economic indicators reviewed in the last chapters make demographically based predictions even less cheerful. Poverty remained high all through the post-1990 era in New York City, and the number of kids in single-parent households expanded all through the period after 1980 to 44% of all children.

Single-parent custody was a particular predictor of dysfunction to the conservatives reading the demographic tea leaves in the mid-1990s:

> Between 1960 and 1990 . . . there was not only an enormous increase in violent crime but also a huge increase in the rates of out-of-wedlock births, the percentage of children living in single-parent homes, the teenage suicide rate and the divorce rate. (Bennett, DiIulio, and Walters 1996 at p. 195)
>
> [F]our out of 10 children go to sleep without fathers who live in their homes and upward of 60 percent will spend some major part of their childhood without fathers . . . we have come to the point in America where we are asking prisons to do for many young boys what fathers used to do. (id. at p. 196)

The notion that prisons will be necessary to compensate for absent paternal authority is far more than an accidental or superficial rhetorical device. It expresses instead the assumption that, at least in current social conditions, the only controls for criminal careers determined by birth and social circumstance are jails and prisons.

From the numbers and social indicators, New York City after 1990 should be a good place to test such theories. Both violent crime and youth arrest rates had expanded dramatically during the 1980s, even as the 15–19 population had declined. So a deterministic model would expect even higher rates when the cohort at risky ages expanded.

So What Happened?

The aggregate crime rate trends outlined in Part I of this book are not a direct test of the criminal propensities of the expanding youth population in the city because even some expansion in youth crime might be counterbalanced by sharp declines among other age groups. Indeed, there was differential movement of different age groups in the late 1980s, when large increases in youth crime were partially offset by declining rates of offense in age groups over 25. So the best test of the impact of an expanding youth population in the city on crime is some analysis of crime trends among different age categories.

The only measure of age-specific rates of crime that comes in police statistics is trends in arrest by age. This is an incomplete and inaccurate measure for two reasons. First, only a small fraction of most crimes result in arrests, and it is often not clear that the crimes that produce arrest are a representative sample of the crimes that do not. The second problem is that when groups are involved in committing offenses, more than one person will be arrested if grounds for arrest exist. Because most crimes committed during adolescence involve groups, a large number of youth offenses result in multiple arrests (Zimring 1981). This means that the percentage of all arrests involving youths will almost always be larger than the true proportion of all offenses that are committed by young offenders. Still, arrest data by age provides the best indication of the extent of crime participation by different age groups at different times, particularly if care is taken in interpreting the statistics.

Figure 4.2 compares the percentage of all arrests that involve persons under 18 in New York City for the peak crime year of 1990 and for 2009.

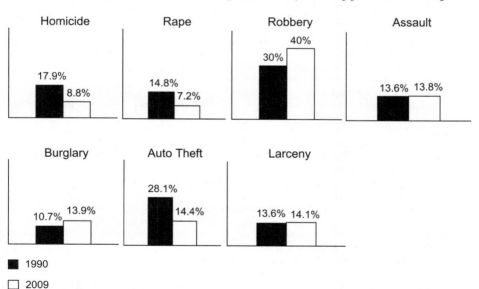

FIGURE 4.2 Under 18 Arrests (as a Percentage of Total Index Offense Arrests), New York City, 1990 and 2009.
Source: New York City Police Department.

The share of arrests under age 18 declines substantially for three of the seven index crimes: murder (8.8 vs. 17.9), rape (7.2 vs. 14.8) and auto theft (14.4 vs. 28.1). For each of these crimes, the percent of all arrests involving persons under 18 is cut in half. For three other crimes—larceny, burglary, and assault—the youth share of total arrests stays about the same (flat for larceny and assault, and a slight increase for burglary). For one offense—robbery—the arrest share of young offenders starts high and then increases from 30% in 1990 to 40% in 2009.

On the issue of whether the overall crime decline has happened in spite of growth in youth crime, the data are quite clear. The arrest volume under 18 is down for everything, of course, but the drop in youth arrests is greater than for adults for the two most serious index crimes and for auto theft, while the youth share of arrests increases substantially only for robbery.[1] Youth crime dropped at least as much as crime among older age groups and probably more. The modest increase in the population of youth in the city was overwhelmed by dropping rates of offenses among persons under 18.

Two methodological points should accompany this important substantive conclusion. The first point is that this was the *second* time that variations in youth population pointed in exactly the wrong direction for future

---

1. The use of under-18 arrest numbers and rates over time in New York City is complicated by a change in the criteria for police reporting adopted by the department in 2001 and 2002. Before the change, whether a police action was reported as an arrest for an offense was determined by regulations from the uniform crime reporting section of the Federal Bureau of Investigation. After 2002, the department used its own understanding of New York Law. The difference in criteria, as described by Deputy Chief Farrell, is as follows: "These (pre-2002) statistics include juvenile reports (apprehension of persons under 16 years of age for New York State Penal Law misdemeanors and violations) and criminal court summonses, which may be issued to persons 16 and over for selected misdemeanors and violations." (Farrell 2010 at p. 1). By its terms, this change would not seem to influence felony arrests, but since reduced charges are possible for categories such as larceny, some shift is possible.

To test whether the changes in youth share of arrests might be a product of the change in reporting for the three crimes where the youth share of those arrested dropped significantly over 1990–2009, I compared the annual changes in under-18 arrest volume during the years covered by the transition (2000–2004) with the changes in arrest volume for these three offenses for the five-year period after the transition was completed (2004–2009). The average annual change in arrests is reported in Table 4.1.

For murder and rape, the changes after the transition was completed are much larger than during the changes in criteria, so a major change in criteria impact on overall arrest trends seems highly unlikely. For auto theft, there are very large declines during both transitional and post-transitional eras. The major changes in auto theft seem unlikely to have been caused by the reporting change, but the almost 3% advantage in the transition era suggests that the drop from 28 to 14% in the official statistics may be higher than the effect that *would* be observed if the reporting hadn't changed.

crime rates, both in New York City and in the national aggregate. The youth crime increases that ignited the expectation for super-predators in 2005 took place while the youth population as a share of the total was dropping. Those who would use variations in youth population as a leading indicator of rates of youth crime are batting zero for two in the quarter century after 1985. Indeed, perhaps the uncharacteristic increase in youth violence when the youth population and adult crime rates were both going down should have been a warning that the late 1980s were atypical and not a signal of permanent structural change.

But even the more recent arrest statistics in New York City are not typical in one puzzling dimension. The offense that *looks* atypical in Figure 4.2 is robbery, which shows a much higher youth share of arrests for both 1990 and 2009. But it is actually the 2009 auto theft share of juvenile arrests and both the 1990 and 2009 burglary shares for under 18 that are much lower than the national average (compare national totals in Zimring 2004 at p. 42).

The New York City Puzzle

New York City is only one of a large number of settings across the United States where the predictions of coming waves of youth crime were turned upside down during the 1990s (Zimring 2005, Chap. 8), but the New York data puts an exclamation point on the decisive failure of demographic determinism in two respects. What Figure 4.2 shows is that a modestly expanding youth population has fully participated in the most dramatic crime reduction on record. So the prediction of increasing rates of offending was not merely wrong but catastrophically wrong.

The second distinctive contribution of the New York story is the absence of *any* increase in penal confinement as even a partial explanation for epic quantities of crime reduction. While the incarceration rate increased

Table 4.1 Average Annual Change in Arrests, New York City, 2000–2004 (Transitional) and 2004–2009 (Post-Transitional).

	Murder	Rape	Auto Theft
Transitional	-0.5%	-4.5%	-15.5%
Post-Transitional	-5.6%	-8.7%	-12.6%

Source: New York City Police Department.

nationally all through the 15 years after 1990, New York City is now locking up a smaller fraction of its youth and young adults in 2010 than in the early and mid-1990s.

So the children of single-parent households that were the "coming storm" of youth crime have grown up on the streets of New York City in an environment of much lower crime. Depending on the crime category one selects, they have either been equal partners in the crime drop (burglary, larceny, and assault) or have contributed more than their fair share (homicide, rape, and auto theft). How and why has this happened?

There have been few attempts in either academic or policy discourse to conduct an extensive autopsy of the demographic predictions of the early 1990s. In the late 1990s Professor Wilson was asked about the implications of the national crime decline on the demographic predictions. His reply: "This is a good indication of what little all of us know about criminology" (Steinberg 1999; Prof. Wilson was trained in political science).

One reason that there is no pressure for explaining the failure of demographic data to improve crime predictions is that declining crime rates have diverted public and policy attention from the crime issue to other questions. Just as people only think about dentists when they have toothaches, only periods of concern about crime generate sustained attention to crime policy. So no matter how inaccurate the prediction about crime policy toothaches, when the problem doesn't materialize as predicted, there is little interest in pursuit of explanations. Nobody is thinking about dentistry when their teeth feel fine.

There is another reason that many of what can be called the negative lessons of New York's crime decline have not been discussed in any detail. The public and the political actors involved with policy are much more concerned with what *has* caused a crime decline than with any negative lessons that the New York experience might teach. The central question about New York City was: What worked? And the consensus answer (not without reason) was that changes in policing were a central cause of the crime decline. Why should other aspects of crime policy—the failures—matter much to the man on the street or to his government?

Appendix B shows some of the large differences between New York City incarceration trends and those in the rest of the United States and shows some cost impacts of the difference. For the present, however, the central finding is that the demographic shifts widely feared in New York City occurred on schedule in the 1990s and first decade of the new century but had none of the predicted effects on crime rates. And the expansion in incarceration that was supposed to be the only defense against super-predators didn't happen either.

B. Crack, Crime, and Violence

A close linkage between illicit drugs and serious crime has been a long-standing assumption in American law enforcement and public opinion for at least the eight decades after 1930. Illegal drug users of all kinds are considered criminal justice problems and those using "hard" drugs— heroin in the postwar years and cocaine since the 1980s—have been singled out as criminal justice priorities. Chronic concern with hard narcotics intensified into publicly defined crisis conditions twice in the last three decades of the twentieth century. The first crises involved heroin, in the early 1970s. The second crisis was centered on "crack cocaine" and generated unprecedented levels of public and governmental concern in the late 1980s and early 1990s. At all times in the post-war years, the overlap between drug offenders and imprisonment in the United States was quite substantial. Since the late 1980s, however, the impact of drug offenses on the prison systems of the United States has broken new ground. There are, as of 2010, more persons in prison for drug offenses than there were persons in prison for all offenses in the United States in 1975 (Zimring and Harcourt 2007, Chap. 3).

Of all the fears about hard narcotics in the United States, the criminogenic effects of drug sales and use are on the short list with addiction and AIDS. As the federal DEA asserts on its web site as number seven in its "Ten Facts on Drug Legalization," "Crime, violence and drug use go hand in hand" (Zimring and Harcourt 2007 at p. 343).

New York City has long had a reputation as being the national capital of hard narcotic abuse. Part of New York's notoriety was simply a function of its dominant size, but relatively large heroin-using subcultures added to the status of the city as a visible symbol of hard drug epidemics. Blumstein and Wallman reflect this long-standing perception in the crack era in the following terms: "A focus on New York City is easily justified by its bellwether role in national drug and violence trends and its hugely disproportionate weight in those trends." (Blumstein and Wallman, 2006rev ed., at p. 9). And New York City played a prominent role in both of the modern drug panics. The heroin crises of the early 1970s produced the so-called "Rockefeller Drug Laws," with mandatory minimum sentences sufficiently abnormal to capture national attention, which remained a prominent part of criminal justice in New York into the twenty-first century. The crack epidemic of the late 1980s also hit New York hard, but resistance from Democrats in state-level government provoked New York's Republican Senator Alfonse D'Amato to successfully introduce a federal drug-related homicide death penalty in 1988 (Zimring 1988). So the politics of drug control and punishment in New York produced the first operational federal death penalty in national government since 1972.

New York City has served as a bellwether not only for trends in drugs and violence but also for the policy responses to drug panics in both the 1970s and the crack emergency of the late 1980s.

The Asymmetric New York Pattern

Figure 4.3 traces trends in two drug-related death rates in New York City over the period from 1985 to 2009. Each of the death categories is an imperfect indicator of one aspect of the drug/crime nexus in the city. The drug overdose death rate is an indicator of trends in illicit drug use in the city. Overdose death rates are concentrated in drugs with more life-threatening pharmacologies—chiefly heroin and cocaine. Other drugs will be underrepresented in death statistics so that overdose deaths will be a poor indicator of trends in use of illegal substances like marijuana that don't

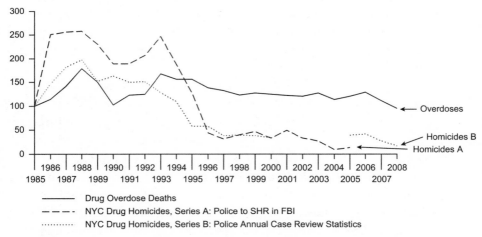

FIGURE 4.3 Trends in Drug Overdose Deaths and Drug-Related Homicides, New York City, 1985–2008.
Sources: New York City Police Department (killings); Bureau of Vital Statistics, New York City Department of Health and Mental Hygiene (overdose deaths).

commonly lead to classified drug overdose fatalities. But the concentration of overdose deaths in heroin and cocaine make variations in overdose deaths a plausible measure of patterns of use for the two drugs of most concern during the decades after 1985.

Two counts of apparently drug-related homicides come from the police. Series A is an analysis of cases submitted by the city police each month to the FBI's supplemental homicide-reporting program. The problems with this data include imperfect knowledge by the police of the facts of homicides and categories of homicide motive that are crude and incomplete. The monthly Supplemental Homicide Report (SHR) data undercount actual drug-related killings. Work by Paul Goldstein in the late 1980s suggests that the police categories undercounted drug related deaths greatly. In 1989, when Goldstein indicated that 53% of New York City killings in the areas he studied were drug related, the official "narcotics" related estimate in the Supplemental Homicide Reports was under 10% (Goldstein et al. 1989). Series B of drug-related killings come from annual case file reviews generated after a change in statistical reporting in 2004. Series B produces much higher numbers of drug-related cases, but the time trends of the two measures are pretty close. Series A is more volatile, with a peak of 258% of 1985 levels. But both measures go up until the early 1990s and then start downward by leaps and bounds. By 2005, the SHR killing rate is down 95% from its peak rate and 93% from the killing volume of 1990. Series B has dropped 91% from its peak and 90% from its 1990 volume. Adjusting for population changes would increase the decline. The trends over time in drug-related homicide are used as a measure of the extent to which drug sales and use are an important generator of criminal violence. The undercount is not a fatal problem as long as reporting is constant, as we expect it was until 2006. So overdose deaths measure trends in the use of (some) drugs, while drug-related homicides measure the impact of drugs on criminal violence.

Overdose deaths are much less volatile, with the highest recorded number less than twice the lowest (1208 in 1988 vs. 670 in 1985). Overdose deaths jump from their lowest to their highest volume in the first three years of the series, then stay relatively flat after 1988. Drug-involved homicides are much more volatile over time, with the highest total in the period from 1985 to 2005 more than 20 times the lowest in Series A and 12 times in Series B.

The peak rates of drug-involved homicide occurred in 1987 and 1988, and the drop in the volume of such killings is steady and steep from

1993 to 2005. The number of drug-overdose deaths in 2004 and 2005 is 90% of the volume in 1990—indicating pretty flat trends in the use of at least the high-lethality illicit drugs. The volume of drug-involved homicides in 2005 is only 5% of the number in 1990. The contrast in measures of drug violence (way down) and cocaine and heroin use (very flat) shows a city where drug violence drops by more than 90% while drug use is relatively stable.

The asymmetry in the homicide and overdose trends over time might simply mean that overdose deaths are not a consistent index of drug use, or even of the use of cocaine and heroin. Or the flat trend in overdose deaths could indicate that the use of heroin and cocaine was itself relatively stable during the past two decades in New York City. The next subsection of this chapter examines several other statistics available in public health and criminal justice to estimate trends in the use of cocaine, heroin, and other illicit drugs, which thus help decide whether the overdose fatality trends are decent indicators of heroin and cocaine use.

Alternative Measures of Drug Availability and Use

There are a variety of different measures available to provide information on the availability and use of illicit drugs at the city level. One widely used measure of drug use at the national level is data from a government-sponsored telephone survey. City-level estimates over time are not available from this, but the New York City Department of Health did compare answers from two surveys (2006 and 2007) for New York City with national totals. As Table 4.2 shows, self-reported use in the last year is higher in New York City than nationally and higher in the most recent surveys than earlier in the decade.

Table 4.2. Past Year Use in Phone Survey.

	New York City			U.S. Total
	2002–2003	2004–2004	2006–2007	2006–2007
Cocaine	2.6%	1.5%	3.9%	2.3%
Heroin	1.0%	0.3%	0.8%	0.1%

Source: Paone, D., Heller, D., Olson, C., and Kerker, B. 2010. Illicit Drug Use in New York City. *NYC Vital* Signs 9(1); 1–4.

The limits of this data are substantial, however. The reported rates of heroin usage are tiny, and even the cocaine frequencies are not large. The comparison of a major city rate with a national survey rate also may confuse a tendency for illicit drug use to be concentrated in big cities with a specific New York City concentration. And the "past year" data in the table concern everybody who reports even a single use of the drug over a 12-month period, so that casual users and drug-dependent frequent users are lumped together. With all those limits, however, the table still reports that cocaine use is four to five times as prevalent in New York City as heroin. While marijuana usage is much higher than either heroin or cocaine, the survey data provide some support for a special focus on cocaine in analyses of hard drug usage and commerce.

But cocaine is a less dominant hard drug when the focus shifts from the prevalence of reported use to the number of hospitalizations caused by drugs. Figure 4.4 shows the breakdown of the 128,545 drug-related hospitalizations reported to the New York City Department of Health Statewide Planning System (SPARCS) in 2005 by type of drug reported.

In this count of drug hospitalizations, cocaine and the opioids together dominate the hospital statistics with more than 75% of all the mentions, but opioids have slightly more mentions than cocaine. And the rank order of the top four drugs is the same in every year between 1999 and 2005 (in 2006, however, cocaine received 44,161 mentions to 43,573 for opioids, a virtual tie).

The larger share of hospitalizations for opioids may reflect hospitalization for the use of non-heroin opioids (such as oral pain killers) and also the greater health emergency risks associated with injectable heroin. And it may also be an indication that the proportion of heroin users who are

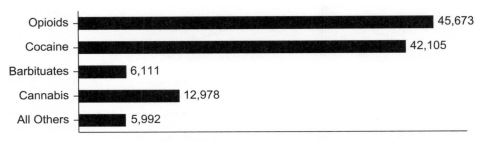

FIGURE 4.4 Drug-Related Hospitalization Incidents by Drug Mentioned, New York City Residents Aged 13 and Over.
Note: Drug types are not mutually exclusive.
Source: New York State Department of Health Statewide Planning and Research Cooperative System, 1999–2006 (updated).

frequent users and drug dependent may be higher than in the cocaine-using population. Hospitalization may measure the incidence of drug use instead of its prevalence.

Figure 4.5 provides annual data on two further types of public health statistics collected in New York City about cocaine use and its medical treatment. The longest time series is for hospitalizations where cocaine was mentioned as a cause of hospitalization at discharge. Data are available from the SPARCS system from 1989 through 2000.

The second set of medical indicators are mentions by emergency room physicians of cocaine as a cause of the medical problem bringing a patient to the emergency room. This data series only starts for New York City in 1994, then stops after 2002 and restarts in 2004 with a new set of case definitions that produces an almost 50% jump in cases during its first year, a second 50% jump in the second year, and warnings from the collectors that comparison of the new data should not be made with earlier "dawn" numbers.

Figure 4.5 reports case volume rather than rates per 100,000, so that a moderate downward adjustment toward the end of the period can be justified by the population increase when a long and constant statistical category is used. The hospital discharge numbers start high, with almost 30,000 cases in 1989 and 1990, jump in the next two years, and then stay over the 1991 volume through 1998. Cocaine hospitalizations then dip 18% over the three years at the turn of the century before returning to levels near their mid-1990s highs by 2004. If hospitalizations are a good measure of current usage, cocaine usage stayed high all through the period and remains high. And the relative usage flatness in the overdose

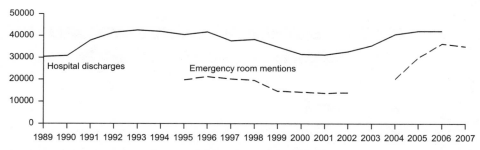

FIGURE 4.5 Annual Number of Hospital Discharges and Emergency Room Visits Related to Cocaine, New York City, 1989–2007.
Source: New York State Department of Health Statewide Planning and Research Cooperative System.

death statistics in Figure 4.4 seems an accurate measure of the incidence of drug use for cocaine when hospitalization and emergency room mentions are the index.

The shorter time series of emergency room cocaine mentions is high and constant until 1998, then drops by about a third for the three years prior to the case definition change. Then the rate jumps by 50% due to the new method in 2004 but also keeps rising in 2005 and beyond. Adjusting for both the 50% increase in 2004 and the increases in population, the emergency room cocaine mentions are still at or near their highest level by 2007. These data are consistent with a cocaine downturn in the late 1990s that is canceled out by upward drift by the middle of the next decade. The flat level of hospital discharge suggests that this measure is somewhat less sensitive to variations in trends than emergency room mentions, but it is not clear which is the better index of trends in cocaine use. More important for present purposes: both measures are inconsistent with major long-term decreases over the full span of the crime decline.

Price Trends

Drug enforcement agencies create estimates of "street price" to measure both availability and cost to users of illicit drugs. Figure 4.6 presents federal drug enforcement administration estimates of street prices in New York City for crack cocaine, powder cocaine and heroin per gram in constant 2007 dollars, which the agency uses to control for inflation.

Cocaine prices decline sharply in the 1980s (while heroin prices increase in the mid-1980s, then turn down and stay down for the 20 years after 1990). Over the period of the crime decline, cocaine and crack prices

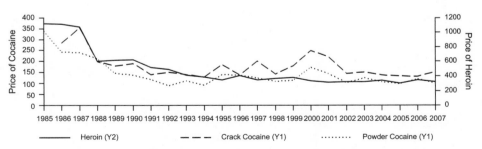

FIGURE 4.6 Price of Illicit Drugs in Constant 2007 Dollars, New York City, 1985–2007.
Source: Fries 2008.

stay low until the mid-1990s, increase in the late 1990s, peak in 2000, and decline after that to near the low for the era by 2003. Figure 4.7 shows price trends for powder cocaine from DEA estimates for five cities over the period 1981–2007. The function of this figure is to put the New York City trends in context. Is the price pattern found in New York typical or singular?

The five-city pattern over 27 years sends a clear message—New York City is typical in its long-term trends and even in the short-term upticks in 1995 and 2000. To the extent there is any identified price difference between cities in annual estimates, New York is on the lower end of the spectrum, but the cities are so closely bunched by the end of the period that the inter-city differences seem unimportant. To the extent that price is a good index of availability, the lesson of Figure 4.7 is that cocaine is about equally available in the five major cities studied, and as available in 2007 as in most of the earlier price eras covered.

For the purposes of this analysis, the figure tells us that neither drug availability nor price sets off New York City from other major cities—drug price trends are not the "New York difference."

Drug Use by Persons Arrested

Our final chapter in the statistical portrait of drugs in New York City concerns the overlap between drug use and crime. A series of federal programs launched during the drug panic of the 1980s investigated the relationship between drug use and crime by interviewing persons in custody who have just been arrested. If the arrestee consents to the interview,

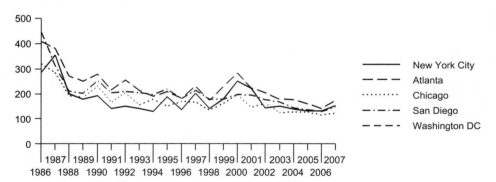

FIGURE 4.7 City Trends in Retail Price of One Expected Pure Gram of Powder Cocaine.
Source: Fries 2008.

he is then asked at its conclusion if he will also submit a urine sample for drug analysis. This program, first called Drug Use Forecasting (DUF), then renamed Arrestee Drug Abuse Monitoring (ADAM), was administered in several different sites, including in Manhattan. There are three ways in which the persons who took these tests were not a representative sample of criminal offenders in New York City. First, only Manhattan arrestees were included in the program, not persons arrested elsewhere. Second, only persons arrested rather than all who commit crimes are in the sample. Third, only those who consent both to an interview and then to a urine test are included. In New York City, refusal rates are high by 1997, relative to other cities and presumably the drug use of refusers is higher than consenters (Adam 1998 at pp. 37–38).

With all those reservations, the drug use data that emerges can provide a good minimum estimate of the prevalence of drug use in arrested persons and if refusal rates stay constant in its trends over time. Figure 4.8 shows the percentage urine testing positive for any of ten substances, nine of which are illegal drugs (the tenth is alcohol).

The prevalence of a defined drug in arrestees hovers around 80% throughout the 12-year period, with no clear time trend or gender difference. Urine tests for cocaine do show a time trend, as shown in Figure 4.9.

Cocaine is present in urine tests about 60% of the time for the first five years, and then drops by a third for the years after 1996. The pattern is the same for men and women but is most pronounced for younger arrestees (Adam 1997 at 1).

Figure 4.10 rounds out the arrestee results with opiates. The prevalence of opiates starts much lower than cocaine and stays nearly constant over the period studied.

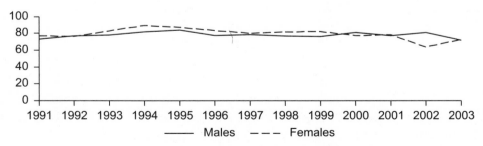

FIGURE 4.8 Manhattan Arrestees Urine Test Results (Any of Ten), 1991–2003.
Source: U.S. Department of Justice, DUF and ADAM programs, 1991-2003.

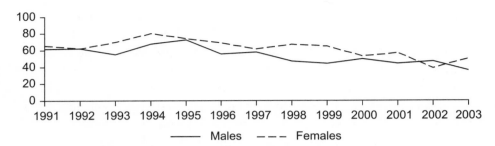

FIGURE 4.9 Manhattan Arrestees Urine Test Results (Cocaine), 1991–2003.
Source: U.S. Department of Justice, DUF and ADAM programs, 1991–2003.

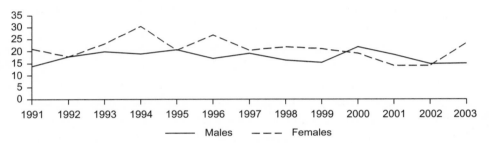

FIGURE 4.10 Manhattan Arrestees Urine Test Results (Opiates), 1991–2003.
Source: U.S. Department of Justice, DUF and ADAM programs, 1991–2003.

Some Common Ground

While each of the measures used in this analysis is biased, there is a surprising amount of congruence in the portrait of drug use in the city over
time. Illicit narcotics remain widely available and widely used in New
York, but cocaine use among younger segments of the population starts to
decline in the mid-1990s, and this is reflected in emergency room mentions (the DAWN system) as well as arrestee urine tests. This downturn
occurs prior to the price increase around 2000 and also seems to persist
when inflation-adjusted prices go down.

The major changes in drug use noted in New York City are observed in
other cities about the same time. But the continued availability of hard
narcotics in New York City does not mean that the locations and methods
of sale did not change in response to police pressure. A major target of
police intervention during the early 1990s was wide-open drug commerce
that drove other public functions away (Bratton 1998 at pp. 227–228). The
time, place, and manner of illicit drug commerce may have changed much
more than the volume of drugs sold and consumed.

Indeed, the New York experience may be an outstanding example of successful influence by the police on patterns of drug trade without any much greater suppression of the drug traffic and use. At least two changes in the conditions surrounding the sale and use of illicit drugs in New York City contributed to the large drop in drug-related homicides. While the cohorts of cocaine users of the 1980s aged into less violent demographic categories, the next generation of young persons in high-risk neighborhoods had much lower rates of all forms of cocaine use. The availability and volume of hard drugs may not have changed much, but the demographics of cocaine use changed in ways that reduced the overlap of cocaine use and arrest for other crime. That demographic change happened in a great many of the urban centers of crack in the late 1980s, and is not closely tied to police policy. The second major shift in New York City is that the police placed successful emphasis on suppressing public open air drug markets. The first drug priority for policing was driving drug trade from public to private space. For a variety of reasons, this may have also reduced the risk of conflict and violence associated with contests over drug turf. The preventive impact on lethal violence seems substantially greater than its impact on drug use. As the next chapter will show, once the police had eliminated public drug markets in the late 1990s, the manpower devoted to a special narcotics unit dropped quite substantially.

To the extent that New York's reduction in drug-related homicides is greater than in other cities, this may signal the success of a new strategy of police-managed harm reduction. This chapter has focused on demographic and drug use trends as potential causes of crime and violence in New York City. The third part of this book will address a closely related issue, what the demographic and drug use trends can teach about the best way to control crime.

And the city's experience on this question is potentially quite important. The city may be winning its war on crime (and on drug violence) without winning the war on drug abuse.

Chapter 5

Policing in New York City

POLICE HAVE BEEN the center of attention in conversations about the city's crime decline almost from the beginning. In part this focus on police was a function of public relations—a mediagenic police chief and an aggressively credit-claiming mayor in the early and mid-1990s. A further reason for the centrality of policing was the absence of any other major changes in criminal justice or city government to compete for credit with policing. But there was also real and substantial change in the number of police, in the mission and tactics of street policing, and in the way that the nation's largest police force was organized and governed. Twenty years into the city's crime decline, changes in policing are virtually the only frequently mentioned cause of the long-range crime decline. And the New York story now has national ramifications—the apparent achievement of the police in New York City has come to play a central role in national discussions of the potential and limits of urban police as agents of crime prevention and control.

While the police have played a dominant role in discourse about the causes of the crime decline in the city, there has been surprisingly little social and behavioral scientific analysis of what happened in New York and why it happened. Statistics generated by the police department have been debated in episodic regression exercises (Kelling and Sousa 2001, Corman and Mocan 2005, Ludwig and Harcourt 2006). But while Chicago was the subject of a major community and human development study of crime in the 1990s (Sampson 2008) and two book-length studies of police organization (Skogan and Hartnet 1997, Skogan 2006), New York—the city with the largest crime decline where police were supposed to have been a central cause of the drop—produced only two studies prepared in the late 1990s—halfway in the 19-year decline (Karmen 2000 and Silverman 1999). A large gap between public importance and scientific understanding is almost always an invitation to urban legends, and the popular myths about New York policing include more than their fair share of tall tales.

My report here cannot compensate for the lack of rigorous evaluation of the organization and impact of the New York City police. This 20-year chapter in criminal justice history demands and deserves major attention and sustained organizational research that hasn't happened yet. Some of the lost opportunities for measuring the impact of changes in policing can never be recovered. But the sooner we start to collect and evaluate the necessary data, the more we will know.

What follows is a four-part down payment on the comprehensive portrait of the New York experience that the two-decade history of policing deserves. The first section of this chapter will provide a short history of police methods and social science understanding of the effectiveness of police circa 1990 in the United States. It describes a crisis of confidence in orthodox theories of policing produced in large part by systematic evaluation efforts that deconstructed decades of received but unproven wisdom. This left the field more open to new leadership and ideas in the 1980s and 1990s than in previous decades, but without proven methods of crime control and prevention. The second section of the chapter briefly describes the three major changes in city policing and when they occurred: changes in numbers of police, changes in organization and accountability, and changes in the strategies and tactics of street policing. These changes were the inputs of the new approach to policing—the series of shifts that were supposed to prevent and control crime. The third section of the chapter shifts focus from how policing changed in the city to the question of whether the sum of changes reduced crime, whether the magnitude of police crime prevention in New York can be measured, and whether the effectiveness of different segments of the multi-part shifts in policing can be separately assessed. The fourth section of the chapter addresses the lessons that can be learned from available data, as well as the things that can't be known until the slow and painful bean counting of policy science displaces storytelling and salesmanship.

The current state of empirical knowledge on the impact of New York policing is tantalizing but grossly inadequate. The circumstantial evidence that some combination of policing variables accounts for much of the New York difference is overwhelming. There was simply nothing else spread over the four major boroughs in both decades—in population, incarceration, economics, or education—that would provide the city a big advantage in crime reduction over other major cities.

But this kind of negative and circumstantial evidence means that there is no good way to apportion the crime control credit among the several very different changes in policing—the larger number of cops, much tighter management of manpower, the sustained intervention in high crime "hot spots," and the much more aggressive tactics of street policing. Some of the changes worked in New York City, but sorting out the specific impacts of different changes is not possible on current data.

A. A Short History of Municipal Police

The changes in organization and strategy that happened in New York City after 1990 came at a critical juncture in the modern history of municipal police in the United States, and both the way the changes were introduced and the difficulty of precisely measuring the impact of these changes on crime can be explained by the special moment in the history of city policing when the city's changes happened. I provide here a short and highly opinionated description of police organization and orthodox beliefs prior to the late 1970s and then briefly describe the assault on that orthodoxy that preceded the generation of new theories of police organization and strategy in the 1980s.

Municipal police were a rather late addition to the evolution of cities in relatively developed countries. The earliest consensus municipal police department was established in London in 1829. City police came to the United States in the middle of the nineteenth century (Silverman 1999 at p. 25). While other criminal justice functions were organized at the state level of government in the United States (such as prisons and court systems), policing was local, either relegated to county government (sheriffs) or city government (municipal police). This degree of localism created a decentralization that often resembled fragmentation. The United States of the 1960s had 51 different prison systems between the states and the federal government but as many as 40,000 different police departments (President's Crime Commission 1967). More recent estimates put the estimated number of agencies closer to 20,000 (Committee to Review Research on Police Policy and Practices 2004 at pp. 48–49).

Localism and fragmentation were only two of many organizational features of policing that made it an especially parochial branch of public administration. While policing had aspirations to professional status throughout the twentieth century, most street police in the United States were not well educated and came from the same cultures and ethnicities as those who worked in municipal fire departments. Policing at the street level was a working-class occupation, and police leadership generally came up through the ranks of police patrol. Adding to the insularity of police administration, lateral movement of police officers and administrators from one city system to another was both difficult and uncommon, so that largely self-governing police organizations were not easy to penetrate or to change absent major scandals (Goldstein 1978, Chap. 9).

With very few exceptions, the training of police and of police leadership was also an "inside job," with police academies training recruits in larger departments and department-generated in-service training provided for specialized functions and administrative advancement. The result of this inward-looking combination of training and administration was often close to a hermetically sealed organization in the dictionary meaning—one almost impervious to outside influences.

There were heroic exceptions to the parochial leadership one would expect from this ingrown culture of policing—August Volmer, Orlando Wilson—but inbreeding was a systemic dysfunction of city police of central concern to critics and reformers, as were racial and ethnic discrimination, lack of diversity, and many of the other common effects of insular white working-class hegemony in mid-century American life (President's Commission on Crime, Taskforce Report on Police 1967.

There were also a set of orthodox beliefs by 1960 about the functions of municipal police and how they could best be accomplished. The functions of the police included investigation, the enforcement of a wide variety of criminal laws, the maintenance of order, and a wide variety of emergency services to the public (Bittner 1970; President's Commission Task Force on Police 1967). The police presence was also believed to have a potential for preventing crime, and the most popular version of police crime prevention practice by the 1960s was what was called preventive patrol, usually the patrol activities of uniformed officers in marked cars conducting routine surveillance of designated geographic zones.

That fragmented and insular municipal police departments did not produce rigorous empirical research evaluating the effectiveness of police performance can hardly be regarded as an organizational surprise. There is no research budget associated with any local police academy, and if there was any form of research imperative in most insular municipal police organizations it was probably the secret-keeping opposite of "publish or perish."

Even sustained analyses by outside social science of police were a late blooming phenomenon, coming in the 1960s and 1970s (Skolnick 1966,

Wilson 1968, Reiss 1971, Bittner 1970). What had been a trickle of observational studies in the period leading up to the President's Crime Commission Report published in 1967 became a flood in the five years thereafter, with at least four of the classic studies of police behavior published between 1966 and 1971 (Skolnick, Wilson, Reiss, and Bittner). Three of these four studies were the product of independent social scientists riding along as observers of police operations, an early precursor to what later was called "embedded observation" by journalists in the military operations of more recent times. These pioneering social scientists could impose their insights and independent judgments on the police behavior they observed, but they couldn't alter that behavior (except by being present) and they could not systematically test the impact of the behavior they observed on the communities being policed. So behavior could be categorized (see, e.g., "Varieties of Police Behavior"), questioned, and related to the theoretical structure provided by the authors, but rigorous evaluation would require the power to alter police behavior and a scale of research far more extensive than a professor and his graduate students could generate.

Two new organizational structures of the 1960s did produce the potential for large-scale and systematic evaluative research on the effects of police on crime and communities. The first was the creation of the federal Law Enforcement Assistance Administration, which funded research through a variety of mechanisms including the National Institute of Justice (Goldstein 1990). The federal program had quite a bit of money but a very broad portfolio of crime and criminal justice issues of interest. The Police Foundation, created by Ford and other foundations in 1969, also had substantial money and only a single subject—police. But both financial agencies had no direct control over how municipal police were deployed. So the ultimate shape of *any* police research depended on finding police departments willing to sign on to a program of transparent and rigorous evaluative research. This was not an easy task in 1969 (and it's no easier in 2011).

The Police Foundation made common cause with a progressive police chief in Kansas City named Clarence Kelly (soon elevated to succeed J. Edgar Hoover as head of the FBI). The Kansas City Preventive Patrol Experiment was a revolutionary collaboration between independent researchers and a major police department to use powerful evaluative methods to assess the impact of conventional police tactics on crime rates. The target of the Kansas City evaluation was testing different levels of routine patrol by police cars on the incidence of crime. The orthodox belief was that routine patrol deterred potential criminals and reassured citizens, but the strategy had never been tested. The mix of progressive police administration and outside evaluators who mounted the patrol assessment in Kansas City were not believers in the effectiveness of preventative patrol "so it is fair to suppose that . . . the null hypothesis was not only the technical objective of the research but its desired outcome as well" (Zimring 2006 at p. 31). Joseph McNamara, who had succeeded Kelly as Kansas City chief summarized the 1974 report of results:

> Three controlled levels of routine preventive patrol were used in the experimental areas. One area, termed "reactive," received no preventive patrol. Officers entered the area only in response to citizen calls for assistance. This in effect substantially reduced police visibility in that area. In the second area, called "proactive," police visibility was increased two to three times its usual level. In the third area, termed "control," the normal level of patrol was maintained. Analysis of the data gathered revealed that the three areas experienced no significant differences in the level of crime, citizens' attitudes towards police service, citizens' fear of crime, police response time, or citizens' satisfaction with police response time. (Zimring 2006 at p. 31, quoting Kelling et al. 1974 at p. vii)

Chief McNamara then provided his readers with a peek at the strategic objective of this preventive patrol demonstration:

> Thus, it is apparent that with the right kind of leadership and assistance, urban police departments have the capacity to mount successful controlled experiments necessary to develop viable alternatives to the obsolete concept of preventive patrol. (Kelling et al. 1974 at p. viii)

The reform program was thus a two-step revolution. First would come the creative destruction of the preventive patrol demonstration. This would be followed by the testing of new theories of policing with collaborative controlled experiments.

Like so many revolutionary movements in the twentieth century, the two-step program of the Police Foundation proved more effective at the destruction stage of its program than in the task of rigorously testing new methods of police service and prevention. For one thing, preventive patrol proved somewhat more resilient than its critics had hoped in 1974—and routine patrol by police cars is still a predominant police strategy in many police departments in the United States in the second decade of the twenty-first century. Orthodoxy dies hard in police organizations.

But beyond this, the experiments of the 1970s were *much* more successful in undermining faith in older methods of policing than in institutionalizing rigorous evaluation of new methods of crime control.

Writing in the late 1970s, Charles Silberman echoed the progressive party line:

> Serious research and experimentation on policing are barely 15 years old; their main contribution has been to destroy the assumption on which most police activity has been based—to demonstrate the extent of our ignorance about what the police can, and cannot, do to reduce crime and improve domestic tranquility. What is needed is not more hardware, communications equipment, or personnel, but more research and experimentation. (Silberman 1978 at p. 252)

That call to experiment was issued a generation ago, and the subsequent changes in police tactics and organization over the past 30 years have been substantial. But an era of controlled experimentation never happened in American policing and we are almost as far removed from experimental policing in 2011 as in 1978, and in New York City as in any other large city in the United States. Why?

Part of the answer concerns the political economy of true experiments in policing and part relates to the odds against positive findings. The reader will recall that no true experiment can take place in a police department unless the department agrees to a transparent shift of authority to determine what the police do in the experimental and control areas. There is a second transfer of power as well—from the police department to the researchers—to determine whether the experiment was a success. And this will usually put the police department more at risk of apparent failure than happened in Kansas City with preventive patrol. In that experiment, the department was rooting for the null hypothesis—and a finding of no significant difference is much more likely in experimental trials than a significant difference favoring the experimental condition. So the deck was stacked *in favor* of the desired result in the preventive patrol exercise. In most experimental trials—where the police are the proponents of the policy to be evaluated—the deck will be stacked against the favorable outcome that the department would wish—so most experiments that police participate in will end up as failures from the department's perspective. Some heavily regulated activities can require running the gauntlet of experimental proof before innovations are allowed on the market—the clinical pharmaceutical industry is the classical example of this, but there is no requirement for experimental confirmation of effect in *any* aspect of public administration—least of all the police. So police chiefs don't have to surrender authority to evaluators unless they want to do so.

The golden age of experiments in American policing was rather short. The Police Foundation followed up its preventive patrol experience with a foot patrol trial in Newark, New Jersey (Kelling and Pate 1981). This was a strategy that the progressive brain trust favored, and citizens in the experimental zones felt safer than in control areas, but there was no significant reduction in crime. So this time, the null hypothesis was not the Foundation's friend. A gun enforcement trial in Kansas City produced suggestive results (see Sherman and Rogan 1995), but later work in Indianapolis found only one of two strategies—the one emphasizing high-risk persons—effective (McGarrell, Chermak, and Weiss 2002). A random experiment into different treatment conditions in Minneapolis showed that arrest of domestic assailants produced a significant reduction in recurrences reported—a celebrated success in the 1980s—but replication of the experiment did not duplicate the result. Experimental evolution of "hot spots" in Atlantic City did replicate successful outcomes, a singular achievement in police experiments (Committee to Review Research on Police Policy and Practices 2004 at p. 238). A second series of experiments in "hot spots" policing was also started in Minneapolis and has produced the single most sustained and successful series of rigorous evaluations of policing techniques (Braga and Weisburd 2010). The relatively discouraging track record for experiments may have driven a wedge between police innovations and rigorous external evaluation. Joseph McNamara had hopefully announced in 1974 that urban police departments had "the capacity to mount successful controlled experiments" but the 30 years after 1980 demonstrated the lack of incentives to engage in this type of research and the disadvantages to administrative control and public reputation of controlled experiment as a method of testing policy innovations.

The only sustained series of successful experiments of police tactics involved a version of problem-solving policing generally called "hot spots" patrol enhancement, targeted either on crack houses or other places with extremely high violent crime or drug activity. A series of experiments in Kansas City and New Jersey provide solid evidence of crime reduction (Committee to Review Research on Police Policy and Practices 2004 at pp. 238–239; Braga and Weisburd 2010).

But these experiments are close to being the exception that proves the rule. The 2004 Committee to Review Research on Police Policy and Practices report on police acknowledges the "strong empirical support for the hot spots . . . approach." But there is no series of controlled experiments reported to test various definitions of community policing, police crackdowns, field interrogations, order maintenance policing, or other tactics (id.). And the principal reason for this equivocal set of conclusions is not the negative outcome of other controlled experiments but the absence of a sustained sequences of these experiments (id. at pp. 224–251). Rather than sorting through the wide variety of policing tactics into "works" and "doesn't work" categories, the Committee to Review Research on Police Policy and Practices finds most of the new theories of policing promising but unproven.

The 1980s and 1990s became an era when a large number of new strategic and tactical innovations were suggested and tried, often without precise definition; but few decisive evaluations were attempted in large urban departments. The usual suspects for conducting controlled research were places like Kansas City, Minneapolis, Jersey City, and Newark. Missing from the list of experimental hosts are the nation's largest cities and biggest police departments. Community policing, problem-solving policing, and order-maintenance policing were prominent ideas in the literature and were introduced in a variety of forms in urban police practice. But the second step in the systematic program of trial and error that Chief McNamara had hailed on the horizon in the post-preventive patrol era he envisioned never came to pass, and New York City is no exception to this rule.

Policing in New York City

The modern history of the New York City Police Department is an odd mixture of reform and reactionary intransigence. The nation's largest municipal police force was never by reputation regarded as a great department and was prone to periodic scandals, intensified by the publicity generated by its media capital status. The department was open to bringing in renowned outsiders into the police commissioner's post long before other agencies—Howard Leary from Philadelphia, Patrick Murphy from Detroit, and Lee Brown from Houston—but New York was usually not hospitable to the reform efforts that they attempted to impose. The Police Department that new Mayor David Dinkins inherited during the crisis of concern about drugs and violent crime in 1989 was not regarded as either energetic or effective (Silverman 1999).

Yet the same accident of political economy that had produced 20,000 to 40,000 different police forces in the United States also limited a big city mayor to concentrating on police for any crime policy initiative. Policing is the only major criminal justice agency that is usually under municipal control. Improvements in the quantity and quality of policing may therefore look like a mayor's best choice because it is his only choice.

The architects of the first major plan to expand the city's police force were Mayor David Dinkins and Police Commissioner Lee Brown, and the announcement of the program was made in August 1990 (McKinley 1990 at B1). The long-range goal was a 5,000 officer net expansion of the force. While the expansion goal was not tied to any overarching policing strategy, the first piece was toward "building a force of foot patrol officers who are specially trained to solve recurrent crime problems rather than just respond to emergencies" (McKinley 1990).

So problem solving and "hot spots" were on Commissioner Brown's mind in 1990. The contribution of the Dinkins-Brown administration to expansion of the police force went well beyond the planning stage. Figure 5.1 traces total police manpower in New York City by year, using 1990 levels as a base. The emphasis in Figure 5.1 is on net manpower so that the transit police and housing police that were incorporated into the department after 1994 are excluded from expansion numbers.

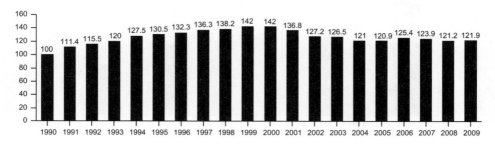

FIGURE 5.1 Trends in Police Manpower, New York City, 1990–2009.
Note: Excluding Transit and Housing Police.
Source: New York City Police Department.

B. What Happened?

The Magnitude and Timing of Staffing Changes

The City of New York began the 1990s as the largest police department in the United States in its main functions, and this department was augmented by two special purpose police forces, one for the transit system and one for housing. There were over 17,000 police in the New York department in 1990 and nearly an additional 5,000 police in two autonomous transit and housing forces. Figure 5.2 shows (for the NYPD) the ratio of police to population for the four major boroughs in 1990. Transit and housing are not included.

The numbers in Figure 5.2 are representative but not a complete account of police resources because transit and housing departments are not included. Using resident population as a measure, Manhattan occupied almost half again the number of police per 100,000 than the citywide average and more than twice the per capita staffing in Queens. One reason Manhattan stands out is the much larger population it contains during the day, with a correspondingly greater need for police service. But while that explains the gap between Manhattan and the outer boroughs, it does not help us to comprehend why the Bronx requires 68% more police per capita in 1990 than does Queens. The obvious theory here is that there is a larger concentration of violent crime in the Bronx. Figure 5.3 explores this by dividing the number of police in each borough by the homicide volume in the borough for 1990.

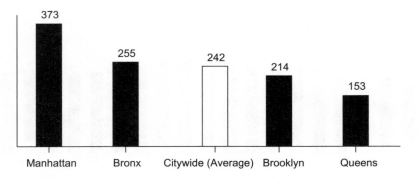

FIGURE 5.2 Police Officers (Excluding Transit and Housing Police) per 100,000 Population, Four Major Boroughs, 1990.
Source: New York City Police Department; see Appendix D.

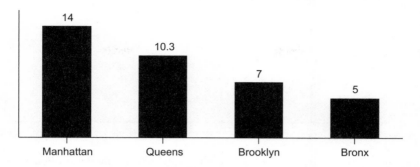

FIGURE 5.3 Police Officers per Reported Homicide, Four Major Boroughs, 1990.
New York City Police Department; see Appendix D.

Using police officers per reported homicide as the measure, Manhattan maintains its city leadership with 14 police per reported homicide, but the Bronx—which was second for that year in per capita police—is dead last in police officers per reported homicide with 5 police per reported killing. Crime density obviously explains the difference in per capita policing between the Bronx and Queens. Even though Queens had the lowest population rate of police presence, it recorded the second highest number of police per homicide, and has twice the police per homicide ratio as the Bronx in 1990.

These two contrasting ways of measuring police workload and the allocation of police resources can both be used to compare the distribution of police to different places and trends in police resources over time. Figure 5.4 shows trends over time in total uniformed NYPD manpower from 1990 to 2007, again excluding the 1995 integration of transit and housing force.

Using police staffing without transit and housing, the police force increased all through the 1990s, from 17,692 at the beginning to the decade to just over 25,000 by 1999, a 44% increase. Seventy percent of that increase was in place by 1995. After 2000, the trend is reversed; the number of police in service drops quickly in the first half of the next decade. By 2005, the net increase in staffing had been cut from the 42% increase in 1999 and 2000 to a 21% increase from 1990 levels, or half the peak rate increase in force, and the number of officers remains close to the 2005 level for the rest of the decade. Adding the transit and housing forces into the picture changes neither the extent of the changes after 1995 nor their timing.

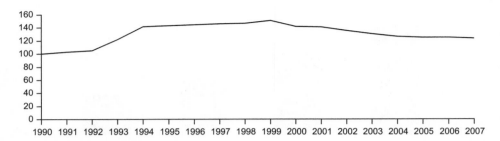

FIGURE 5.4 Trends in Uniformed New York City Police Department Personnel, 1990–2007.
Note: Excluding Transit and Housing Police.
Source: New York City Police Department; see Appendix D.

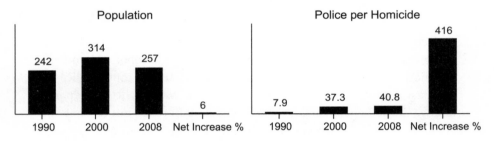

FIGURE 5.5 Two Measures of Police Staffing, New York City, 1990–2008.
Source: Staff (NYPD; see Appendix D); crime (NYPD; see Appendix D); Population (U.S. Department of Commerce, Bureau of the Census).

But if we shift the focus from population to serious crime as a measure of workload, the time trends are much more encouraging, as shown in Figure 5.5. The percentage increase in police per population after 1990 is down to single digits by 2008, but the homicide indicator shows a much more dramatic expansion in the 1990s, and the high ratios even increased a bit more during the manpower reductions after 2000 (adding 9.4%).

Figure 5.6 shows the pattern of police assignment for staff other than transit and housing for the four major boroughs. The largest increase during the 1990s was in Queens, which had the lowest 1990 population rate of policing, and two-thirds of the Queens increase was retained in 2009. The lowest increase of the four boroughs during the 1990s was Manhattan, with the highest base rate in 1990, and most of Manhattan's 1990s personnel increase was lost by 2009.

Brooklyn staffing growth was the second lowest of the four during the 1990s, but Brooklyn retained just over half of its peak rate increase in

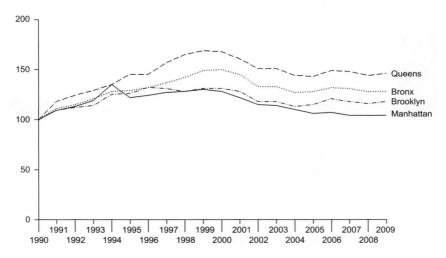

FIGURE 5.6 Trends in New York Police Department Staff by Borough, 1990–2009 (Transit and Housing Excluded).
Source: New York City Police Department; see Appendix D.

2009, while Manhattan lost 80% of its increase. The high-crime Bronx, which started the 1990s with the second highest per capita police coverage, increased staffing by half during the 1990s and retained just over half of that increase in 2009.

The division of the city into these four major population centers provides only a limited view of how the allocation of police resources may have changed in the era of Compstat administration. To some extent, the inter-borough comparison of manpower after 1990 suggests that the new regime evened out the extreme values of 1990 manpower represented by Manhattan and Queens. But the continued emphasis of officers for the Bronx also indicates that continued concentrations of crime attract higher levels of personnel. Finally, the reduction of Manhattan police to levels under the 1990 ratio per 100,000 residents suggests that sustained success in crime reduction (see Figure 3.3) may result in allocating police to other places in the city.

Trends by Function

Limited information is available on trends over time in the different types of police work. Figure 5.7 shows the distribution of police officers by function for 1990, the beginning of the city's changes (except for the housing and transit force where 1995 totals are provided, the first year after they were incorporated into the NYPD).

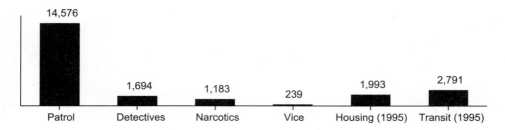

14,576

| 1,694 | 1,183 | 239 | 1,993 | 2,791 |

| Patrol | Detectives | Narcotics | Vice | Housing (1995) | Transit (1995) |

FIGURE 5.7 Police Officers by Function, New York Police Department, 1990 (Patrol, Detectives, Narcotics and Vice) and 1995 (Transit and Housing). *Source:* New York City Police Department; see Appendix D.

About two-thirds of the police manpower in the city were assigned to the NYPD patrol division staff in 1990. Patrol is the dominant function of all municipal police, and many of the transit and housing police are also on specialized forms of patrol (Silverman 1999 at p. 167). About 1,700 officers were in the detective services and 1,200 in specialized narcotics. A much smaller unit was detailed to vice, and the housing and transit forces provide another group, estimated at just under 5,000 officers, who were in autonomous administrative units until 1994.

Figure 5.8 shows trends over time in deployment of the four police functions continuously under NYPD control for the 19 years after 1990, using the 1990 staffing level for each function as 100 to emphasize trends over time. There is no adjustment in the figure for shifts in population.

The number of patrol police increases by one-third between 1990 and 1995, then stays close to the 1995 level for the rest of the decade, drops by 8% in 2002 and stays close to the 2002 level for the rest of the decade. By 2009, the level of patrol staffing was 22% greater than in 1990, and the patrol function had held on to more than two-thirds of its 1990s gains.

While patrol growth was concentrated in the early 1990s, the number of detectives grew in 10 of the 11 years after 1990. The 2,709 detectives in service in 2001 was an all-time high, with the 60% growth representing twice as much expansion as the growth in patrol. By 2009, the detective force remained 41% above its 1990 level so that both detectives and patrol retained 60% of their peak gains.

Both the specialized narcotics and vice operations show atypical patterns over time. The narcotics unit grew faster than anything else in the department during the 1990s, from a base of 1,183 to over 2,800 in 1999, a 137% increase in nine years. But narcotics staffing then dropped very quickly as well, back to 1,180 in 2006, three fewer officers than had been

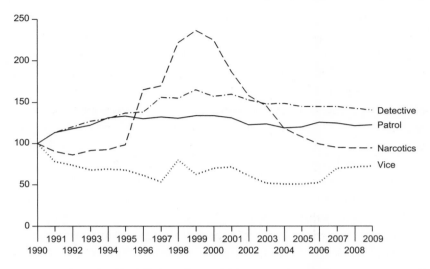

FIGURE 5.8 Trends in Staff for Four Police Functions, 1990–2009.
Source: New York City Police Department; see Appendix D.

in the unit in 1990, and some further shrinkage followed in later years. While patrol and detective retained two-thirds of their peak gains from the 1990s, the narcotics operation gave back all of its substantial increase and more. The small vice unit dropped substantially even while general force levels were increasing, then drifted lower to a 50% decline by 2004 and 2005, with some recovery starting in 2007.

These contrasting patterns provide some evidence of priorities in the department. The expansion in patrol forces and the retention of two-thirds of patrol growth in the face of the economic pressures of recent years is a vote of confidence from police management for patrol operations. But why then do the detective staffs grow faster and retain much more net growth (41% v. 22.6%)? My suspicion is that part of the increase in detectives is a function of the changing mix of police responsibilities, with surveillance, anti-terrorism, and crime analysis work creating the demand for a larger number of higher skilled officers. Then, too, as new officers gain in skill and seniority during the 1990s, there is probably a "supply side" push for larger numbers of desirable detective positions to retain and reward a maturing police force.

The first 17 years of the personnel history of the vice unit tells a pretty clear story of limited management confidence in this branch of police

function. From 1990 to 2006, what had been a low status police speciali-
zation got even lower, with only marginal increases in staff in recent years.
For all the rhetoric of "zero tolerance" and "order maintenance," the control of vice must have been among the department's lowest priorities all
through the period under study. Since public prostitution and gambling
are priority targets in "broken windows" policing programs, the downgrading of vice is one indication that this branch of "quality of life" enforcement wasn't at the top of the department's goals. A number of other
indications of this will be mentioned later in the chapter.

But what of the rise and fall of the special narcotics unit? This unit had
double the growth during the 1990s of any other major department—127%
vs. the 60% growth of detectives—but this was followed by the biggest
drop of any other major unit, a 58% decline in the six years after 1999. Did
the department's priorities change that markedly? Or did New York City
win its war on illegal drugs and then withdraw its troops?

One very likely explanation is that the police had succeeded in achieving
the two major strategic objectives that animated the narcotic unit's expansion—driving drug markets off the streets and reducing drug traffic–
related violence. Perhaps reducing the level of drugs sold and ingested
were not high strategic priorities, so that trends like drug treatment levels
and overdose deaths (see Figures 4.4 and 4.5) were of lesser priority.
Indeed, the almost 60% drop in narcotics unit strength is strong circumstantial evidence that the open air market and lethal violence aspects of
drug traffic were the department's chief priorities all along. In this sense,
the personnel shifts in post-Compstat management may be an important
window into management priorities.

Figure 5.9 completes the time trend study of police units by examining
force levels from 1995 onward for the newly integrated housing and transit police. There is a substantial difference in trends over time for these
units, both in the short and long run. Both units lost manpower in the
three years after integration, but the housing police lost almost twice as
much manpower between 1995 and 1998 as the transit police (18.7% v.
10.1%). But then the housing police increase 9.3% over the 11 years after
1998, while the transit police drop a further 20%. Why these contrasts?

In the short term, the above-ground overlap between housing police
and non-housing patrol units may have produced more extensive trims
as the two forces were integrated. After that, the department's emphasis on "hot spots" and disadvantaged areas may have made the terri-
tories covered by housing police a higher priority. Thus, housing gained

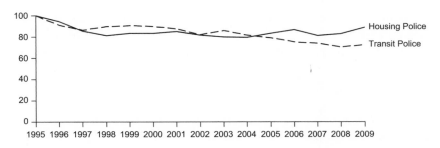

FIGURE 5.9 Trends in Staffing for Housing and Transit Police, 1995–2009.
Note: 1995 = 100.
Source: New York City Police Department; see Appendix D.

personnel, even while the rest of the department went on a manpower diet after 2000.

The relatively sharp loses for the transit police (28% after 1995) may have been the price of success. If the police department was concentrating on the largest remaining areas of violent crime in the city, the 20% drop in transit police after 1998 may best be considered a departmental compliment. Certainly, observers cannot use personnel trends in transit police as a way of uncovering the real priorities of the police, as I tried to do with vice and narcotics manpower. The across-the-board success of safety efforts in public transport make the transit reduction in force an unreliable indication of which crimes and which victims were most important to the police because all the news from transit was so good. Transit crime was still very important, but this was one "mission accomplished" announcement of the era that wasn't premature.

Strategic and Tactical Changes

A wide variety of changes in how patrol resources were deployed in New York City were at the center of the regime initiated by William Bratton and crime analyst Jack Maple and continued for the years afterward. Crime analyses and mapping were used to target particular problem areas where patrol, detective, and narcotics units might be emphasized. In part, the new allocation of street police resources under Bratton was relatively uncomplicated. His deputy commissioner for crime control complained about standard practice under previous administration:

> [W]hen night fell, the NYPD went home. During almost any twenty-four hour period, shootings in the city peaked between 8pm and

4am, but the vaunted Narcotics Division went off duty at 7p.m. . . . The warrant squads . . . didn't hit any doors until at least 8am and they took weekends off too. The robbery squad were off weekends. . . . Unfortunately, the bad guys work around the clock. (Maple and Mitchell 1999 at pp. 22–23)

An early priority of the new regime was putting police in service where and when "the bad guys" were at work!

Much of the coordination between patrol, detective, crime analysts, and other specialists that were part of the Bratton/Maple program were integral to problem-solving policing as practiced in other departments. But the New York force combined these approaches with the dramatic increase in manpower.

The Embrace of Aggressive Tactics

A further shift worth independent mention was emphasis and rewards for aggressiveness in street policing. The labels given to aggressive street work vary from site to site—it was called "field interrogation" in San Diego, proactive policing in other locations, and "preventive policing" by William Bratton, but the basic methodology is trying to take control of potentially threatening situations by street stops of suspicious-looking persons, by frisking after stops for weapons or contraband, and by making arrests for minor offenses as a way to remove perceived risks from the street and to identify persons wanted for other crimes.

While statistics from New York City in the 1990s showing expansions in arrests for motor vehicles, alcohol, gambling, and truancy offenses may look like an investment of resources in maintaining the city's "quality of life," that was *not* the arrest strategy outlined by the Deputy Commissioner for Crime Control Maple:

I'm not a big fan of curfews, because too often they're selectively enforced according to a kid's skin color. But a curfew could be an excellent tool if the penalties are applied only to juveniles on parole, probation or otherwise have criminal records. Those offenders should be remanded to court; the other kids who are out unreasonably late should be brought home. (Maple and Mitchell 1999 at p. 157)

The instrumental use of stops and arrests for preventive enforcement against bad guys is illustrated by a traffic tactic:

Most cops aren't really that good at catching people dealing drugs or
trafficking guns. But we do know that many of the gangsters of this
era roll around in cars that have blacked out windows and very loud
radios . . . and because those indicators are offenses in themselves,
the cops don't have to worry about accusations of inappropriate profiling. (Maple and Mitchell 1999 at p. 160)

The problem with using a predicate offense—alcohol, loud radio noise
in a car, marijuana—as a justification for selective enforcement of non-
serious crimes is that it really does become the moral equivalent of racial
profiling. A much larger percentage of the African American and Hispanic kids picked up for truancy and curfew will be in the parole, probation, or "criminal record" group that the Maple New York City strategy
singles out for punitive treatment. African American and non–African
American respondents report similar rates of marijuana use, but (as we
shall see) the African American percentage of New York City marijuana
arrests is much higher than the white rate. And the obvious reason is that
young men of color live in poor neighborhoods and also more often look
to police like potential street criminals. If that is the motive for differential
treatment by the police, it has very substantial racial and ethnic impact. If
"the units enforcing quality of life laws must be sent where the maps show
concentrations of crime and criminals, and the rules governing stops have
to be designed to catch the sharks, not the dolphins," (Maple and Mitchell)
the differential punitive impact of the policy on dark-skinned persons on
the streets in low-income areas is inescapable.

The Strategic and Organizational Features of Compstat

One further organizational change that came in the Bratton-Maple era
was a tighter organization of police manpower and the use of crime information and statistics to inform tactics, manpower deployment, and enforcement priorities. The analysis process that was called "Compstat"
used crime statistics for planning purposes and also as a method of evaluating patrol performance. As a management system, this was apparently
centralized and top down in its authority structure. Information from the
field was necessary and valued, but authority and strategic choices came
from downtown at One Police Plaza. Intermediate stops up the city's organizational chart for detectives and other special agencies were eliminated,
but not to decentralize so much as to create a more direct linkage from the
top command down.

The tighter top-down organization of the police department in the era of Compstat is usually justified as an efficient method of coordinating crime control, but that is only one of two major functions that the New York team achieved with centralized and crime-centered organizational meetings (Bratton 1998, Maple and Mitchell 1999). It is important to understand that the design and execution of Compstat, New York style, was not just about crime control.

Here is Eli Silverman's list of Compstat goals from his 1999 study of the New York reforms:

> Enforcing accountability and improving the crime-fighting ratio of 'full suit' to empty suit' [in police manpower] required crime information, graphic crime mapping, revised crime strategies, empowered precinct commanders, street-level creative problem solving, and breached unit barriers. Compstat emerged as the catalyst and arena for those developments. (Silverman 1999 at p. 99)

What is noteworthy in Professor Silverman's long list of Compstat functions and goals is that some of the crime-fighting virtues to be pursued seem to be suited to decentralized power and authority, things like "empowered precinct commanders" and "street-level creative problem solving." Yet the organizational emphasis of the program is, Silverman tells us, very centralized:

> Compstat gathers all NYPD informational arrows in one quiver, targeting crime conditions for all key decision makers at their crime fighting meetings . . . The top brass convene to discuss crime on a regular basis, and the scheduled crime strategy meetings engage both top echelon and each borough's precinct COs once every four or five weeks. (Silverman at p. 109)

Why so much central command input and authority? The critical objective here is one that Silverman mentions at the front end of his Compstat objectives, namely "enforcing accountability" in the nation's largest and most bureaucratic municipal police department. The modern history of New York police prior to 1992 was the importation of progressive outside police administrators into the city's top job, where their efforts to reform the force were frustrated by a labyrinthine bureaucracy, unsympathetic police administrators, and no effective method of enforcing central priorities on field staff. Compstat was not merely a method of gaining control over crime in New York City, but also a strategy for the equally difficult task of getting control of the New York Police Department.

Marijuana and Policing Priority: A Cautionary Tale

The use of stops and arrests as instruments to control suspicious persons and street situations means that statistics on patterns of minor arrests must be very carefully considered before assuming that they represent the priorities of police policy. Some of the biggest mistakes that are evident in claims about what the New York department did and how it reduced crime stem from failure to read the intentions of the people like Maple and Bratton who designed the New York program as well as the statistical patterns that suggest that they meant what they were saying.

Figure 5.10 will serve as a graphic introduction to the dangerous art of inferring policy from trends in minor offense arrests. The figure reports the annual total of marijuana arrests in New York City from 1978 through 2008, as reported by Harry Levine and Deborah Peterson Small in a report for the New York Civil Liberties Union (Levine and Small 2008).

The first 14 years of the time series after 1978 show relatively small numbers and minor variations, then misdemeanor marijuana arrests start to take off in 1994 and 1995, from less than 5,000 in 1993 to an all-time high of more than 50,000 in 1999. Because private possession of small amounts of marijuana is not an offense in the state of New York in non-public places, these marijuana arrests are predominantly street and public space events. Why the skyrocketing rates during the mid 1990s?

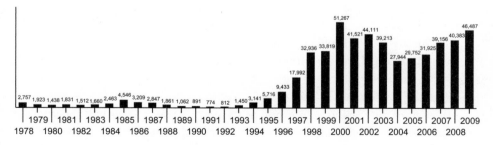

FIGURE 5.10 Misdemeanor Marijuana Arrests in New York City, 1978–2009.
Source: New York State Division of Criminal Justice Services, Computerized Criminal History System (June 2009).

Did marijuana become a law enforcement priority during this very late stage of the drug war? There is no evidence of this in the discourse of police leaders or political figures. These misdemeanor arrests were certainly not the work of the narcotics unit or of the department's detectives, indeed the number of "fingerprintable" marijuana arrests remains higher in the years after 2006 when the police department has already cut its narcotics division back to 1990 strength than even during the peak narcotics force years of 1997 and 1998 (see Levine 2010). These arrests are police on patrol concentrating effort in high-crime areas and with persons whom police regard as potential offenders for more serious crimes. But the threshold offense of marijuana provides the patrolman a method of obtaining fingerprints and removing the suspect from the street. Fundamentally, these arrests are attempts not of drug control but of crime control.

The critics of this use of a threshold marijuana charge emphasize the disproportionate involvement of African American and Latino suspects in New York City's misdemeanor marijuana arrest dragnet. Levine and Small correctly report that survey research shows marijuana use is slightly higher among whites than among African American youth and significantly higher for whites than for Latinos (Levine and Small 2008). But African Americans—who comprise 28% of the city's population—absorb 52% of the city's misdemeanor marijuana arrests, while non-Black Latinos are 31% of the arrests, and whites (35% of the population) were less than 10% of marijuana arrests in the years 2004–2008 (Levine 2010). Instead of the equal risk that marijuana use surveys might suggest, African Americans are arrested at seven times the rate of non-Hispanic whites, with the Latino rate in the middle. How does this happen?

The racial and ethnic disproportions are a natural result of the two-stage selection process that uses stops and minor arrests as crime prevention tactics. The first stage of selective control is concentrating police attention and resources in areas where serious crime is high. The larger the concentration of police in high-crime areas, the more likely that the persons arrested will be minorities of color at the lower end of the economic ladder. This doesn't mean that racial disproportion in arrests is a necessary by-product of "hot spots" policing, but it *does* mean that using street stops and arrests as prevention strategies in such areas will concentrate the impact of the stops and arrests on minority youth.

The second stage of the selection process that concentrates stops and minor offense arrests on racial and ethnic minorities is restricting the use of these tools to persons who look dangerous to a street patrolman, trolling for "sharks" (in Jack Maple cop speak) and "not the dolphins." Blacks and Latinos, who were 84% of the marijuana arrests in the decade after 1996, were certainly not 84% of the people who possessed or smoked marijuana, but Blacks and Hispanics were about 90% of the persons arrested for robbery and burglary in New York City in 2007 and 2008 (see Table 5.1). So if the street patrol officer is concentrating on potential robbers and burglars when selectively enforcing marijuana laws, he or she will select "the usual suspects" not for pot but for street crimes more concentrated among minorities.

Table 5.1 compares the racial and ethnic distribution of arrests for two street felonies—robbery and burglary—with the racial and ethnic distribution of persons arrested in the city for marijuana offenses. By combining a national estimate of marijuana use in the last month with the population of the city in 2007, I also add an estimate of how marijuana use would be distributed in the city's three largest population groups (SAMHSA Survey 2007).

White non-Hispanic persons are less than 10% of marijuana arrests in New York City, while they constitute about 40% of the pot smokers. Blacks are about one-third of the smokers in the three groups, yet they are over half of the persons arrested. But there is a very close fit between the proportion of persons of each ethnic and racial group arrested for the two street crimes—robbery and burglary—and the proportion arrested for marijuana.

Table 5.1. Percent Distribution by Race and Ethnicity of New York City Robbery, Burglary, and Marijuana Defendants in 2006 and 2009 and Estimated Percent Distribution of "Last Month" Marijuana Users, New York City 2007.

	Robbery Arrests[1]	Burglary Arrests[1]	Marijuana Arrests[1]	Marijuana Users[2] (estimated)
White Non-Hispanic	6.3%	8.4%	9.6%	40.2%
Black	60.9%	52.6%	55.7%	34.2%
Hispanic	30.6%	37.6%	33.0%	25.6%

Source:
[1] Computer data provided by the New York State Criminal Justice Agency
[2] Based on a population distribution of 33% white non-Hispanic, 23.9% Black, and 25.6 Hispanic (see Table 3.3). Use in last month reported in SAMHSA survey.

The small percentage of white non-Hispanics arrested for marijuana is within a point and a half of the percentage arrested for burglary and 3% more than the white robbery arrest share. The huge disproportion of Blacks arrested for marijuana is nested halfway between their over-representation in robbery and burglary, so the 55.7% is probably almost equal to the average racial concentration for these two crimes, and that is also the position for Hispanic marijuana arrests, almost halfway between the 30.6% for robbery and the 37.6% for burglary at 33%.

The natural inference from these patterns is that the persons selected for marijuana arrests are in the neighborhoods and fit the profiles in the police view of potential robbers and burglars. Managing street risks rather than combating the evils of marijuana is the patrol agenda. The alternative explanation for the race and ethnicity patterns of Table 5.1 would not be one extraordinary coincidence but three extraordinary parallels between the profiles of arrested populations.

A final demonstration of the large gap between the people who use marijuana in New York City and those arrested for possessing it concerns gender. The best survey of youth marijuana rates is the National Survey of Adolescent Drug Use and Health. Combining these surveys for the years 2002–2007, the report shows that males say they have used marijuana in the past month at 7.5% compared to 5.8% for females (NSDUH Report 2009 at Table 1), a percentage distribution of 56% male to 44% female in a 50–50 gender distribution. Figure 5.11

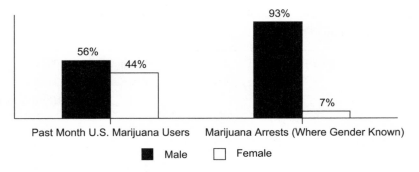

FIGURE 5.11 Male to Female Ratios in National Adolescent Marijuana Use Surveys, 2002-2007.
Note: N = 91,936; 3,691 records had no gender indication.
Sources: National Surveys on Drug Use and Health (from SAMSA), January 8, 2009 (Male Past Month 7.5%; Female Past Month 5.8% = 56.4% Male); Arrests by Gender from the New York State DCJS Computerized Criminal History System as of April 2010.

compares this with the gender breakdown of total marijuana arrests in New York City.

While the gender distribution of marijuana users is close to 50–50, the gender distribution of arrests is 93% to 7%, which generates a use-corrected difference in risk by gender of about 10 to 1. This is only circumstantial evidence that the police are going after robbery risks, but it is conclusive evidence that they aren't trying to go after marijuana as a threat to the quality of life.

A second example of the instrumental use of minor offenses as a selective crime control tactic comes from Silverman's study of Compstat:

A good case in point was a creative approach to bicycles, which, beginning about 1996 were used in robberies, shootings, and drug transactions. A commanding officer identified laws regulating the operation of bicycles. Through lawful bicycle inspections, enforcement swept up nineteen guns within that one precinct by the end of the summer. This success was heralded at a Compstat meeting and resulted in a citywide adoption of this strategy. The approach has subsequently resulted in the confiscation of hundreds of guns and large quantities of narcotics from this previously "invisible" criminal element. (Silverman 1999 at p. 190)

This tactic is exactly what many in the NYPD call "quality of life" enforcement. But the object of the campaign is guns, not bicycle safety, and I therefore do not think that 12-year-old private school student bikers are the focus of the effort. Whether or not this set of tactics reduces violent crime, it is a far cry from the symbolic communication strategy described in "Broken Windows" (Wilson and Kelling 1982). And when talking heads use the "quality of life" label to describe this policy, it lends further confusion to definitions and concepts of police work that are not wonderfully clear in the first place.

An Acid Test for "Broken Windows"

Detailed patterns of arrest in New York City allow us to test whether police are using these arrests broadly to enforce "quality of life" offenses or selectively to facilitate searches and record checks with persons who they think are street crime risks. Figure 5.12 compares arrest rates over time in New York City for two non-predatory offenses that are usually regarded as classic examples of offenses against public order, gambling and prostitution.

While arrests for marijuana went up tenfold (see Figure 5.10), trends for these two arrest rates differed markedly over time.

It is an understatement to say that arrests for these public order offenses follow different tracks in the years after 1990 in New York than for marijuana. Marijuana arrests jump in the mid-1990s to a peak more than ten times the 1990 volume (see Figure 5.10) and stay very high. Whatever their function, the police continue to use these arrests at historically high rates. The gambling pattern shows large increases between 1991 and 1997, stays higher than its 1990 level until 2001, then drops off suddenly and continues to decline through 2009. By that last year in the series, gambling arrests are only at 35% of their pre-Compstat 1990 level and down 88% from the peak rate of 1997. The most plausible interpretation of a near tripling of arrest rate followed by a greater than 85% drop is that police used gambling arrests as part of an aggressive patrol for some time but didn't find the persons brought in on such charges to have the records, warrants, or other indices of danger that were the targets of the policy. But the one interpretation that can't explain either the five-year increase or the precipitous decline that followed is any consistent policy of trying to reduce gambling that was designed to maintain public order. If all we had to compare with the marijuana pattern was the ups and downs of New York gambling enforcement, a "broken windows" or "quality of life" explanation for the contrasting patterns would seem quite improbable.

But prostitution arrest data in Figure 5.12 are critical to the proper analysis of the real priorities in New York arrest trends. Prostitution is the *perfect* control for testing whether "quality of life" or preventing street

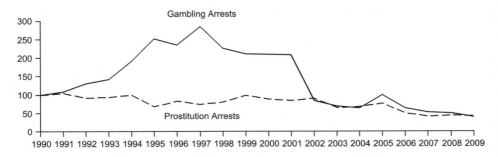

FIGURE 5.12 Trends in Gambling and Prostitution Arrests in New York City, 1990–2009.
Note: 1990 = 100 (gambling arrests in 1990 were 2,686; prostitution arrests were 9,953).
Source: New York City Police Department; see Appendix D.

crime is motivating police arrests for a wide variety of other public order and vice crimes. Very few women are arrested for robbery and burglary in New York, so the usual gender of prostitution suspects disqualifies them for being a street crime prevention target audience. Figure 5.13 shows the difference in gender between robbery and prostitution arrests for U.S. cities in 2007.

At the same time, publicly visible prostitution would appear to be a classic affront to public order that sends "broken windows" signals to law-abiding citizens that legal standards are not enforced, (see Kelling and Sousa 2001 at p. 5) so "Broken Windows" co-author George Kelling-mentions prostitution as one of two main examples of "broken windows" crimes.

And the New York City trends for prostitution arrests couldn't be clearer. This particular "broken windows" offense never attracted any of the additional resources that New York City deployed after 1990. The rate of prostitution arrests *never* gets higher than the 10,457 recorded in 1991, even as the police force is expanded and the new regime in policing comes to power. There is no period of increase to parallel the mid-1990s expansion for gambling or the sustained explosion of marijuana misdemeanors in the mid-1990s and beyond. Instead, the rate of prostitution arrests stays just under its 1990 base rate until the manpower cutbacks in 2001–2002, then declines to less than 40% of the 1990 base rate.

So prostitution never had any enforcement priority in the police expansion and had a sufficiently low priority in the era of manpower reductions

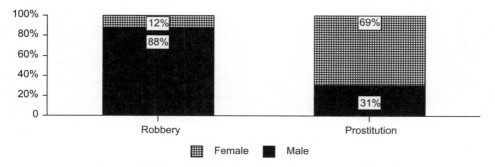

FIGURE 5.13 The Gender Gap between Street Crime and Prostitution, U.S. Cities, 2007.
Source: FBI, Uniform Crime Reports.

for arrests to drop by more than half. Why was prostitution never a priority while marijuana misdemeanor arrests skyrocketed and stayed very high? The only plausible answer is that order maintenance and quality of life were labels but not real motives for the pattern of arrests and deployment of police resources. It isn't just that the statistics in Figure 5.12 make the Jack Maple explanation plausible; they prove him right. And any attempt to rehabilitate "quality of life" accounts of New York City policing must begin with an alternative explanation of the sharply contrasting trends in Figure 5.12.

Stop and Frisk

Street police frequently stop, frisk, and require identification from persons in public places. The rationale for these interventions is suspicious activity and potential public danger including weapons. Each of these non-arrest interventions in New York since 1986 should, by departmental regulation, be reported within the department on a form known as a UF-250 if a frisk took place. Figure 5.14 shows the count of UF-250 stop and frisk incidents by year.

The volume of official stop reports increases from 41,438 in 1990 to 581,382 over the two decades covered, a 14-fold increase. There is no reason to doubt the high volume of stop-and-frisk events in 2009, but there are a number of indications that the data for a great many earlier years was substantially undercounted. The earlier volumes of stops seem suspicious because 90% of the reported increases happen after 1997 and 80% of all the official increases take place after the level of police manpower started its

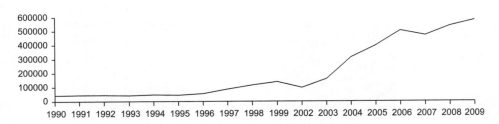

FIGURE 5.14 New York Police Department Documented UF-250 Stops, 1990–2009.

Sources: 1990-1998: http://www.usccr.gov/pubs/nypolice/ch5.htm#_ftn6 Memorandum from Director Central Records Division to Executive Director Support Services Bureau, Apr. 5, 1999, p. 1; 1999 est. based on New York State Attorney General's Report; 2002: Baker 2007; 2003-09: NYPD web site, John Jay Primer Report; 2010: NYCLU.

decline. The marijuana arrests, it will be recalled, reached peak levels during the late 1990s when manpower was at its peak. Why the discontinuity in time trends for these two similar manifestations of aggressive street patrol?

The distribution of stop subjects by race and ethnicity parallels the concentrations found in marijuana arrests and robbery and burglary suspects, with 87% of the stop targets reported as African American (56%) or Hispanic (31%) (New York City Police Department 2010). The negative impacts of stop and frisk include the discomfort and limited mobility of the stop and information retained by the police department on the incident and the identity of the subject. Retaining information in stops was restricted by state legislation in New York in 2010 (N.Y. Crim. Pro. Law Sec. 140. 1 2010).

The New Regime in Summary

The data available in public records provides limited but important insight about the strategies and priorities of policing in New York City. The size of the department expanded substantially in the 1990s and then dropped back somewhat when police are measured against population, But when available police are measured against crime rates, the resources of the NYPD remain impressively larger than 20 years prior, even after manpower cuts. The department introduced and institutionalized a centralized data-driven crime statistical and mapping program that is both an important element of enforcing accountability to central authority across the police department and a major weapon in crime detection and patrol strategy.

The strategic features in the 1990s program include: (1) crime reduction as a central priority, (2) sustained resources allocated to hot spot identification and control, and (3) very aggressive street police behavior in target areas, including stop and frisk and minor offense arrests targeted at suspicious street behavior or persons. Both the written record of the architects of the department's program and the statistical patterns of staffing and allocation of resources by function and geography establish a consistent pattern of these priorities.

There is no clear indication in either the design or execution of the Maple/Bratton Compstat regime of either the priorities of "broken windows" policing set out in the 1982 article or any broad measure of enforcement aimed at zero tolerance. Traffic stops of dark windowed cars in the Maple/Bratton strategy is not a traffic enforcement technique but a method of combating gun traffic and drug marketing. Many elements of the huge number of street arrests for marijuana misdemeanors are very controversial, but there can be no doubt that the driving force behind the tenfold increase in marijuana arrests is not a police commitment to reduce marijuana possession in public, or to make citizens feel better about their safety because marijuana smokers have been removed from the streets. And the low priorities of vice units, prostitution arrests, and gambling arrests in recent years seem to be the opposite of broken windows priorities.

The gap between NYPD priorities and broken windows policing circa 1982 is even greater when considering the community areas where the two strategies concentrate effort. Wilson and Kelling were not big fans of "hot spot" priorities in their 1982 "broken windows" analysis, wanting to concentrate resources in marginal areas, rather than the highest crime zones "where the situation is hopeless" (Wilson and Kelling 1982 at p. 16). Compstat in New York is driven by the numbers of the most serious crimes in the city—homicide, robbery and rape—so the priorities *must* be in the highest serious crime areas. Citizen feelings of safety in the Compstat universe are a by-product of lower crime levels when police put out the fires in the city's most impacted zones.

Even the most famous example of "order maintenance" priority during the transit police era was actually an ingeniously instrumental use of minor crime enforcement to discourage and apprehend "bad guys." Apprehending persons jumping turnstiles to avoid paying a subway fare was not only another Jack Maple technique for using minor infractions to go after "sharks" but it also removed a perverse incentive. The subway had been charging admission to everybody else but providing free entrance to prospective purse thieves and armed robbers.

With such basic differences in major goals and priority targets, how can we explain the rather frequent conflation of the order maintenance focus of "broken windows" with the crime-centered crusade of Compstat? In part, the brevity and imprecision of the original "broken windows" presentation invites readers to fill in the blanks in the 1982 magazine article with their own preferred meanings. The colorful phrases and insights in the Wilson and Kelling article become something of what psychologists call a projective technique—an expression of faith that police performance does matter in cities that gives the reader the opportunity to provide his own portrait of what types of police activity generated the good news.

In policy and political discussion, the issue is often reduced to debates about whether police activity reduces crime so that *any* police activity that works is taken as evidence that *everything* the police might do will be effective. (This same "all or nothing" view would generalize from a negative result of a police experiment—i.e., if routine car patrol doesn't prevent crime, then *no* form of police activity can prevent crime (see Braga and Weisburd 2010 at p. 8).

Two other psychological tendencies may be at work in awarding "broken windows" tactics credit for the crime prevention from the Compstat program. The first is that periods when crime is declining promote optimistic assumptions about the capacity of police to reduce crime, just as periods of rising crime make observers pessimistic about the preventive impact of street policing. While Wilson and Kelling may have been doubtful about the impact of foot patrol on crime rates in the "nothing works" atmosphere of the early 1980s, the size of the crime declines of the 1990s might have provoked more optimistic assessments (see Kelling and Coles 1996; Zimring 2006 at pp. 35–37).

And the dramatic success of New York City is an open invitation for policy entrepreneurs of all kinds to see their own fingerprints on the causes of this municipal miracle. Any set of changes as eclectic and multifaceted as New York's recent changes in policing probably had elements of most any set of new policing ideas of the last generation. It is only human nature that this conspicuous success would lead to multiple claims of paternity.

But does the evidence really support the crime prevention prowess of police in New York City? And, if so, *which* of the city's police innovations can rightly claim credit for reducing crime?

C. What Works?

This section addresses two separate questions about the impact of police on crime in New York City and uses different types of evidence to address each question. The first question is the more general one: Did the package of changes in policing reduce crime in the city and by how much? My "yes" answer to the question of aggregate police impact comes from the crime analysis in Chapter 1 of this book and the survey of other crime and criminal justice–related conditions in Chapters 3 and 4. I argue that the package of changes in the quantity and quality of policing should get credit for what I have called "the New York difference"—a crime decline close to 35% for some offenses—by a process of elimination. There are simply no other changes in policy, social conditions, or economics that could plausibly explain the city's much better than typical performance in the crime drop years of the 1990s and in the nine years after the general decline stopped. But this is not a conclusion based on direct observation of one or more features of police behavior reducing crime, it is an inference based instead on the absence of any plausible rival theories to account for a crime decline twice as large and twice as long as the national norm.

The second question is which of the many changes in policing in New York have produced the city's significant crime reductions. Was it the increased number of police, alone or in combination with new tactics and new management? Was it the crime centered management system, alone or in combination with increases in manpower and tactics? Was it the new tactics, and if so, which ones? Hot spots, gun emphasis, stop and frisk aggressiveness, instrumental arrests, coordination with civil enforcement? But clear evidence of the independent influence of *any* one factor in New York's portfolio of changes will often have to come from somewhere other than New York City, because all of these interrelated changes happened together. Some tactics have such specific targets (public drug markets, guns) that data on specific effects can be produced, although not independent of the extra manpower and change in management and aggressiveness that were the context of their introduction in New York. And patterns of change over time both up and down in variables like manpower provide limited opportunities for attempting to measure their independent impact. But isolating the separate impact of policing variables is an extraordinarily difficult task, and the methods by which changes have been introduced and evaluated in New York does not help outsiders to make such assessments with rigor.

After discussing the case for police as the cause of the "New York difference" and the probable magnitude of that difference, I will consider in some detail efforts to assess the impact of several specific elements of changes in policing—additional police, hot spots and gun specific focus, and aggressive stop and frisk and instrumental minor arrest policy.

A Process of Elimination

The search for non-police causes of the New York difference outlined in Chapter 3 did not produce any citywide changes in population, economy, or criminal justice that might explain a major crime decline, but there *were* changes in the population of Manhattan that is a plausible alternative explanation for part of that borough's extra measure of crime decline. Manhattan was the one borough in the city where the proportion of the population coming from high-risk demographic groups went down in the 1990s and after, so some of its crime decline could be the result of population change. And Manhattan also experienced very large increases in resident income not paralleled in the other major boroughs. One of the disadvantages of using a process of elimination as the primary method of determining a cause of the New York difference is the need to eliminate the impact of elements like population change.

The best way to control for any extra measure of reduction in Manhattan that may have come from demographic or economic change is to estimate the citywide police effect by using the large median crime decline in the three major boroughs that did not have risk reductions or income increases in their populations. This assumes that Manhattan would have had a decline equal to the average for the rest of the city without its population and economic changes. Figure 5.15 presents these citywide estimates.

The range of declines in Figure 5.15 is from 54% for larceny to 93% for auto theft, close to the citywide averages not excluding Manhattan, but slightly less. The next step in estimating the individual impact of policing in New York City is to eliminate the impact of the crime decline of the 1990s that was a national phenomenon and presumably also drove down crime in New York City. Table 5.2 provides one approach to the issue by comparing the crime declines in Figure 5.15 with the median crime decline over 18 years after 1990 in the rest of the ten largest cities. The difference between the average city experience and

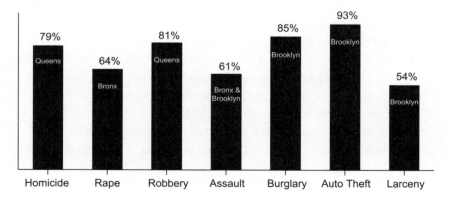

FIGURE 5.15 Median Crime Decline for Three Major Boroughs without Demographic Dividend or Extraordinary Economic Growth, New York City, 1990–2009. *Source:* New York City Police Department.

Table 5.2 **Estimating Police Impact by Comparing Median Non-Manhattan Crime Decline with Median Crime Decline in the other Nine Largest U.S. Cities.**

	Median Crime Drop among the other Nine Largest U.S. Cities* (1990–2009)	Median Crime Drop in Major Boroughs Excluding Manhattan (1990–2009)	Presumptive Policing Difference
Homicide	-64%	-76%	12%
Rape	-49%	-64%	15%
Robbery	-49%	-81%	32%
Assault	-57%	-61%	4%
Burglary	-53%	-85%	32%
Larceny	-52%	-54%	2%
Auto Theft	-72%	-93%	21%

*This is calculated by using the first larges rate of decrease out of the next top ten biggest cities, since San Jose and Detroit have moved in and out of the top ten largest American cities between 1990 and 2009.
Source: New York Compstat; 10 Cities (Uniform Crime Reports).

the non-Manhattan New York City experience is what the table calls the "presumptive policing difference."

The New York experience as measured in Table 5.2 is a larger decline in all seven crime categories, but the magnitude of the New York advantage is much greater for robbery, burglary, and auto theft (32%, 32% and 21%) than for larceny (2%) and assault (4%). The estimates for homicide (12%) and rape (15%) are in the middle. The two crimes with much lower presumptive policing impact are heterogeneous offenses with a mixture of public and private settings. The estimates for these crimes are quite close to zero. The three crimes with vastly larger presumptive policing impact—robbery, auto theft, and burglary—include two classic street crimes (robbery and auto theft) and a third offense where public access is important (burglary). So a much larger policing influence for these crimes is quite plausible. And the middle position of homicide and rape, a mix of stranger and acquaintance offenses, also is consistent with a middle position on policing influence.

But the crisp precision of a specific estimate of policing influence from Table 5.2 is misleading, of course. Even if the method used in this exercise were beyond reproach, the confidence intervals that one should impose on each of these estimates are not small. And the notion that the difference between New York and the average large city is a good measure of police effects is an approximation at best. Why not compare New York with the next best city instead of taking an average value? So the specific estimates in Table 5.2 are a best estimate for which the margin of error is very substantial. Still, the unanimity of the statistical advantages and the higher advantage for classic street crimes are consistent with policing effects.

While the margin estimated for policing is much smaller than the total crime drop, it would also be the biggest effect of municipal police impact on record. Figure 5.16 shows both the scale of estimated policing impacts on crime and the large differences by type of crime by expressing the estimates of aggregate police crime reduction taken from Table 5.2 as a percentage of remaining offenses in New York in 2009, instead of that table's use of 1990 rates as a denominator.

For the three street crimes with the highest police impact, the intercity comparison estimates far more police prevention since 1990 than current crime levels. New York police have prevented twice as much robbery and burglary as the city now experiences, and police efforts have eliminated more than three times the volume of auto theft that now takes place in New York. The prevention estimates for assault and larceny are insignificant by this measure. But almost as much rape and homicide have been prevented by police effort as remain in the city.

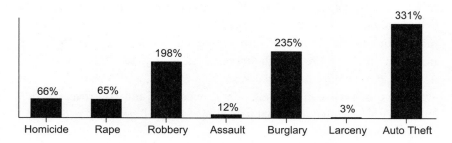

FIGURE 5.16 Policing Crime Reductions 1990–2009 as a Percentage of 2009 New York City Crime.
Source: Data in Table 5.2; New York City Police Department for 2009 crime rates.

Assessing the Impact of Particular Features and Practices

If observers could clearly identify which elements of policing were responsible for specific levels of crime reduction, that would be much more useful than concluding that the gestalt of manpower strategy and management changes probably reduced crime. For instance, specific estimates of how much crime resulted from increased manpower would help determine the costs and benefits of this expensive step. A whole host of highly specific strategies—such as targeting street drug markets, and gun enforcement emphasis—could be evaluated for their effectiveness and cost in New York City and for adaptation to other places. And it would be edifying if the contribution to crime control of two pervasive changes in New York policing—Compstat information and organization and aggressive police street interventions—could be separately evaluated. Highly specific findings about what works and what doesn't in New York City would be of great practical and theoretical value.

But the way in which changes were introduced, documented, and evaluated in New York conspires against reliable estimates of the effectiveness of individual variables in the two decades of police history after 1990. Most changes were citywide when introduced, and many aspects of the new regime happened together. New levels of manpower came into the department with new levels of aggressiveness and new enforcement priorities—and the new information and management systems coordinated these efforts. How can we measure Compstat effects independent of the manpower and the new tactics? If the only information available on the effectiveness of police strategies comes from New York City after 1990, the identification of the most promising elements in the police changes could only work for tactics with very specific indicators—and the biggest and most pervasive changes couldn't be assessed. Even with reliable findings from evaluations outside New York, the specific effectiveness of most innovations in the New York setting cannot be measured. And that is an important limit. Even though it seems clear that *something worked* in policing, that doesn't mean that *everything* worked, and certainly not that everything worked equally well. When expensive and controversial policies can't be isolated and separately assessed, intelligent policy planning can't take place.

My effort to evaluate individual effects will take place in two unequal installments. I will first examine published statistical analyses that announce conclusions about the impact of specific elements of the New York police changes on crime briefly in this chapter and in detail in Appendix C. Then, I will present my own analyses on what is shown in 19 years of experience about the individual effects of five elements of the city's policing changes: (1) police manpower, (2) hot spots emphasis, (3) removing drug markets from public places, (4) aggressive street policing, and (5) management and information systems.

There are three separate questions that empirical research could address: (1) How can the totality of New York's crime decline be explained? (2) What factors might explain the substantial difference between New York's crime decline and that of other American cities? and (3) Which of the many different changes in policing can claim credit for preventing crime?

Because there are no convincing explanations for the general crime decline in the United States during the 1990s, there is also no plausible model for explaining the almost 40% national crime decline (see Zimring 2006; Rosenfeld 2004). What this means is that the 50% or so of New York's crime decline that was a tailwind from the national downturn cannot be modeled or explained. If we don't know why crime dropped in Toledo, Ohio, we also can't explain half of the New York decline. Yet unfortunately most of the research on New York attempts to create models of the totality of crime. This mission is in my view doomed.

A second issue, explaining the New York difference, is more easily addressed, but has not been a focus of much research prior to this study. The last section, building on Chapters 3 and 4, argued that the average decline in non-Manhattan boroughs that exceeds the average for other large cities can only come from police changes.

A third issue is whether specific elements of New York policing can be studied in isolation to assess their contribution to crime prevention. As we shall soon see, most of the attempts to control for all other changes in policing while isolating one element—manpower levels or arrest risks or stop-and-frisk levels—cannot be done in New York City because too many changes happened together.

There have been several attempts at statistical analysis of crime data in New York City to make inferences about the influence of particular police practices on rates of crime. Appendix C describes nine published and unpublished studies of policing and crime in New York City and provides my detailed criticisms of each of them. Most of these exercises found some evidence for effects of police policy, although the crimes and magnitudes varied widely. All of the studies had major difficulties identifying plausible measures of single aspects of policy and controlling for the influence of other policy variables. The large number of studies that used variations in precinct level police and crime data could not control for the police department's selection of the hottest "hot spots" for special effort.

While the current crop of regression exercises adds some circumstantial evidence that police efforts reduced crime in New York, there is no strong and specific evidence in the published record on which of the many simultaneous changes in New York policing can be linked to measureable units of crime prevention. The next section of the chapter summarizes the evidence I have collected to the most prominent changes in policing.

Testing for Specific Policing Effects
Does Size Matter?

The diversity of published statistical studies on the relationship between police force size and crime rates was discussed in the previous section and Appendix C. In the Eck and Maguire count, a larger number of statistical comparisons of crime rates and police strength found no significant effect or more manpower associated with more crime than found the negative correlation consistent with additional police reducing crime, but there were twice as many significant negative correlations as there were significant positive correlations. With this much uncertainty about whether extra police prevent crime, the magnitude of any such effect is doubly uncertain (Eck and Maguire 2000).

What can the New York City experience add to the empirical evidence on this question? Most statistical studies examine natural cross-sectional differences and modest changes over time in municipalities. The large additional manpower added in New York City in the 1990s was the biggest deliberate policy change of its kind yet documented, so this large a change has a much better chance of yielding visible and significant findings. Further, the drop in police numbers after 2000 again creates a visible change in policy to measure against crime trends.

Two Ways to Measure Crime Decline

Figure 5.17 shows the pattern for police manpower and homicide trends in New York City after 1990 with both homicide and police manpower rates during 1990 set at 100 so that each year after that shows relative change.

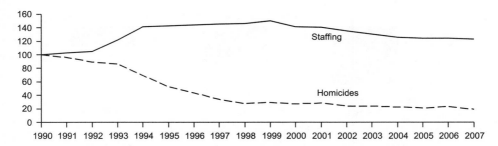

FIGURE 5.17 Trends in New York Police Staffing and Homicide by Year, 1990–2007.
Note: Staffing Percent Change from 1990, Homicides 1990 = 100.
Source: FBI, Uniform Crime Reports (homicide); New York City Police Department; see Appendix D (staffing).

Homicide rates trend downward all through the period covered by Figure 5.17, but the sharpest drop happens in the middle and late 1990s, when the city is at its peak rate of police manpower. So the concentration of the decline in the expansion era makes a case for additional manpower as a primary cause. And Chapter 1 shows the same pattern of the steepest drop in the 1990s for other index crimes in New York. But there was no national pattern of dramatic increase in police numbers and there was a nation-wide crime drop in the 1990s, so not all of New York City's crime decline during the 1990s should be attributed to the idiosyncratic changes that one city made in policing. How best to measure how much of New York's decline in crime was not a part of a national trend?

Figure 5.18 compares the average crime decline in New York City to trends in the other nine of the nation's ten largest cities for 1990–2000 and for 2000–2008. All seven index felonies used throughout Chapter 1 are measured, and the median rate (5th city) is compared to the New York City rate with the difference labeled the "New York difference."

The seven-crime average drop in New York was 63% during the 1990s, much larger than the 45% New York drop recorded in the police-reduction years after 2000. But the seven-crime average drop in the next nine largest cities was almost twice as big in the 1990s as during the years after 2000, so that the New York City difference was actually the same (21%) during its era of fewer police and during the era of police growth.

The post-2000 pattern in Figure 5.18 is a textbook case of why compar-ison cities are necessary, and also of the value added when periods of per-sonnel reduction can be compared with the sharp expansion that

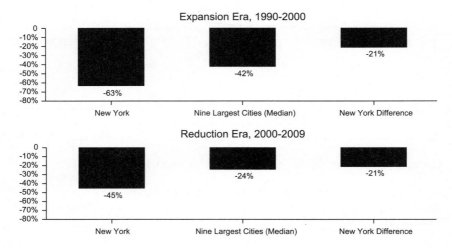

FIGURE 5.18 Percentage Crime Changes in New York and other Large U.S. Cities in Two Time Periods.
Note: Expansion and reduction in staff per 100,000 population.
Source: FBI, Uniform Crime Reports.

characterized the 1990s. But how far does this data go toward completely deconstructing the evidence that more police manpower reduced crime in New York?

I don't think the mechanical assumptions that Professor Levitt made in his 2004 dismissal of other types of police change as agents of crime reduction can survive Figure 5.18. And any theories which assume that the impacts of police manpower shifts must be short term in their preventive effects are also in serious trouble. But a careful review of the pattern in New York City leaves room for more nuanced theories of police strength as an important agent of crime prevention.

The level of patrol strength remained high all through the decade after 1999, even if lower than its peak rate per 100,000. So there may only have been very subtle visible changes associated with a decline from 141% to 121% of 1990 patrol manpower. Further, there may be longer lasting residual effects of peak period patrol intensity. This isn't known. Finally, there is one measure of police manpower on which there was no decrease in manpower during the period after 2000, the ratio of police per crime reported in Figure 5.6. The ratio of police to homicides and other street crimes like auto theft and robbery *did not* decline on a sustained basis after 2000 because rates of these crimes declined more in the period than the number of police. So on this measure of available police resources, there was an increase in police even in the force reduction period of 2000–2009.

What can't be done with historical data on police and crime in New York City is to decisively test any of these more complex theories of police manpower effects. A mechanical police per population estimate of crime prevention productivity doesn't work well in comparisons of the two eras of staff changes. Whether the alternative theories I mention in fact explain the pattern of crime in the two eras is unknowable. More disciplined experiments in manpower intensity (in the brief Kansas City and Newark tradition) might help determine the length of manpower effects and the better measure of the level of police resources as between crime and population. For the present, the proper measures of resources and the effects of variations in resources on crime are not known.

Increased Efficiency?

One thing is quite probable, however, and that is that the preventive impact of police manpower has to depend on what the police do and how effectively they do it. For that reason, a complete separation between levels of police manpower and the content of police activity is a fool's mission. And this raises yet another possible explanation for the strong relative performance of New York City even as the numbers of its police diminished—the force may have become more effective in using its resources to prevent crime. Under these circumstances, the marginal impact of each police officer—crime prevention productivity—will increase over time, and New York can perhaps maintain its comparative advantage over other cities with a smaller force.

So a large part of comprehending how well the NYPD performed throughout the two decades after 1990 must involve judgments about the effectiveness and the costs of the wide variety of new tactics and methods that came to New York in the 1990s. But this, as we shall soon see, is also a difficult task.

The Evaluation of Strategies and Tactics

I will organize my view of major policing innovations in New York City under three headings: (1) proven successes, (2) probable successes, (3) open questions.

Two Proven Successes

The two important tactical measures that almost certainly reduced crime in New York City were (1) the emphasis on hot spots for enforcement, aggressive street intervention, and sustained monitoring; and (2) the priority targeting of public drug markets for arrest, surveillance, and sustained attack.

The "hot spots" logic is that highly specific locations become the site of repetitive patterns of violent crime and should be a priority for long-term surveillance and special patrol. New York City has been practicing "hot spots" targeting with energy, resources, and very aggressive street interventions. There has been no publicly available evaluation of these efforts in New York City, so that if our evidence was restricted to New York City's limits, the tactic couldn't be regarded as a proven success. What pushes the "hot spots" approach over the top is the careful evaluations in other locations of the tactical approach (National Academy of Sciences Committee to Review Research on Police 2004), combined with the extensively documented emphasis on this approach in the NYPD. We know the approach works (from outside sources) and we know from New York that it was often used, well supported, and aggressively pursued. The evaluations in other places are a necessary condition of any confident conclusion about the effectiveness of the New York version of the strategy (see Braga and Weisburd 2010).

There is some overlap between the "hot spots" emphasis just discussed and the campaign to eliminate public drug markets in New York City, because open air drug markets are often very hot spots for a variety of crimes and drug-related lethal violence. So the external evidence on hot spots provides some support for assuming the success of this particular program. But the NYPD in its early Bratton/Maple era put very high emphasis on open air drug markets, and the New York effort was a leading example of a specific New York priority rather than an adaptation of an often-documented strategy. And the evidence of New York effectiveness here included a more than 90% decline in police nominated drug deaths from the early 1990s to 2005 (see Figure 4.4). So the decision to place a high priority on disestablishing open air drug centers is an independent contribution to the decline of life-threatening violence in New York City. Because the police code for one measure of drug-related homicide (the SHR) undercounted the share of these offenses, the number of lives saved in consequence of this program could be much more substantial than the SHR volumes would estimate and closer to the volume of decline of series

B in Figure 4.4, several hundred fewer drug killings each year from one program emphasis.

Probable Successes

Compstat information and planning systems pervade all of the strategic changes in the NYPD and have become an indivisible part of everything else the department does. But how then can observers separately evaluate the value added by the information gathering, mapping, periodic meetings, management by crime statistical objective, and other features of the Compstat regime?

My judgment here is that Compstat probably made a measurable contribution, but this is not a certainty. What separates judgments about the distinctive contributions of Compstat from the two strategies I judged "proven successes" in the previous section is the absence of rigorous external evaluation from other settings that encourages confidence in hot spots and the absence of a set of specific indicators (such as drug-related killings), that provide evidence that the open air drug market attacks had differential impact. The Compstat program that New York put in place had no clear operational model that had been assessed, and the best evidence that Compstat added value was the size of the crime decline—but this didn't provide a distinctive fingerprint that pointed to Compstat and not to increased manpower or aggressiveness or hot spot interventions.

Then why do I believe that it is probable the Compstat provided clear added value to the crime prevention efforts of the police? One powerful reason to suspect an independent Compstat effect is the magnitude of some of the estimated crime-reduction effects in New York City. The estimated total policing impact on robbery and burglary is a one-third reduction in citywide rate—well beyond any previously noted police effects on big city crime. Auto theft is down by more than 90%. With so much additional prevention to explain, the unprecedented and high intensity information management system is an obvious candidate for some of the credit. While there is no evidence of Compstat effectiveness from other places, that is because Compstat hadn't been around to evaluate. There is also no evidence *against* a high level of value added for mapping, management, and information reforms, and this is to some extent a distinction between Compstat and aggressive patrol tactics like field interrogation and stop and frisk. The absence of evidence in the case of Compstat is completely explained by the novelty of the effort. This is no substitute for rigorous evaluation, and better assessment of the impact of Compstat style reforms is a high priority for future evaluation efforts. With Compstat-style changes occurring in many police departments and with a Los Angeles effort close in design and authorship to the New York version, first rate evaluation is an important next step in operational reform of American policing.

A second operational emphasis that merits classification as a probable success is the NYPD's efforts to get guns off the streets. The very first of the department's ten strategy documents issued in 1994 was "Getting Guns off the Streets of New York" so there is little doubt of the high priority that removing guns represented (Silverman 1999 at p. 205). There are two indications that a variety of gun programs reduced gun violence in New York City—the number of gun homicides dropped more quickly than for non-gun homicides (Fagan, Zimring, and Kim 1998)—and a number of gun-specific interventions have produced promising results, in at least one case, Chicago's Ceasefire, with rigorous evaluation methods (Papachristos, Meares, and Fagan 2007). Then why stop short of regarding the post-1994 gun emphasis in New York a proven success?

The first reason is that New York City's gun program differs from the Chicago program that showed strong results, and there is some hazard in generalizing across the different methods. And the national homicide decline in the 1990s was also somewhat larger for gun than non-gun killings (Zimring 2006). Finally, while programs like Compstat were new to the NYPD, there had been emphasis on gun enforcement in street settings for many years. A somewhat thicker evaluation of New York's post-1993 gun emphasis is needed before the evidence can be regarded as conclusive.

A third probable success is the additional manpower, as already extensively discussed. Particularly as New York used their new infusion of manpower, size probably mattered. And productivity may also have increased over time as the force gained experience and the level of crime decreased. But the size of the effect for New York isn't known, and the New York effects could not, in any event, be assumed to transfer to other departments using extra police in different ways.

Open Questions

When the particular history of New York since 1990 is combined with other studies of police and crime, there are two strategies of policing on which the data don't produce plausible indications of value added in crime prevention—aggressive street intervention and "quality of life" or "broken windows" in New York City.

One important element of almost all street patrol activities in the 1990s and beyond was the very aggressive use of stops by the police, stop and frisk procedures, and arrests of suspicious persons for minor crimes to remove them from being an immediate threat and to identify persons with outstanding warrants (Maple and Mitchell at pp. 154–161). The push for aggressive patrol tactics increases the number of stop and frisk events and is the motive for arrests on minor charges, which permit removal and fingerprint and warrant checks. This aggressiveness has been a part of most street policing in New York City since 1994, including such successful and probably successful efforts such as hot spots, the open air drug market offensives, and gun patrols. The police administrators who designed the New York program believe that these aggressive tactics add significant value to patrol efforts, and so do most police officers. Do they? We don't know.

And the lack of knowledge about aggressive street tactics is not like Compstat, where the practices were new and evaluations hadn't happened. Aggressive street policing is almost as old as street policing—as the NAS Panel on Fairness and Effectiveness in Policing warns us, "Tough law enforcement strategies have long been a staple of police crime-fighting" (Fairness and Effectiveness in Policing 2004 at p. 228). But the efforts to study precursors to New York's recent policy such as San Diego's "Field Interrogation" or the correlation between traffic stops and crime have not been frequent, and the strategies of comparison over time or between areas have not been strong. The Committee concluded that with respect to "undifferentiated intensive enforcement activities, studies fail to show consistent or meaningful crime or disorder prevention benefits" (Fairness and Effectiveness in Policing at p. 250), compare also Weiss and Freels (1996) with Wilson and Boland (1978).

This combination of long practice and mixed evidence of effectiveness casts a shadow on aggressive policing as a general strategy, but might the New York City brand of aggressive policing be different? The answer here is undoubtedly yes, but it is difficult to know how the New York difference affects the crime prevention value added of stops and arrests. Some critics have suggested that the aggressive street stops have a limited additional yield of gun confiscations (Fagan 2010), and no data is available on what value added is produced by stops and minor offense arrests in hot spots and drug market operations. The marginal contribution of street stops and arrests can best be measured by systematic variation of police aggressiveness in executing these strategies, the methodological equivalent of a

Kansas City Preventative Patrol Experiment for aggressive street level enforcement. This hasn't happened yet, and no plans for this type of evaluation are planned.

The gap that consigns aggressive intervention tactics to the open question rubric is the absence of good data on the effect of the strategy. There is no doubt that the NYPD used aggressive street tactics throughout the Compstat era. By contrast, there are at least three separate reasons to doubt that "quality of life" or "broken windows" policing contributed to the decline in New York crime. The first problem is the lack of evidence that the department ever tried to enforce "quality of life" offenses as a consistent priority. Prostitution is one of the two classic "broken windows" crimes that George Kelling mentions in his 2001 statistical study (Kelling and Sousa), and yet the rate of prostitution arrests never went up in the Compstat era and is now a small fraction of its long-term volume. What makes trends in prostitution arrests an important test of the motives for the increase in other misdemeanor arrests is that its gender profile makes it a lousy method of fingerprinting robbers and burglars. The rise then fall of gambling arrests also suggests that police lost their enthusiasm for the men they arrested for gambling after the mid-1990s, perhaps because they produced low yields of persons at high risks of street crime or outstanding warrants. So disaggregating misdemeanor arrests casts serious doubt on the department's dedication to enforcing laws against minor crimes.

A second reason to doubt the crime control efficacy of "broken windows" priorities is the continued crime decline experienced in the city after 2000. From 2000 to 2009, the rate per 100,000 of prostitution arrests in New York City fell from 110 to 50, or 54%. The gambling arrest rate fell from 70 to 12.9 or 82%, perhaps in part influenced by a reporting change in 2001. And even drug arrests fell slightly from 123 per 100,000 to 109, or 11%. During this rather radical turn away from enforcing non-drug quality of life offenses, New York City maintained its comparative advantage in crime decline over the trends in other large cities.

There is a third reason to doubt the connection of "quality of life enforcement" to the size of the New York crime decline—the lack of evidence from other cities; the Committee to Review Research on Police Policy and Practices reported a gap between sentiment and evidence in these terms:

There is widespread perception among policy makers and the public that enforcement strategies (primarily arrests applied broadly against offenders committing minor offenses lead to reductions in serious crime. Research does not provide strong support for this proposition. (Fairness and Effectiveness in Policing 2004 at p. 229)

Is it possible that New York City's version of arrest for minor crimes might be different? Yes, but even if the wave of misdemeanor arrests during the 1990s contributed to the first years of the crime decline, that would rehabilitate only the "shark hunting" instrumental use of minor arrests against dangerous looking persons. The reason that a devotion to the across-the-board strict enforcement of public order offenses didn't contribute to the crime decline is that it never happened.

D. Policy Choices in an Age of Indeterminacy

The results of this survey provide a mix of good and bad news for the police planner and urban mayor anxious to apply the lessons from policing in New York City to another big city in an era of scarce public resources. The best news is that police and police strategy can make a difference in big-city crime. The estimates of the independent impact of changes in policing in New York City exceed 30% for robbery and burglary, 20% for auto theft, and are also substantial for homicide and rape. This is based on circumstantial evidence rather than direct observation, and the margin of error in the estimates is not small. But police make a difference. Wise investments in preventive policing can produce very significant public benefits.

But which exactly are the wise investments in preventive policing? Two of the New York City strategies are proven successes and obvious choices for cities with the special problems they addressed—hot spots emphases and tactics, and the destruction of open air drug markets. If you have these problems, New York's experience is directly on point.

There are two other aspects of the New York program with less conclusive evidence of success but highly favorable risk/benefit profiles. The most important of these is a data driven crime mapping and patrol strategy management program with many of the elements of Compstat. The magnitude of the independent contribution of this program in New York is not known, but the additional elements of the approach are not hugely expensive, and some of the manpower savings in generating greater patrol accountability can help to pay for the program.

A gun emphasis program also seems like a good bet for most big cities, but here New York City's success may have been assisted by its low rates of civilian handgun ownership. Even when there were a substantial number of handguns on New York's streets, the number in homes was much smaller than in other big cities. So removing guns from the street may have worked because handguns were harder to replace than in Seattle or Cleveland. Los Angeles, a second city where William Bratton reorganized the police, may serve as a better model for the effectiveness of gun removal programs in higher handgun ownership cities.

The third "probably successful" element of the New York story—the extra value of larger numbers of police—is a much more difficult policy decision because of its substantial cost. Extra police officers are much more expensive than computers, even when a few crime-mapping sergeants are added to the computer bill. The additional manpower in New York City probably added significant value to the new tactics and organizational changes, but how much value was added cannot be assessed by combing through the history of the city's changes. What is needed is another rigorous division of areas pursuing the same best practice tactics with different levels of manpower, except this time the different manpower levels would have to be maintained for long periods—years rather than months. Without better data, the question of whether and to what extent extra patrol resources make good tactics more effective is a twenty-first-century guessing game.

Unlike the decision to create Compstat style mapping and information, adding manpower is a *very* expensive act of administrative faith. While the field needs more rigorous evaluations of manpower levels to make rational cost/benefit decisions, the atmosphere of optimism that is generated by success stories like New York City is not likely to inspire rigorous evaluation of manpower variations. Police chiefs lose control to evaluators when careful evaluations are designed, and the risks to favored tactics that controlled experiments represent is almost as great as in the 1980s. It will take a police strategist with the courage of his convictions to allow the definitive work on manpower effects that the field requires.

What about the aggressive use of stops, frisks, and pretextual minor arrests that New York City uses extensively in every aspect of preventive street policing. Most New York City police decision makers believe that this adds significantly to the impact of the programs. But the evidence for aggressive stop effectiveness in other settings is not strong, and there is no way to separately measure the value added by aggressive intervention in New York City. Kelling and Sousa, it will be recalled, found a correlation between misdemeanor arrests and crime reduction in New York precincts but didn't measure felony arrests or control for the impact of the department's selection of high problem areas for special efforts. Other studies previously discussed found less broad effects or evidence that regression from high historical rates explained the relationship. Could misdemeanor arrests independent of felony arrests be a good measure of differential aggressiveness in police patrol? The problem here is that the different precincts are all under the control of a central administration that is trying to produce evenness in policy. If they succeed, there is no documented variation to study.

And aggressiveness in policing is a costly strategy because it imposes real disadvantages on exactly the minority poor who can least afford additional handicaps. It would be a complicated calculus of public cost and benefit if this kind of intervention is necessary to the kinds of impacts documented in Table 5.2. But to institutionalize a continuation of this kind of policy without a rigorous test of its value cannot be justified. Not knowing whether these tactics provide substantial increments in prevention is regrettable in 2011. It will be inexcusable in 2016. But here again, an era of optimism about the impact of policing is not the ideal time to design transparent experiments.

Of all the undocumented elements of New York City's policing changes, the marginal value to crime reduction of a variety of aggressive tactics—stops, searches, misdemeanor arrests—should be at the very top of the priority for rigorous evaluation efforts but it isn't. The absence of any conclusive evidence that any of these tactics, or all of them jointly, contribute to crime reduction is not the equivalent of a negative finding. Pretextual arrests may add significant value to street policing efforts in New York City, and so might high volumes of stop-and-frisk. And the marginal impact of specific measures in the New York scene may be substantial.

But two elements of the best way to evaluate these tactics make it unlikely that we will have definitive answers to questions about the value of aggressive tactics in the near future. The first problem is that by far the best test of aggressive enforcement New York style will take place in New York City. One cannot abstract stop-and-frisk from the complex of information, patrol, and policy in New York City to test it comprehensively in Newark or Miami.

The second problem is that changes in the aggression content of police tactics will have to be sustained for substantial periods of time before observers can be confident that previous levels of aggressiveness have worn off as treatment effects. Not only do we not know the marginal impact of high levels of pretextual arrests but we also do not know the half-life of these unknown effects. So testing down in police aggressiveness—the only way to introduce a meaningful control in New York City—would have to reduce the prevalence of a crime-fighting technique that police believe in for a long period of time. That has rarely happened in the history of rigorous evaluation of police measures (perhaps in Kansas City) and it isn't likely to start in New York City.

So any real test of particular aggressive tactics will involve a choice of inferior strategies—either weaker methods in New York or better methods in urban settings that cannot duplicate the combination of policing ingredients that produced an unprecedented cumulative effect. Given the huge importance of the issue, the best choice might be to invest in both imperfect strategies and hope for triangulation of proof.

Because police planners and big city mayors read newspapers (or scan the Internet), they may also have questions about the role of "quality of life" or "broken windows" approaches in the New York approach. On this issue, the data is pretty clear. Large increases in some minor crime arrests like marijuana were a pretextual effort to identify and remove street criminals rather than a crusade against marijuana. Some crime-connected behaviors such as fare jumping in the subways were special targets of police effort. But the classic "broken windows" offense of prostitution never attracted any additional resources even as New York City increased its police force. That is apparently why gambling suspects were not a high yield for warrants or serious criminal records after which the arrests dropped by 88%. Either the very announcement of zero tolerance solved the city's prostitution problem, or sex for sale and many other affronts to public order were not the priority for New York police at any time in the era we have been examining. Some other city might try an orthodox version of broken windows policing, but New York didn't. The central mission of New York policing was the prevention of serious crime, and this mission was accomplished.

PART THREE

Lessons and Questions

The first two sections of this book presented most of the empirical data analyzed for this study. Part I measured the decline in crime in New York City since 1990 and compared New York's current conditions with the circumstances of crime and public safety in other cities in the United States and elsewhere in the developed world.

Part II organized a statistical search party for what I call "the New York difference," the gap between a 35%–40% single-decade drop in crime that was a widespread if somewhat mysterious phenomenon in the United States and the New York crime decline that was twice as long and twice as large. What pushed this city into the unprecedented condition of 80% drops in most street crime? There were no obvious changes in population, economy, education, or criminal justice sanctions that seem likely candidates to explain the double dose of crime decline. The two preoccupying theories of crime causation in the late 1980s—fatherless high-risk youth and widespread availability of illegal drugs—did not change radically over the two decades of crime drop, and New York reduced its rate of incarceration while imprisonment and jailing continued to increase elsewhere in the United States. There were large changes in policing, and some combination of new cops, new tactics, and new management appears a likely cause of much of New York's advantage over other cities. Which aspects of the many changes in the size and character of police in New York can claim credit for the big additional drop in crime is a surprisingly difficult question to answer.

This last part of the book tries to summarize the nature and importance of what can be learned from New York City as well as unanswered questions that need to be addressed. There are three chapters in this concluding segment, but the order in which they appear is a minor variation of long-standing academic custom.

Chapter 6 addresses a series of what I call open questions about what caused the 80% crime decline, as well as what its effects are likely to be on New Yorkers. Having a chapter on unanswered questions lead rather than conclude this last part of the book is my violation of customary sequence.

Since all academics workshop at the altar of the need for further research, a long and expansivelist of unanswered questions is usually the grand climactic of a scholarly tome, the professor's march to his next big grant. But not here.

The list in Chapter 6 of unanswered questions and necessary research is very important, but one reason that so little work is now being done on the subject is the failure of many to understand the game changing importance of lessons from New York City on our priorities for crime control and on our understanding of crime and social structure in America. So Chapter 6 urges substantial further research but defers to the analysis and arguments in the final two chapters, which emphasize what we do know about the importance of New York's experience.

Chapter 7 compares the mix of crime-control strategies in New York City over the past 20 years with the assumptions and the resource priorities of crime control in the rest of the United States over the last generation. New York City has proved that mass imprisonment is neither a necessary nor a sufficient condition to control urban crime. It has also demonstrated that drug violence can be controlled without major changes in the incidence and prevalence of illegal drug use.

Chapter 8 considers what New York City teaches about crime and the American metropolis. The central contrast in New York City was this: a very modest set of changes in urban populations and institutions contributed to a very large change in crime. The city's timing may have been quite fortunate, but the stark contrast between such modest inputs and such large outputs calls into question long-standing assumptions about the depth and intractability of the cultural and structural determinants of violence and serious crime in America's major cities. It has long been thought that the big cities of the United States were hard wired to produce high rates of lethal violence and robbery. Because crime rates proved to be so malleable in a polyglot metropolis like New York City, it is now clear that chronically high homicide and robbery rates are not an essential part of modern city life.

Chapter 6

Open Questions

THE MISSION OF this chapter is to identify a series of important unanswered questions that are priorities for future research. I will organize the "need to know" list around five main headings: (A) The Unsolved Mystery of Particular Cause; (B) Four Questions about Crime Rates in the Future; (C) The Dynamics and Limits of Preventive Policing; (D) Where Have All the Criminals Gone?; and (E) The Impact of Lower Crime on High-Risk Populations and Areas.

None of these is a small question, and most of the specific issues discussed in these pages are new to social science. The reason for this is the surprising novelty of the New York experience. Most criminal justice experts are unprepared by training and theoretical understanding to think about how much lower rates of crime can fall in New York because we didn't think it could fall as far as it has. One reason why there is a long and daunting list of new questions to address is that New York City has deconstructed the common understanding of how crime rates can be reduced and with what limits.

The more than 80% drop in most safety crime is as close to the miracle of the loaves and the fishes as criminology has come in the past half-century. The changes in crime policy and institutional structure in New York have been modest, and the changes in crime have been huge. That essential contrast between modest impacts and big effects was not merely hard to comprehend when it was happening, it is quite difficult to understand in 2011.

'Til Human Subjects Wake Us?

And one important reason the statistics in the first five chapters of this study cannot produce a deep substantive understanding of how crime rates declined is that the statistics in Part I of the book are a critical step removed from the processes that generated the change. There is an ample supply of numbers in this volume, but there are no human subjects being observed. We thus can be relatively certain about what happened but far less informed about how it happened. Indeed, most well-informed observers still harbor skepticism about the power of anything government can do to produce the game-changing results on the scale of New York since 1990. Homicide is down 82% but the population, cultures, and opportunities of New York's urban poor have not changed much at all. How can that be?

The only sure prescription for such an epic case of cognitive dissonance is direct observation of the behaviors we think caused changes and careful study of how and why individual citizens in New York City came to behave differently. But my book stops short of this important work. So a large reservation about exclusively statistical methods serves as a preface to all of the other questions this chapter will discuss—that we cannot fully understand either the nature of urban crime or the best methods to control it without deep knowledge of what happened in New York and how it happened. And deep knowledge can only come by tracking actual human beings through the streets and institutions of New York City.

A. The Unsolved Mystery of Particular Cause

Chapter 5 reported that a substantial minority of the New York City crime decline, about 40% of the drop in robbery and burglary and a quarter of the huge decline in auto theft, was probably the product of the city's changes in policing. A more modest fraction of the homicide decline—about 15%—seems tied to the police changes. There is also a small fraction of the crime drop in Manhattan which may be the result of population changes in the 20 years after 1990 that redistributed that borough's population toward groups with lower crime rates.

The bad news is that more than half of New York City's crime decline is not tied to particular causes. A majority of the city's 20-year decline is part of the larger pattern of crime decline during the 1990s. My earlier work on the general crime decline concluded that it "was a classic example of multiple causation, with none of the contributing causes playing a dominant role" (Zimring 2006 at p. 197). My cautionary conclusion about the national pattern extends to the half and more of the New York City decline that is a part of that broader trend:

There is reason to fear that many of the professional observers who were embarrassed by failing to predict the crime declines of the 1990s are now prone to overestimating the predictive powers that might seem to have been conferred on the profession by good news.

Sustained crime declines encourage people to believe they know what drives crime trends, just as stock market booms convince investors that they are financial wizards. In both investment and government, doing well is too easily confused with knowing what you are doing. (id. 2006 at p. 199)

About half of the total New York crime decline was a result of being in the tailwind of a 1990s process where the operating causes were outside of the city and very difficult to identify. The usual tendency is for observers to assume that the causes of visible changes in crime are whatever changes in policy or practice have been receiving public attention. In New York, the natural tendency is to credit the entirety of the crime decline to police activities.

The really bad news about the mystery of what generated the national crime decline is that there is no obvious prospect for solving the mystery in the foreseeable future. If there are cyclical forces driving crime trends in North America (see Zimring 2006 at pp. 200–201) they have left no visible fingerprints. What drives crime cycles?

The danger in attributing all of the New York decline to policing effects is that changes of that magnitude cannot be replicated anywhere else. In the long term, modest and accurate estimates of police impact are of greater benefit to policing advocates than overenthusiastic ticker tape parades.

But unknown causes of crime declines cannot be intentionally reproduced. So the disadvantages of the mysterious 1990s national pattern are an important limit on our capacity to make many cities much safer.

B. Four Questions about Crime Rates in the Future

How Low Can Crime Go in New York City?

When a trend over time breaks unprecedented ground, one natural question for observers is how much further the trend might have to go before constraints of the kind that limited previous movements can be expected to set in. These types of trend-limit conversations are quite familiar in discussion of market phenomena—stock prices, the housing market, and economic growth rates are three prominent examples from recent years. Pushing toward new levels (either up or down) invites speculation that processes of equilibrium might soon catch up with trajectories that have moved in only one direction for long periods. The rhetorical centerpiece of many such discussions in 2011 is the great housing bubble of 1996–2007 in the United States—and the suggestion is that there are natural forces equivalent to gravity that will interrupt and reverse long trends. That's what we should have known about house prices. Are there such processes for crime? And how close might New York City be to testing such limits in its downward spiral of crime rates?

There are at least two important ambiguities involved in the common version of the "how low can it go" discussion. One concerns whether the subject is New York's crime decline or its current rate of various different crimes. As Chapters 1 and 2 showed, the size of the crime decline in New York is already record-breaking for at least four crimes—homicide, robbery, burglary, and auto theft. And the auto theft pattern, with the citywide rate at one-sixteenth of its 1990 total and each major borough with 90% or more in rate decline, is the single largest two-decade drop documented in felony crime statistics.

But the crime rates now prevalent in New York City are not for the most part the nation's lowest. Homicide rates are lower in San Jose and Honolulu. Robbery rates are lower in many American cities. So there is certainly no lower limit on possible rates of crime in big cities that New York will test soon.

But are there natural limits on the capacity of a particular city to experience crime declines over time? New York's homicide rate of 5.6 per 100,000 may be higher than San Jose's, but New York's rate has dropped more than 80% while San Jose homicide was always much lower and has only declined 22% since 1990. San Jose has a 2008 reported robbery rate that is a small fraction of that in contemporary New York notwithstanding New York's 84% decline. Why should the decline from previous rates constrain a metropolis like New York City from further drops?

The implicit assumption that animates the conclusion that a big drop might leave less room for further declines is that the population or environment of a particular city has relatively fixed proclivities for particular offenses, and these fixed proclivities might limit the possibilities of further declines. After all, one of the best predictors of this year's rate of homicide or burglary in a city is last year's crime volume. The reason New York has historically had more robberies in this analysis is that it has more robbers, or a different set of cultural attitudes, or a more robbery-prone environment. And this may limit the size of the decline that should be expected in New York.

Of course, the limits one would imagine from theories of fixed proclivity have long since been passed in New York City, and the size of the decline to date is already evidence against a notion of natural limits. Yet the social and environmental determinants of behaviors like life-threatening violence and rape *must* be important. And there may well be thresholds below which more fundamental social change is necessary than has happened so far in New York if rates of crime and violence are to continue downward.

A second ambiguity in the discourse about how low New York's crime rates can fall is the distinction between predicting future crime levels and the discussion of the limits on possible decline—are we discussing how low New York's homicide and robbery rates *can go*, or how low they *will go* next year or in the next decade? To argue (as I will) that crime rates can decline further in New York City is rather different from predicting with any confidence that homicides will fall below 400 next year, or in five years, or ever. Understanding the social and structural tolerance of further crime declines is an important and complicated matter in its own right. It is best to keep this issue separate from conversations about predicting next year's homicide totals. So the topic of the moment is how low New York crime rates can go without any explicit predictions of actual trends for next year or 2020.

The Paradox of Leadership

Many of the qualifications and uncertainties in the previous discussion would not be necessary if the question was whether Saint Louis or Chicago could easily tolerate substantial drops in their crime rates. Why is that? We *know* that Chicago could tolerate very large crime declines without fixed social or environmental limits because New York City has already demonstrated such extensive downside tolerance. If New York homicide could drop 82%, why not Chicago? The reason that the further capacities to decline in New York are harder to estimate is that it has already gone further than any of its peers. If crime goes down again in New York in 2012, that will break new ground for an already record-setting decline. So every further decline in New York City is a journey into the unknown.

How Low Can Crime Go in Other Cities?

New York City is a leading indicator of the kind of crime decline that other cities in the United States could experience without major changes in population, economy, or punishment. But this doesn't mean that Philadelphia

or Baltimore can expect 80% declines from their current rates of homicide, burglary, and robbery, because most U.S. cities have already incorporated the downward trends of the 1990s in their 2011 crime statistics, but
the "New York difference" attributal to policing is an achievable target for
major cities all over the country, and that appears to be about 15% of homicides, and about one-third of robbery and burglary rates and more than
20% of auto theft rates for cities that haven't yet introduced major changes
in policing. Further, because there are no clear indications that New York
City has yet touched bottom, those "New York difference" estimates are
the minimum. If New York goes lower, that will increase the decline that
other cities might emulate.

And the New York experience is also a leading indicator for the mechanisms that other cities can use, with emphasis on the proven and probably successful elements of street policing. Even though additional police
manpower is a gamble on current evidence, it is probably a gamble worth
taking for many cities. Well-documented and self-conscious emulation of
New York tactics can rather quickly increase information about the consistency and magnitude of policing prevention effects. One hopes that the
confidence police in other cities will feel about the validity of tactics will
translate to the courage to allow transparent evaluation.

But the potential that other cities have to experience declines in crime
are no guarantee that crime drops are imminent. Crime rates *can* go down
substantially in St. Louis without major social change, but whether this
potential will be realized is uncertain.

Diversity or Uniformity in Crime Specific Patterns?

The first 19 years of New York's crime decline produced some unevenness
in pattern, but there were three strong similarities in pattern across areas
and crime classifications that are worthy of note. First, the rate of all kinds
of crime fell more in New York City than in other places. While the absolute magnitude of the declines in auto theft (93%) and larceny (68%) were
quite far apart, the relative magnitude of the declines when compared
with other cities were usually closer. For at least five of the seven traditional index offenses, the New York decline was significantly larger than
the median for big cities.

The second close-to-uniform tendency for New York crime was the length
of the decline. Most New York City crimes went down well into the twenty-
first century and this was long past the consensus end of the national crime

drop in 2000. The third element of near uniformity in New York City was the broad geography of the crime decline among the four major boroughs in the city. *Each* of the four major boroughs in New York would be among the ten largest U.S. cities if it were an independent entity, ranging from fourth (Brooklyn and Queens) to seventh in size (Bronx). And if these constituents were broken out into independent entities, *each* of them would have the largest crime decline when compared to the other nine of the major cities. The only real crime decline competition for each of the four major boroughs of New York City is with the other three boroughs (compare Figure 1.4 with Table 1.3 in Chapter 1). That is amazing.

Two important non-uniform patterns in the crime decline were the higher comparative advantage for New York in street crime—robbery, burglary (street access), and auto theft—and the persisting difference in relative rate for violence and property crime. Chapter 5 estimated the New York difference from the big-city average decline in burglary, robbery, and auto theft at many times the city's advantage over the biggest cities' average for assault and larceny. Homicide was almost midway between the two crime categories. If this pattern holds in New York, and if similar differences appear in other places where street policing initiatives are put in place, it will suggest major differences in the susceptibility of different crimes to effective police enforcement efforts.

The other important differential in New York City crime as of 2011 is the large difference (at least by Western standards) between New York City's property crime rates (very low) and its violent crime rates (low only by U.S. standards). The violent crimes of robbery (84% decline) and homicide (82% decline) and the nonviolent crime of burglary (85% decline) had very similar rates of decline over the period since 1990. But the starting rates for robbery and homicide were so high in New York City relative to large foreign cities that even with comparable rates of decline to burglary, the current rates of homicide and robbery remain high by Western standards. We saw in Chapter 2 that both Montréal and Toronto have rates of burglary and auto theft substantially higher than New York City but rates of robbery that are one-half the rate in New York. New York City's auto theft rate would be the lowest of any big city in Canada, but its homicide rate would be by far the highest of any big city in Canada.

This long-standing concentration of violence in the United States persists even amidst record-setting crime declines. Because property crime is more common than serious violence, this means that the aggregate concentration of criminal offenders might well be higher than New York in places like London and Toronto, but the rate of violent offenses still remains much higher in New York. Is there a different kind of criminal in New York?

Perhaps the distinction between crime and violence when New York is compared with other cities is evidence that culture is an important restraint on the capacity to control crime. But we now also know the cultural barriers to crime prevention can be easily overstated on the New York evidence since 1990. Recall that homicide (down 82%) and robbery (down 84%) are down almost as much in New York as burglary (down 85%). So any cultural limits on this huge change over time are not in obvious evidence. Yet the very evenness in decline between robbery and burglary locks New York City into its traditional profile of being more inclined to violence versus other property crime than other Western capitals. Robbery and homicide would have to drop *much more* than burglary for the ratio of burglary to robbery and homicide in New York to approach the ratios found in other Western capitals.

That hasn't happened yet. So the relative high concentration of violence remains a legacy of traditional American patterns rather than the result of violent propensities being harder to suppress than non-violent property offenses.

One question is whether more specific patterns of police or punishment policy might generate differential preventive effects on serious violent crime. The impacts to date have been street crime specific, but have had generalized impact across the property/person crime boundary. If this pattern continues, so will the New York City tendency toward higher rates of violence by comparison with the rest of the developed world.

The End or Reduction of Cyclicality in New York City Crime?

For the 40 years after 1960, the city of New York was fully participating in the up and down cycles of crime rates in the United States, with crime rates increasing sharply from the mid-1960s to the mid-1970s, fluctuating in the down-then-up national pattern in the 1980s and then way down in the 1990s, when the rest of the United States was in decline. Figure 6.1 shows the New York City versus U.S. patterns for rates of criminal homicide (which is much less suspicious than early New York City underreported robbery and burglary rates).

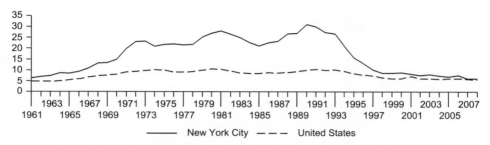

FIGURE 6.1   United States and New York City Homicide Rate, 1961–2008.
Source: National Center for Health Statistics, National Vital Statistics Report & Bureau of Vital Statistics, New York City Department of Health and Mental Hygiene.

While the 1990s homicide rate was a departure from the national pattern in the magnitude of the decline, it was not distinct from the overall pattern. Since 2000, however, New York homicide has seen definite if more modest downward trends (excepting September 11, 2001 deaths) while the first seven years of the new decade were trendless nationally. While the statistical distance between the United States and New York patterns since the turn of the century is not large, the consistency of the New York City decline does raise the possibility that New York might now continue on a time trend less clearly connected to national patterns than in previous periods.

But the evidence to date of New York City's immunity to national trends is quite weak. While the New York City pattern over the years since 2000 is consistent and downward, there is no clear national trend pattern to compare it to, and there are substantial variations in crime rates in many cities. With no strong cyclical impetus nationally, the first decade of the twenty-first century is one of the worst periods one could pick to test the susceptibility of any particular city to national trends. And there is no obvious theoretical reason that New York might opt out of national trends because of its more substantial policing effects. There might be some muting of national trends—on the way up because of a less inviting environment for street crime and on the way further down because of lower rates at the baseline—but even this is conjecture.

So little is known about what factors drive crime cycles that any theoretical predictions are a hazardous occupation. The best test of New York's future participation in national level trends will come from a strong national push either up or down in the coming decades. That hasn't happened yet.

C. The Dynamics and Limits of Preventive Policing

Observers in New York City have learned one critically important but very general lesson about police in big cities—that the way police define problems, develop information, and deploy resources on the street can have a major impact on levels of crime and on citizen safety. Police matter, and they matter a lot more than many experts thought as recently as 20 years ago.

And because police matter, the public importance of specific information about what works and what doesn't work in street policing is greater now than at any earlier period in the United States. But there is also a very large gap between what we need to know and what we now know about policing. The two biggest unknowns from the previous chapters' analysis of New York City were: (1) the specific contribution of different levels of manpower to effective strategies like hot spots, public drug market elimination, and firearms interception campaigns; and (2) whether and by how much high levels of stop and frisk and pretextual minor offense arrests increase the effectiveness of concentrated enforcement programs. In each case, the high cost of a program element—the money for cops and the regressive burdens on minority youth for the aggressive focus—requires a specific calculus of cost and benefit before informed decisions can be made at the critical margins of police policy. That specific calculus is missing in 2011. Can we expect more precise findings any time soon? Probably not, and that is a problem.

All the political, economic, and institutional barriers to transparent evaluation of specific elements of preventive policing are as powerful in 2011 as in earlier years. Police departments are still parts of municipal government without any strong investment in transparency or in ceding power to outside evaluators. The very successes that have made specific findings about what works best more important have also insulated successful police chiefs from the pressure to prove that their tactics work in policy evaluations. A highly successful police chief is probably in a better political position if he insists that the entire range of his department's activities should be judged as an indivisible gestalt than if he exposes specific elements of his current policies to controlled evaluation.

It is not just that important gaps remain about the costs and benefits of particular elements in preventive policing; the greater importance of the questions in light of positive general indications in New York and elsewhere makes the gap between what is known and what is needed *larger* in 2011 than a decade before. And the economic and political incentives that are common in big-city policing argue against any spontaneous program of visible and rigorous evaluation in most successful metropolitan departments. If there have been any such evaluations to date in places like New York City and Los Angeles, they are well-kept secrets. And there is nothing in the current structure and governance of metropolitan policing that promises important progress soon.

What may be necessary to produce rigorous and specific evaluations is a much more aggressive federal role in funding high-quality research on critical issues in street policing—not with the small dollars and eclectic priorities of federal crime research efforts after 1975, but with high standards and big money. Even then, the most prominent and successful departments may hold back from full involvement. Atlantic City, Kansas City, and Newark may be easier to integrate into a program of rigorous evaluation than New York City or Los Angeles, and this pattern may generate issues of quality control and generality of findings. If increments in manpower or aggressiveness don't add value in a Kansas City evaluation, Los Angeles and New York City might insist that Kansas City didn't do it right. So the impact of even strong evaluations on police practices is not a sure thing.

Many but by no means all of the important open questions about police effectiveness are susceptible to Kansas City preventive patrol style evaluations. Both the extra manpower and police aggressiveness issues would fit a randomly assigned area comparison strategy, but one limit of that design in Kansas City in the 1970s was the length of the experiment. Particularly with manpower variations, much longer treatment and comparison periods are probably necessary. And careful documentation of how police attempt to increase the productivity of street police resources is also a high-priority target, first for observation then for evaluation.

Without federal intervention and support, the transfer of police technologies will continue and accelerate, but no police department has either the resources or the priorities to engage in rigorous evaluation. Consultants will cultivate a set of believed best practices for information gathering and dissemination and will adapt these practices to a departmental client's local conditions and resources. For some types of police methods—computer mapping and highly specific problem solving approaches—trial and error and local adaptation may not be grossly inefficient. But there will be no core of science-based evaluations for many critical questions. This will render whatever police wish to do less vulnerable to science-based criticisms, but it will reduce public discussion about the effectiveness of police services to global judgments based on crime statistics. The specific impact of many controversial and high-cost aspects of police strategies will remain unknown. The number of experts will expand, but not the level of expertise.

The critical issues of manpower impacts, of how best to increase productivity in street policing, and about whether and when aggressive street tactics pay dividends in additional prevented crimes cannot be answered with the resources and political priorities of municipal police forces. Either new levels of government will begin to participate in an evaluation enterprise, or the capacity of those who observe and participate in policing to obtain reliable answers to specific questions will fail to mature, even as the police role in public safety grows more important.

D. Where Have All the Criminals Gone?

From the perspective of the dominant theories of both crime causation and crime control in the United States after 1970, the statistics on crime, population, and incarceration in New York City after 1990 literally do not add up. Crime rates drop dramatically while incarceration rates edge up, then stabilize, then decline. The high-risk populations in three of the city's four major boroughs increase over time.

This pattern is a direct challenge to what I will call the theory of "supply side criminology," which predicts and explains the volume of crime in a population area by determining the number of chronic or high-rate offenders unrestrained in a community and assumes that they continue to offend at relatively fixed rates until they age out of crime or are removed by incarceration. When Richard Nixon quipped that "the chief cause of crime is criminals," he was keynoting a perspective that produced cohort studies showing concentration of serious offending among relatively small segments of the youth population (Wolfgang, Figlio, and Sellin 1972). These were the youth who became the criminals who were the chief cause of crime. Other predictive work focuses on distinguishing "adolescence limited" from "life course persistent" offenders by background and personal characteristics (Moffit 1992) or measuring the length and intensity of what were characterized as "criminal careers" (Greenwood and Abrahamse 1982; Blumstein, Cohen, Roth, and Visher, eds., 1986).

When criminologists and psychologists posited relatively fixed proclivities among small segments of the population, the obvious policy lesson that commentators and legal actors applied to this model was selective incapacitation of high-rate repeat criminal offenders. Whatever else prisons might or might not achieve, the physical restraint of otherwise active offenders would reduce crime, even if criminal proclivities were relatively fixed. Imprisonment for incapacitative purposes thus became the dominant crime control program in the United States by default (Zimring and Hawkins 1995, Chap. 1). "The fundamental notion of incapacitation is taking a slice out of an individual criminal career" (Blumstein 1983 at p. 874).

For a relatively long period of time, incapacitation was not merely the dominant mode of crime control endorsed by a broad segment of the policy community but the only mechanism where most observers thought that investment of additional resources would reduce crime. One reason that other strategies didn't seem practical was the assumed inexorability of criminals at large continuing to offend unless restrained. What else could work?

The New York City puzzle from this perspective is that crime went down for a longer period of time and by a much larger amount than any notion of fixed proclivities by active offenders would regard as possible. If the number of robberies went down 84%, did the number of robbers also drop by four-fifths? Where did they go? If the number of people who used to commit robberies didn't go down much if at all, why did their robbery commission rate go down so much?

The limited data available make it quite clear that both the timing and magnitude of the decline in serious crimes in the city could not be accounted for by outmigration or incapacitation. Figure 6.2 tracks the homicide rate and incarceration rate by year in New York City.

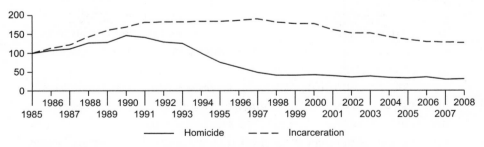

FIGURE 6.2 New York City Homicide and Incarceration Rate Base 100 (1985). *Source:* Bureau of Vital Statistics, New York City Department of Health and Mental Hygiene; New York Department of Corrections and U.S. Census (daily inmate population, New York City).

The rate of incarceration of city residents rises modestly in the early 1990s as discussed in Chapter 4, topping out in 1997 and turning downward. The 11% increase in people locked up was associated with a decline in killings five times that large. After 1997, however, the number of prison and jail inmates sent back to the city exceeded the number removed from the streets in every year, and homicide rates continue steadily downward. Over the eleven years after 1997, the prisons and jails sent 20,000 more persons back to the streets of New York City than they admitted (the 2008 total was 46,479 compared to 66,765 at the 1997 high point, a difference of 20,286). Using some of the more optimistic incapacitation estimates of the era produces very large volumes of extra felony crime that New York City should have experienced as a result of these reductions in incarceration. Ed Zedlewski argued for an annual per person imprisoned crime savings of 187, which should produce an extra 3,793,498 felonies in New York City in 2008 attributable to the reduction in incapacitation in 11 years (Zedlewski 1987). In fact, New York City only reported 355,000 index felonies in 1997 (with more than 66,000 persons locked up), so the 20,200 additional releases would have to multiply crime in New York City by more than 1,100% for Zedlewski's numbers to hold. But instead of increasing elevenfold, the number of offenses went down 44% as the population increased.

Part of the problem with these wild numbers is the implausible assumptions about incapacitation that were in vogue in the 1980s and 1990s (see Zimring and Hawkins 1995, Chap. 7). Dr. Zedlewski's 187 crimes per person year of incarceration would generate about 467 million crimes avoided every year by American prisons and jails in 2010, more than 10 times the crime rate. And supply-side criminology doesn't require such exuberant crime reduction claims. The basic assumptions of supply side criminology—concentration of serious offenses among a small population group and relatively fixed proclivities to commit crimes—can project more realistic annual individual crime rates and estimated incapacitation savings. Perhaps five or six felonies a year instead of 187.

But the entire 19 years of New York crime experience is *fundamentally* inconsistent with the basic assumptions of supply-side criminology, and no tinkering with numbers at the margins can resolve the conflict. Eighty percent reductions in street crime with no significant change in population structure, age distribution, or incarceration just doesn't mesh with an expectation of fixed proclivities toward crime commission over time. The obvious answer to the question of "Where have all the criminals gone?" in New York

City is they haven't gone anywhere, but the same population has sharply different rates of crime commission. But how and why did *that* happen?

The statistics available are strong circumstantial evidence that there were substantial reductions in rates of crime commission by non-incarcerated persons, but what is missing is direct observation of changing patterns of behavior. We know that youth auto theft, homicide, and burglary arrests are way down, but not why this happens and how it developed over time in city neighborhoods.

There are aggregate data on persons released from prison of some relevance to these questions. Figure 6.3 shows trends in return to prison within three years of persons committed from New York City and released from prison for more than two decades by the reason for their return.

The proportion of released prisoners returned to the system is relatively stable over the period since 1985, but the percentage of released persons convicted of new offenses in New York City first goes up in the 1980s and then turns down by almost two-thirds, from 28% to 10%.

One central puzzle in the pattern of Figure 6.3 is the sharp contrast between crime conviction trends and non-conviction returns to prison. Crime conviction patterns within three years in New York City closely reflect trends in felony crime rates, going up in the late 1980s, peaking at 28% in 1990, then dropping by 64% per 100 released prisoners over the sustained crime drop years. But the rate of non-conviction prison returns goes up substantially during the period after 1995 so that total return rates for all reasons are relatively flat. Why?

One possibility is that both trends reflect changes in general parole policy, perhaps a new statewide policy favoring technical returns. Figure 6.4 tests this theory by comparing the new conviction rates within three years of prisoners released to other cities over the same period of time.

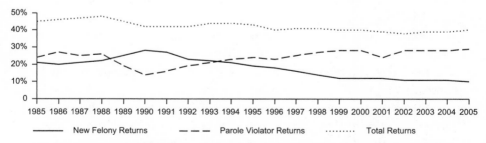

FIGURE 6.3 Percentage of New York City Prisoners Released Who Return within Three Years by Reason for Return.
Source: State of New York Department of Correctional Services.

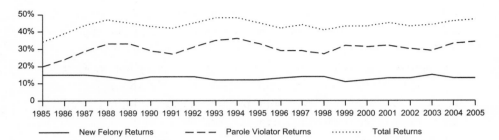

FIGURE 6.4 Percentage of Other Area Prisoners Released Who Return within Three Years by Reason for Return.
Source: State of New York Department of Correctional Services.

The reconviction rates and return rates for these prisoners from other cities do not show either the late 1980s increase or the sustained decline that the New York City data display. So there is no apparent shift in parole agency policy. And the current reconviction rates in the four major boroughs, each with its own independent district attorney, are quite close in recent years, ranging only from 8.9% (Brooklyn) to 11.9% (Manhattan) with the citywide average at 10.3%.

One implication of these changes in parole return policy over time is that the drop in incarcerated city residents would have been even greater than the 20,000 noted if policy had staged constant for non-conviction return rates. The second potential implication of these data and the most important is that experienced felons have pretty fully participated in the decline in serious crime in New York City. If the 64% drop in conviction rates reflects a 64% drop in crime commission rates, it would be a record-setting documented positive change in crime commission rates for a prison release cohort. And if there were increases in police efficiency as well, then a 64% drop in felony reconviction might signal a greater than 64% decrease in crimes committed by this group. How and why did this happen?

Less complete data on a second high-risk group was available from New York City—persons placed on probation after felony conviction. Figure 6.5 shows rates of rearrest for felony for populations placed on probation for the 11 years beginning in 1995.

There are two important limits on the data available for this group. Only arrests are reported, so that the evidence of criminal participation is less convincing than the reconviction rates for the parole releases. More important, the series starts with a 1995 probation population, so that the first three-year baseline rate of rearrest is completed only in 1998. This is after

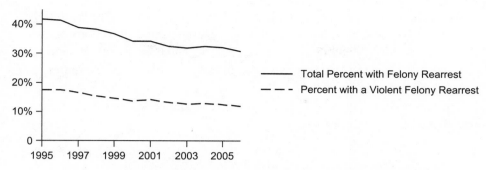

FIGURE **6.5** New York City Probationer Felony Arrests within Three Years of Sentence, 1995–2006, and New York City Misdemeanors and Felony Arrest Trends, 1995–2009.
Source: New York State Division of Criminal Justice Services, Office of Probation and Correctional Alternatives.

the crime rate has fallen for most index offenses by more than 70% of the total crime decline over the two decades.[1] This means that the time series starts about halfway through any reduction of individual crime propensity that is tied to the general environment in the pattern of Figure 6.3 and 6.4. So the pattern of decline that will be in evidence in this limited window will be about half the total that might be expected over the entire crime decline era. For this limited period, the declines are close to half the drop noted for the prison release series. The prevalence of felony arrests is down 26% from 1998 to 2009, while violent felony arrest rates drop 32%, precisely half the 64% drop reported in the prison group over the longer time series. So the size of the decline noted in Figure 6.5 is consistent with the larger drops noted in Figure 6.4 once adjustments are made for the smaller time covered by the trend data.

To ask how individual crime rates decline this quickly is again to bump into the limits of aggregate data. The problem with all these statistics is that they are after the fact of the behavioral changes that underlie these remarkable percentage reductions. There is little direct observation of changing patterns of street life in formerly high crime neighborhoods. There are anecdotes from drug scene workers of younger persons mixing marijuana and alcohol instead of crack in mid-1990s street recreation and socialization (Johnson and Golub 2000) but no cohort studies or

---

1. By 1998, the drop in New York crime had reached 88% of the 20-year total for homicide, 45% for rape, 73% for robbery, 55% for assault, 71% for burglary, 72% for larceny, and 75% for auto theft. Compare Uniform Crime Reports for 1998 and 2009.

sustained ethnographic observation of drug-using youth cultures. So the evidence of variability is overwhelmingly present, but observations of the dynamics of variability are not available to corroborate the statistical patterns. We know that what we used to call "criminal careers" are much easier to alter than had been believed, but what is now required are much thicker accounts of the preventive and diversionary processes that accomplished this in New York City.

E. The Impact of Lower Crime on High-Risk Populations and Areas

Violent crime is one of the most regressive taxes operating in the United States, with almost all of its negative effects concentrated among low-income minority groups and residential areas. The dark-skinned poor pay twice for high rates of violent crime—with rates of victimization many times higher than middle-income white and Asian groups and with rates of imprisonment vastly higher than non-minority populations. So large declines in serious crime should generate double benefits. Homicide in 1990 was by far the leading killer of young African American and Hispanic men in New York City. An 80% reduction in each year's death rate from homicide has a non-trivial effect on the life expectancy of minority populations if it is sustained throughout their young adult years of maximum homicide exposure. The incarceration rate of young men of color is also a high multiple of that for non-minority city dwellers, and the impact of incarceration early in adulthood on life chances for family formation and economic careers cannot be good. So the substantial reduction in imprisonment probably helps social and economic career development.

But the punitive bite of aggressive street policing *also* has differential impact on minority males in poor neighborhoods, and the numbers on this third regressive tax are not small. Figure 6.6 shows that even while felony arrests were falling in New York City, misdemeanor arrests continued to increase substantially. So the number of arrest and stop-and-frisk encounters is near its peak now, even with a lower crime rate and a somewhat smaller police force.

The reader can recall from Levine and Small (2008) that more than 80% of the misdemeanor marijuana arrests in the city were of minority males. And arrests are only the most formal end of aggressive police intervention. There were 581,000 stop-and-frisk incidents reported in 2009,

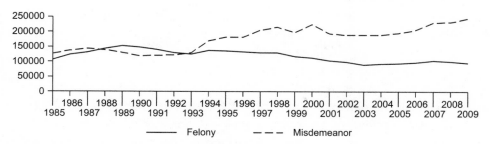

FIGURE 6.6 New York City Adult Arrests, 1985–2009.
Source: New York State Division of Criminal Justice Services, Computerized Criminal History System (as of 4/2010).

and the great majority of these are concentrated on minority males; indeed, the 55% African American proportion for stop-and-frisk is almost identical to the percentage African American that Levine and Small report for marijuana. These encounters cannot be a happy part of city life for the young men who suffer through them. What effect do they have on attitudes, aspiration, and achievement?

What are the criminal justice exposures and life course experiences of youth starting middle school in New York City in 1985, 1990, 1995, 2000, and 2005? How, when, and why does growing up in a lower crime environment make a difference in their lives? No single cohort can provide answers to such questions because their unique experience can't be compared to any experiential baseline. But looking at the ten years after 7th grade in 1985 versus in year 2000 can tell us about the ways in which different aggregate risk environments have impact on individual lives.

There are also important issues concerning how lower rates of crime are distributed among populations at risk. We usually assume that already incarcerated offenders do not have declines in their personal rates of predatory offending anywhere near the drop in crime generally. The data in Figure 6.3 suggest, however, that the crime rates of mid-career offenders are quite sensitive to upward and downward variations in general crime rates.

It is unlikely, however, that whatever environment changes or events that divert would-be offenders from acts of serious crime leave visible signs in individual life histories. A burglary or robbery that didn't happen might be a result of subtle changes in street settings and group experiences. But the signals and circumstances that cumulate in prevention are apt to be quite subtle, and are not prone to leave obvious behavioral fingerprints in the life histories of those who now stop short of serious crime. With the possible exception of shifts in drug of choice, there is no obvious list of precursor behaviors the reduction of which can be expected to reduce predatory crime rates.

Many of the statistical indicators used in this study identify particular questions and populations that would produce important qualitative research. The parole outcome data in 6.3 highlight the participation of mid-career offenders. The youth arrest trends analyzed in Chapter 4 make the comparative study of low school-achieving male cohorts an important human subject research project. The cocaine shifts after 1996 make inter-city comparisons in drug use patterns over time into a potentially signifi-cant avenue of inquiry. The traditional high concentration of violence in housing projects makes changes in those environments an important part of the larger picture.

It will not be easy to reconstruct many of the subtle and interrelated changes that took place in New York City over the years after 1990. We do know the populations and neighborhoods of the city where change was most important to crime, and these are the places where crime rates were highest (Chapter 8 of this book will give extensive statistical justification for that focus). And no matter how incomplete the final account that some researchers can compile, we can do much better in compiling the history of changes in New York City than we have done.

With such an imposing list of unanswered questions and unknown quantities, how much can we say about the nature of urban crime and the potential for its control on current evidence? Quite a lot. Chapter 7 shows how thoroughly the data from New York should change strategic assump-tions about crime control and the priorities of drug control. Chapter 8 addresses the fundamental shifts in social understanding that are pro-duced by the variability of crime in New York City.

The lessons of New York City about the nature of urban crime and the best methods of controlling crime are a mandate to change the priorities and policies of a misspent generation. In Norval Morris's great phrase, "We know better than we do."

Chapter 7

Lessons for American Crime Control

THE SUBJECT OF this chapter is different in an important way from a summary of what crime control strategies worked in New York City and how these techniques can help other cities. My topic instead is what the entire two decades of New York experience teaches about the major assumptions Americans have been making about methods to control crime and violence. To begin, I will argue that the entire four-fifths decline in New York safety crime has important implications for thinking about crime control, even though over half that crime drop has no clearly established cause. This chapter will show that it is more important to know that robbery rates can go down 84% than it is to know that police strategies apparently were responsible for about 40% of that decline. The volatility and variability of crime rates is a major signal to policy analysts, independent of a complete account of contributions to a decline.

The second reason why this chapter is broader than "what worked in New York City" is because my central concern is how the New York experience since 1990 challenges and changes the dominant assumptions of crime control in the United States after 1975. To do this, one must compare the data from New York with the assumptions and orthodox beliefs of people who have been making policy for a generation in cities, in states, and on the national scene. The major assumptions and priorities of American crime control over the last generation thus become the essential frame for reexamining what lessons the New York experience might suggest in rethinking principles of crime control in the United States. So the chapter will begin with another of my short and opinionated histories of crime-control strategy in the last decade of the twentieth century.

The summary will cover areas of both consensus and dispute. It will revisit some of the issues examined in Chapter 4's discussion of New York City debates, but this time with national focus and numbers. In some cases, there was substantial consensus at least among policy makers about appropriate control strategies and the reason that they were indicated, so my summary will stress the major elements in the dominant view. What I called "supply-side criminology" in the last chapter is one example of a dominant set of consensus assumptions. In other domains, there were sharp and basic disagreements on both the nature of the problem and preferred solutions. Illegal narcotics was one such hotly contested topic by the early 1990s, and my short summary for this kind of topic will try to identify the key empirical and value differences that characterize the conflicting schools of thought.

The second section of the chapter will then explore the potential impact of what has happened in New York City and how it happened on the assumptions that underlie crime-control efforts, the tactics that are preferred, and the results that are anticipated. What happened in New York City has undermined fundamental conceptions about the variability of crime rates and of crime propensities of offenders and thus poses a serious challenge to incapacitation as the chief weapon of policy to reduce crime. The timing and results of the police strategy in New York toward drug markets and drug violence are quite different, if not frontally contradictory of the William Bennett version of the all-out war on use of illegal narcotics in the 1980s. And the police success in crime reduction with modest manpower and strategy changes should generate hope rather than envy from other supervisory and facilitative agents who earn their livings trying to reduce the criminality of high-risk youth and adults. The biggest surprise in New York City is the degree of changeability and variability that is characteristic of the most dangerous people in the worst neighborhoods of America's biggest city. This is very good news for probation officers, drug treatment programs, parole agents, and youth workers.

A. Crime Control Policy in the United States: The View from 1992

The diversity of emphasis one might expect to find in a nation with 51 different penal and prison systems and thousands of different counties and municipal governments should produce large differences in patterns of priorities and investment in crime control. Certainly, a federal union that includes Vermont and Texas, New York City and Helena, Montana, should not all believe the same things about appropriate methods of crime control or allocate resources between methods of control in identical fashion. So both the intensities of crime policies and their components do vary from state to state and by demography and politics. At any given time, there can be about a 10-to-1 ratio in the United States between the state with the highest and that with the lowest rate of imprisonment (Zimring and Hawkins 1991 at Figure 6.1, p. 149; Zimring 2010). Yet national fashions *do* exist, and the states and cities follow very similar patterns in policy choice over time. Imprisonment is a striking example (which will be explored later in the chapter) where states could have pursued different paths over the 35 years after the 1972 low point for state and federal prisoners. Instead, every state in the United States expanded rates of imprisonment as never before, and the variation in growth rates in 1972–2007 is not obviously different from the pattern produced by a normal distribution around a single growth rate of 400% (see Zimring 2010, Part III). The common structure of mass media, national politics, and social and economic interdependence often produces much more uniformity of opinion and value than the division of political power by levels of government would require. So there is value in looking for shared attitudes and priorities on issues like crime control, notwithstanding the regional, demographic, and state-to-state differences that also persist in the United States.

I target the search for crime control assumptions and priorities to the early 1990s because that was the period just before New York's crime drop entered the discussions of crime policy—it seems an obvious "before" for an analysis that compares new perspectives from New York to the conventional wisdom on crime control to be found earlier. But the selection of the early 1990s as a historical moment in crime policy also requires some comment on the mood and rhetorical tone of crime control discourse in that era.

The first half of the 1990s was not a happy time to be in the crime control business. The predominant public mood was a mixture of fear, frustration, and anger. The great expansion of crime and violence in the United States in the decade after 1964 had been followed by relatively shallow fluctuations down from the high 1974 rates, followed by return up to the 1974 highs for homicide in 1980, and then near it again in 1991. The last crime increase of this period, from 1985 to 1991, was the most frustrating period for both the general public and for professional observers. Crime rates had dropped swiftly in the early 1980s, and two contemporary trends seemed to promise that more good crime news was on the horizon.

The percentage of the total population in the high crime rate youth group was declining steadily after 1975, a partial compensation for the baby boom fueled explosion of youths that had accompanied the crime expansion after 1964. And the smaller cohorts of youth and young adults were aging into a criminal justice system that had become substantially more severe. The prison population had already doubled by 1988 in the United States from its 1972 lows and was adding new inmates in the period after 1985 at a record pace. A smaller cohort of youth should have meant fewer young offenders, but the rate of arrest among youth went up so fast that the youth crime volume skyrocketed. Larger imprisonment should have reduced both the volume of street criminals and of street crime, but it didn't.

Not only did rates of violent crime go up (mostly young offenders in big-city minority areas), but the middle of the 1980s also produced by far the most intense drug panic of the postwar years. While powder cocaine had a sustained career as a drug of abuse in the late 1970s (the peak year for reported cocaine use in the United States is still 1979), the advent of crystallized "crack cocaine" in smokable and affordable doses brought available cocaine intoxication to big-city ghettos in a way that provoked fear nationally. In the four years after 1985, crack spawned a new vocabulary of drug-specific anxiety ("crack pipes," "crack houses," "crack fiends," "crack babies," etc.), a multi-billion dollar federal "war on drugs," and a huge increase in drug-related incarceration, even by the extraordinary standards of the general prison boom. Drug offenses went from less than 7% of state prisoners to 21%, even as the non-drug prison population grew radically. In the federal system, drug offenders became a majority of all prison admissions and then a substantial majority (Zimring and Harcourt 2007, Chap. 3).

Public attitudes about crime and drugs were angry and negative, but this did not for the most part produce any reexamination of the strategic choices that had dominated crime policy from the mid-1970s onward. Rising crime was not seen as evidence of incarceration's failure but rather of its insufficiency. While the first doubling of the U.S. prison population after 1972 happened without much legislative initiative, the years from 1993 onward witnessed at least three discrete waves of legislative programs of mandatory minimum penalties for serious or repetitive offenders: first came "Three Strikes and You're Out" mandating long-to-life sentences for third felonies if the first two offenses had been serious, sometimes even if the third and triggering offense was minor. These three strikes laws were passed by initiative or legislation in half of U.S. states and the federal system between 1993 and 1996 (Zimring, Hawkins, and Kamin 2001, Chap. 1). This was followed by federal and state "truth in sentencing" laws which require serious or violent offenders to serve a stipulated minimum share of their nominal prison terms before they can be released from incarceration. This was followed in some jurisdictions with 10-20-30 legislation designed to impose mandatory minimum sentences for commission of violent crimes with firearms (Zimring, Hawkins. and Kamin 2001. Chap. 9).

In the short term, at least, the frustrating failure of crime and drug policies to achieve progress in the late 1980s and in 1990 did not undermine the support for incarceration and punitive drug programs. The apparent failure of increasing prison time to reduce robbery, burglary, and rape was seen as a need for still longer prison terms being authorized or required, perhaps in the pattern of a customer with a hangover ordering another installment of "the hair of the dog that bit him."

By 1995, both public anger and punitive legislation were more dominant in the politics of criminal justice then in any period since World War II. The major legislative landmarks of the era were California's three strikes and you're out law (Zimring, Hawkins, and Kamin 2001), the federal Crime Control Act of 1994, and the 1996 federal law announced as the "Anti-Terrorism and Effective Death Penalty Act" (28 U.S.C. § 2241 et seq.).

Doctrines and Disputes

The important questions of crime control policy have never been completely un-contentious in a country as politically diverse as the United States and with different regions and cultures. And by the early 1990s there was a deepening division politically on one of the four topics to be discussed in this section—drugs—where the radical assumptions and excesses of the drug war had generated some cognitive counterinsurgency. But on three of the four topics central to American strategies of crime prevention, consensus was still intact, despite the frustrations and failures of the years after 1985. The issue areas addressed, in the rough order of their public importance, are: (1) the hegemony of incapacitative incarceration as the primary method for controlling serious crime; (2) the dispute between legalist and harm-reduction priorities for control of illegal narcotics; (3) the low esteem of prevention as a public crime control policy; and (4) the relative unimportance of police to crime control.

Incapacitative Incarceration

Imprisonment is the most common punishment for the most serious crimes and criminal offenders throughout the world. But its pervasive presence as a serious criminal sanction does not mean that all governments that use prisons have no other important strategies to control crime. In most developed nations, the prison tends to be a universal but non-exclusive instrument of crime control.

What separated the United States in the decades after 1975 from the rest of the developed world was the scale of imprisonment in most U.S. jurisdictions and the fact that incapacitation by incarceration was the only method used with any confidence to control street crime. Figure 7.1 compares the growth in the volume of arrests reported by the FBI for the seven "index" felony offenses over the period 1975–2000 with the growth in the volume of prisoners.

The growth of imprisonment dwarfs any minor growth of felony arrests throughout the period. While the institution of imprisonment can serve a wide variety of penal purposes—deterrence and retribution in addition to incapacitation—it is incapacitation that represents the prison's largest comparative advantage over non-incarcerative sanctions such as fines, community service, loss of privileges, and supervision. The doors lock from the outside, and this prevents crimes in the community for the duration of the period of confinement. And the operation of incarceration as a crime prevention or community safety tool does not depend on the potential offender's sensitivity to threats (as does deterrence) or his concern about stigma (as does prison as an instrument of retribution). As long as the person locked up would have offended if not incarcerated, those offenses will be avoided, independent of the offender's will or social conscience.

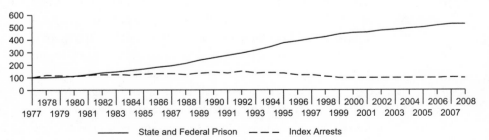

FIGURE 7.1 Trends in United States Crime Index, Index Arrests, and State and Federal Prison Population.
Source: FBI, *Uniform Crime Reports,* Prepared by the National Archive of Criminal Justice Data and Bureau of Justice Statistics.

What the substantial prevention of crime as a result of incapacitation *does* require is the capacity to find and lock up persons who would otherwise commit crimes in the community at a high rate and for a long time. There are such persons, although the number of such habitual or high-rate offenders has been questioned for a long time (Morris 1950), and the capacity to identify and selectively sanction them is also the subject of lively debate (compare Greenwood and Abrahamse 1982 with Blumstein, Cohen, Nagin, and Visher 1986, and Greenwood and Turner 1987).

The very emphasis that criminal justice policy had been placing on imprisonment for incapacitation in the 1970s and 1980s probably produced sharply diminished effectiveness for that strategy. The first problem is diminishing marginal returns. If prosecutors and judges lock up only 100,000 offenders because of the crime they would otherwise commit, they will try to select the most dangerous members of those groups they process. But when the number to be locked up is doubled and then doubled again, the additional offenders selected will be much less obvious risks than the first group of candidates selected. The wider the net is cast, the smaller the additional increment of crimes avoided for each thousand prisoners added.

A second feature of mass incarceration to incapacitate also produces smaller returns as sentences increase. When a judge sends offenders off to prison for two years, the period of incarceration will be close to the period when the prisoner was an active criminal. It is far more likely he would have continued committing some crimes if left in the community for the two years after his crime was committed than if the same offender were imprisoned for two extra years after already serving 18 years since his last period in the community. Predicting a 23-year-old active offender will continue to offend at 25 is no sure thing, but it is easier than assuming that extra crime will be saved by sending the same 23-year-old to prison for an extra two years far into the future, for 20 years rather than 18! So adding additional confinement onto long prison terms will only save extra crimes if we can successfully make particularly long-term prediction of dangerousness.

The policies embraced by the penal legislation of the early and mid-1990s were clearly incapacitation based on the assumptions of earlier habitual criminal laws—with very long terms imposed for repeat offenders. But the same features that most clearly illustrate the incapacitative basis of the strategies also show that the extremities of the policies—the large number of persons and the length of the terms confined—made the preventive potential of these add-on penal regimes quite attenuated. In this sense, the wholehearted commitment to incapacitation in the 1980s created conditions that guaranteed every additional dollar or prison year invested in the 1990s would yield a sharply diminished return.

But the people who created mandatory 25-year-to-life sentences for shoplifters in "three strikes and you're out" were trapped by the same absence of alternatives that had produced the prison explosion in the first place. Crime rates had risen, so something had to be done. The only "something" that fit the notion of persistent offenders who must remain active unless locked up was penal confinement. And all the earlier extensions of who went to prison and for how long meant that extending the incarceration gambit further had to come at the extreme margins of any prediction of dangerousness. The same assumptions of permanent criminal proclivities that deprived those who opposed escalations of imprisonment of a counter-strategy also pushed the hard-line advocates to imprisonment terms that looked close to "reducto ad absurdum" extensions of previous crackdowns.

The peculiar pattern of mid-1990s legislation was produced not because imprisonment for incapacitation had become the dominant method of crime control in America but because it had for the most part been recognized as the *only* method of controlling crime that fit the notion of persistent high-rate offenders.

The Drug Control Debates

The consensus monopoly of incapacitation as a street crime policy was two decades old and still powerfully in place by 1992, but the hard-line premises and "all or nothing" ideology of the first years of the war on drugs had a much shorter career of unchallenged domination. To be sure, the punitive emphasis and prison-centric premises of criminal justice generally were applied with great force in drug cases. Drug-related incarceration shot up tenfold in California prisons in the decade after 1981 (Zimring and Hawkins 1992) and the federal system became dominated by drug admissions (Zimring and Harcourt 2007 at p. 219). But imprisonment was never the only strategy adopted in the national drug war—the late 1980s approach to drug control was to try everything, and there were a large number of components of "everything"—including major investments in federal drug policing, local police drug incentives such as confiscation of drug-related property and money, financial assistance to

drug user treatment programs, massive investments in drug supply reduction efforts in foreign countries, and interdiction at borders and in
transit nations. So the portfolio of prevention strategies was much more
diversified for drugs than street crime. But the theoretical foundation for
what the government was doing in drugs was weaker and the competition
among different strategies of intervention was much stronger. Prison was
competing with drug treatment and foreign crop eradication for priority
and money.

There was no bedrock foundation for regarding drugs as a criminal
harm to parallel the obvious hurt inflicted by the robber, the rapist, and the
burglar. The drug abuser was only hurting himself unless and to the extent
that drug abuse was contagious or imposed external costs. Locking up the
burglar protects the homeowner who otherwise suffers invasion. Who exactly is protected when the drug user is behind bars?

There were two competing answers to this question in drug control
discourse, with different implications for priorities in enforcement of the
criminal law. The legalist view of William Bennett, the first director of the
National Drug Control Office, argues that all deliberate use of illegal drugs
is harmful because it undermines the legitimacy of the government's authority to decide what citizens can or cannot use to alter their moods. In
this view, taking or selling illegal drugs is a species of treason, and the
specific physical harms and benefits of the drug being taken are unimportant. So all illegal drugs are from this perspective not only harmful but
equally harmful. The high-functioning drug taker may be even more dangerous than the devastated crack fiend on a public sidewalk because the
high-functioning user is more likely to be admired and emulated (National Drug Control Strategy 1989 at pp. 4, 7–8).

The opposite view is now more frequently called the strategy of *harm
reduction*. In this view, the only drugs that should be prohibited are those
which inflict harm to users far out of proportion to the benefits they provide. And that is not only the basis for the criminal sanction, but also the
primary aim of criminal law enforcement—to reduce the harms associated with illegal drugs. Drugs with little or no aggregate harm associated
with their use should have low priorities or not be criminal.

The first five years of the crack era drug war did have some differences
of opinion in public discussion, not only including harm reduction but
also advocacy for general withdrawal of criminal punishment for adult
use of narcotics, but federal and state legislation was intensely hard
line—mandatory minimum penalties, very long prison terms, and the

first federal death penalty authorized by Congress in decades, New York Senator D'Amato's legislation reserving execution for murders related to the drug trade (Zimring, *New York Times*, September 16, 1988, p. 19).

By the early 1990s, the waves of drug panic and emergency penal legislation had abated. A serious recession had pushed drug control off its late 1980s pinnacle as the problem more citizens regarded as the nation's most serious, and a many-sided debate about the appropriate ends of drug control policy and the most effective means to achieve them was underway.

The legalist position that all drugs were equally threatening to the national welfare had never captured the national imagination and suffered as well from an inconsistency in its proponent's presentation of it. While William Bennett argued that all illegal drug users and uses were equally threatening, the poster drug for the National Drug Control Strategy was always, and loudly, crack cocaine. And the harms of crack addiction or use that proved the case against it were the hopelessly addicted young persons spawning crack babies and making the streets of America's big cities hazardous. All these consequences were the collateral harms that harm-reduction advocates wanted to center policy around removing. But the legalists were using them instead as examples of why all drugs were equally terrible (see Zimring and Hawkins 1992, Chap. 1).

Harm-reduction advocates frequently used drug dependency and addiction as arguments for public investment in drug treatment. And this was a second important difference between the policy climate of the drug abuse debate and the incapacitation monopoly for street crime—drug treatment as "demand reduction" was attractive as an alternative method of reducing drug abuse. By contrast, once there was widespread acceptance of the assumptions of supply-side criminology, there was no alternative prevention scenario to prison for public crime-control efforts. Early education and parenting training might reduce the eventual flow of career offenders with relatively fixed proclivities, but for tomorrow's crime rate or next year's, it was incarceration or surrender.

If crack cocaine was the poster child for the legalist anti-drug crusade, medical marijuana proved to be its Achilles' heel. Marijuana for all uses had by the 1980s the most benign social reputation of all illegal drugs and the largest rate of "ever used" prevalence to go with it. For an advocate of a legalist "all drugs are terrible" perspective, the physical and behavioral effects of marijuana were a particularly difficult foundation for scaring the public. But *medical* marijuana was even more a public relations disaster for legalist advocates. The people asking to use the drug were sick and infirm, often older or HIV-positive and suffering from nausea and lack of appetite. So the people who were asking for access to this drug were as far from a predatory criminal threat as one could get. The medical marijuana argument was that the prohibition did more harm than good for this deserving group. And the argument was a winner in Arizona and California initiative elections and in several state legislatures (Zimring and Harcourt 2007, Chap. 3).

While it is obvious why the opponents of the drug war and legalist drug policy would concentrate on campaigns like medical marijuana, why didn't this simply provoke a tactical withdrawal from the legalists, a concession on medical uses while discouraging other uses of marijuana and other more dangerous drugs? The problem with any concession is the "all or nothing" character of the major premise of the legalist position. Carving an exception for medical marijuana amounts to admitting that the original breadth of the criminal prohibition was a mistake. And once the government has been proved wrong on one illegal drug or user class, then the entire of the rest of the list of users and uses is open to question. As soon as government prohibition and punishment are not beyond question, the entire of the legalist premise has been undermined. So the medical marijuana movement undermined unquestioning acceptance of the harmfulness of all legally prohibited drugs.

A second round of anti-legalist campaign was the advocacy of drug treatment as an alternative to prison. California's Proposition 36 in 2000 expressed a public preference for treatment instead of incarceration for several types of California drug offenders.

With all these theoretical problems on display, the one area where hard-line legalists continued to prevail was in criminal sentencing. Each year from 1990 onward, the United States celebrated a new historic high for the number of persons imprisoned for drug offenses in state and federal prisons. The hard-line imprisonment policy outlived the hard-line consensus on drugs by at least 15 years.

The Low Regard for Prevention

An important contrast between the street crime and the drug control policy arenas in the early 1990s was the presence of alternative methods like drug treatment in the drug dialogue, while imprisonment stood alone as a response to serious street crime. One reason that the prison had no serious competition for public efforts to control street crime was the low esteem in the 1990s of primary prevention programs as credible street crime control. The early intervention strategies that had produced hopeful results—Head Start in Michigan, nurse visits to prospective and new parents in England—were not regarded as a viable alternative to incapacitation for reducing crime. The clearest example of the non-credibility of "soft" programming in the 1990s was the characterization of community-based programs proposed in the 1994 federal crime legislation as "midnight basketball"—which the Republicans delighted in considering as a non-credible alternative to building more prisons with federal money. But why were "keep them off the streets" efforts like midnight basketball laughable? The contemporary understanding was that recreational diversions from crime were not punitive enough to reduce crime, but why was that? If high-risk youth could be transferred from drug-infested streets into YMCA basketball courts three nights a week, wouldn't that exert downward pressure on the crime rate?

Midnight basketball didn't require the multi-year waits for crime reduction that made frightened citizens skeptical of visiting nurses and Head Start programs. Why would they fail? The same deterministic notion of fixed proclivities toward committing crime that served as the foundation for long-term incapacitation by imprisonment also cast doubt on any program that would try to voluntarily divert "life course offenders" with constructive recreation. Perhaps an "adolescence limited" offender or two might be attracted to the gym, but the hard-core group— the ones we were building prisons to house—would scoff at spending valuable predatory crime time in sports. And even if their Fridays were spent shooting baskets, they would be back robbing innocent citizens the next day.

The notion that "career criminals" or "juvenile super-predators" are hard-wired to persistent criminal offending undermines the preventive promise of programs to redirect or divert likely offenders, so the central conception of supply-side criminology was a major setback for confidence in prevention programs. And I will soon show that the same hard-wired image of the criminal offender was also an impediment to believing that changes in street policing could substantially reduce crime.

What made any situational strategies to remove criminal opportunities or divert the energies and attention of potential offenders look ineffective was the idea that the proclivities of serious offenders to commit crimes do not vary with modest changes in circumstances or opportunities. This image of the persisting criminal offender far overshot the empirical data on "criminal careers" but was nevertheless a powerful *idée fixe* in both policy analysis and political debate.

The Irrelevance of Police to Crime Control Policy Design

One remarkable feature of the debates about crime policy and crime control in the late 1980s and early 1990s is the unimportance of police manpower and strategies to most discussion of improvements in street crime control. Little or no attention was paid in federal and state discussions of reducing crime to the ways in which police might prevent crime or the ways police performance might be improved.

One of the reasons that police were missing persons in the crime policy discourse of the 1980s and early 1990s came from the allocation of responsibility for police in the levels of government in the American federal system. The state legislatures that drafted penal codes and maintained prisons had no major responsibility for most police budgets or administration. A governor or state legislator can initiate changes in the penal code and legislate to build new prisons or close old ones. But city police are not either supported or controlled by state government. The federal government has authority only over the FBI, the drug enforcement authority, and other specialized police forces totaling about 10% of the nation's law enforcement. And the lack of direct legislative responsibility at the federal or state level is one reason that so little attention gets paid to police as crime preventers in Congress or state legislatures. The legislative attention span quickly departs from considering activities that are beyond legislative control.

But there were reasons other than levels of governmental authority that police issues had so little attention in discussing crime control options in the early 1990s. The conventional wisdom was that police didn't make much difference in preventing crime. To be sure, apprehending offenders was the necessary start of the process of removing them from predatory opportunities and thus preventing their future crimes. So police were a necessary but not a sufficient condition for launching the incapacitative machinery that was the main event in American crime control. But what of the attempts of hundreds of thousands of police and sheriffs to engage in one of the many varieties of what William Bratton was to call "preventive policing"—the car patrols, foot patrols, community policing experiments, the problem solving and hot spot approaches?

The lack of attention to these elements as major possibilities in crime control efforts may have been simply an absence of peripheral vision that encompassed the full range of prevention possibilities, but I suspect that more than an oversight was the cause. And I don't think that data sets like the Kansas City experiment were the important obstacle to betting on preventive policing. A major deterrent to thinking that patterns of police street patrol could prevent large volumes of crime was the same image of career criminals with fixed proclivities to offend that made a laughing stock of midnight basketball. Almost all the preventive activities of police are situated and limited in time and geography. The police can occupy a street corner for an hour or (in hot spot interventions) a week. Any crime opportunity that is also limited in time and space can become an offense not committed as a result. But the life-course persistent offender with fixed propensities to commit crimes can vary the time and place of his offenses to avoid the situational constraints imposed by the police. So there may have been important links between predominant theories of the nature of serious crime and the predominant conceptions of appropriate ways to restrain and prevent it.

Figure 7.2 shows the impact of the crime-control choices of the generation after 1972 on the growth of two classes of government crime control personnel, police and correctional staff. As the figure shows, the modest growth in police was dwarfed by the explosive growth of correctional employees in the 35 years after 1972. During the thirty-five years after 1972, the corrections staff growth was almost three times that of police, 196% to 59%. In 1972, the police outnumbered correctional staff by more than three to one (the ratio was 3.32). By 2007, the ratio of cops to guards had fallen to less than 1.5 to 1 (1.49).

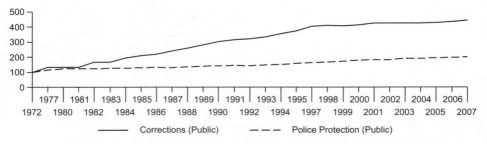

FIGURE 7.2 Trends in United States Federal, State and Local Corrections and Police Protection Employment Estimates; (1972 = 100).
Source: U.S. Census Bureau's Annual Survey of Public Employment.

The decision by the Clinton administration to feature federal financial aid for 100,000 additional urban police was an important political milestone not only for the 1994 federal crime bill itself but for the American politics of crime control. Increasing police in the city is an anti-crime effort with intuitive appeal to most citizens and it is consistent with a punitive attitude toward offenders (unlike basketball leagues). The 100,000 cops idea effectively ended the rhetorical monopoly of imprisonment on crime control and fought the sentencing enhancements and prison construction programs of the Republican Congress to a draw (both were adopted) (Windlesham 1998). And all this happened prior to any real indication of powerful policing effects from New York City or anywhere else. The renewed interest in police came before rather than after the widely reported declines of crime associated with policing.

B. New York's Lessons

The world of 2011 is different from that of 1992 in many ways that this chapter will not consider. My mission here is to consider the ways in which what has happened to crime and crime policy in New York City has or should have altered our understanding of the costs and benefits of a whole series of strategies to control and prevent crime. What we already know from 20 years of New York experience provides game-changing perspectives on all four of the articles of conventional wisdom discussed in the previous section. This section will outline New York City lesson plans for crime control on incapacitation, on drugs, on police, and on prevention.

The End of Incapacitative Hegemony

The incarceration of serious criminals had a monopoly position on crime policy in the United States of the early 1990s, but the beliefs on which that hegemony were based have now been disproved. That does not mean that the United States will lose its world leadership in imprisonment rates soon or ever, or even that New York State will continue its decline in prison population on a sustained basis. But it does mean that incapacitation is no longer the only credible method of crime control in the United States and the major assumptions that had generated the monopoly status of imprisonment have been disproved.

There are three distinct lessons from New York City that change the relative status of incapacitative imprisonment. The first is the fact that the most successful episode of big-city crime decline in the twentieth century took place in a city where increased incarceration was never a prominent feature of the era when crime went down. Figure 7.3 compares trends in imprisonment from New York City with imprisonment trends for the same years in the United States as a whole.

The modest growth in New York City imprisonment in the first years of the crime drop was about one-third of the national average, and then a substantial decline set in. Appendix B estimates that the total incarceration actually occurring in New York City in 2008 was more than 50,000 fewer than would have been consistent with the national trends. So the kids who didn't brush with Crest had many fewer cavities. This huge crime success story took place without even average use of the incapacitation machinery of criminal justice, and that alone calls into doubt the status of incapacitation efforts as a necessary condition to large crime declines.

The apparent success of New York City without correctional expansion since 1990 has also changed the portfolio of criminal justice investments in the state. Figure 7.4 compares the relative growth of police and correctional staff in two eras for New York State. I use state-level data since most New York City prisoners are housed upstate. So the numbers probably understate somewhat the changes attributable to the city itself.

During the first 18 years after 1972, the number of correctional staff tripled, with a growth rate more than 20 times that of police statewide. During the second period, correctional staff growth was under 1% while the growth experience of the police was more than 30 times as great. Given the stickiness of public employment, this large a turnabout is quite remarkable.

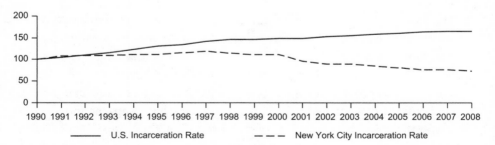

FIGURE 7.3 Trends in Incarceration from New York City and the United States, 1990–2008, and New York Crime Trends, 1990–2008.
Source: New York Department of Corrections and U.S. Census, Daily Inmate Population New York City; New York Police Department Comstat Unit.

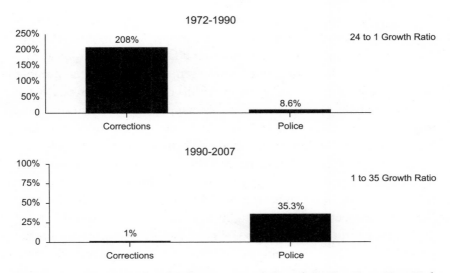

FIGURE 7.4 Correctional and Police Personnel Growth in Two Eras, New York State, 1972–1990 and 1990–2007.
Source: U.S. Bureau of the Census, Annual Survey of Public Employment, 1972–2007.

The second aspect of the New York experience that undercuts the monopoly status of the prison as crime prevention is the apparent success of city police in achieving major reductions in robbery, burglary, and auto theft. The push for 100,000 urban police to reduce crime in the 1994 legislation debates was based on hope rather than experience. But New York City provides evidence that street policing can and has reduced crime independently of increases in imprisonment. Whereas the previous choices often seemed to be prison or no prison, a competition between prison and policing for crime prevention dollars is equivalent to the alternative paths to harm reduction that exist when drug treatment programs came to compete with expanding imprisonment. Again, the primary impact of a police option is the end of the incapacitative monopoly that lasted a generation in the United States.

The Volatility and Variability of City Crime

But the most important data from New York City that undermine the credibility of incapacitation as crime control is the stunning demonstration in the city's crime decline that even with population stability, crime rates are highly volatile and variable. The rhetorical question I asked in Chapter 6 was, "Where have all the criminals gone in New York City?"

The apparent answer was that they had not gone anywhere, neither to prison in increasing numbers nor to New Jersey. When robbery and burglary rates drop by more than 80% without large increases in incarceration or out-migration, the crime volume generated by the same number of high-risk persons also drops by four-fifths or so. But this is exactly the sort of variability that isn't supposed to happen when most crime (the two-thirds of arrests generated by 6% of the boys) is committed by high-volume offenders with fixed criminal proclivities. What has to have happened in New York City undermines the credibility of assuming that persons sent to prison in year one would have continued to commit high rates of offenses for a long number of years. If even those who have been convicted of crime have highly variable and unpredictable rates of expected future crime, the benefits of locking them up fall greatly because there is a much smaller and more uncertain volume of crime avoided by the incarceration.

We have already seen clear evidence of variability of individual crime rates in environments of lower general rates in Chapter 6. The felony reconviction rate of those released from prison who had come from New York City dropped from 28% after three years in 1990 to 10% after three years in 2005, a 64% decline. That's good news from almost all perspectives but very bad news for proponents of incapacitation as crime control. Locking up the 1990 group for that extra three years would prevent almost three times as much crime as locking up the same number of persons from the 2005 release group for a similar period. Their differential reconviction rate reflects lower total crime and greatly expanded chances that additional custody would extend to many inmates who would not commit many crimes in the community.

If the assumptions of fixed criminal proclivities over long periods of time that motivate incapacitative confinement had been true in New York City, the crime declines that the city experienced with no large population change would have been impossible. The variability in individual crime rates that had to happen to produce these massive drops all but guarantees that the assumptions about fixed proclivities that drive most incapacitation expectations are simply not true. In this sense, the huge crime declines that happened in New York City are not merely an indication that incapacitative crusades are unnecessary to reduce crime but also a demonstration that the foundational assumptions of incapacitation were vastly overstated. The demonstration of volatility and variability of crime rates in New York City goes to the heart of the basis for expecting sustained, substantial, and predictable incapacitation benefits from the confinement of most convicted criminal offenders.

The variability of individual crime rates that was demonstrated in New York is also the most plausible explanation for the irony that New York City, the most prominent non-participant in the incarceration boom after 1990, is also the site of the most successful crime reduction of that or any other era.

What the materials in Appendix B illustrate is the comparative cost consequences of increased policing and less than average incarceration in New York City. When the actual incarceration numbers in New York are compared with the number locked up if national trends had been followed, by 2007 the city was imprisoning or jailing 58,000 fewer persons than it would have if keeping up with the U.S. time trends. At a modest $25,000 per person year, the public savings of that many fewer prisoners was twice the cost of the expansion in policing.

Drugs: The Triumph of Harm Reduction in New York

When the trends over time of drug indicators and crime statistics in New York City is measured against the conflicting claims of legalist and harm-reduction advocates, the support for harm reduction is overwhelming. The target for legalists is drug use itself, and the legalist assumes that all illegal drugs were created (nearly) equal. The central measure of success or failure is trends in the prevalence and incidence of drug use. From the perspective of legalist drug control, the years after 1990 in New York were a very mixed picture. Using hospital and death data as an index, the use of most types of illegal drugs was stable during the 1990s and beyond, and recent trends in survey reports of usage and emergency room mentions are up. As far as these data indicate, New York City is not winning its war on drug use.

From a harm-reduction perspective, however, New York City policy was a brilliant success. Public drug markets were gone by the late 1990s and the number of drug-related killings reported by the police (always an undercount) dropped by more than 90% from the early 1990s to 2005. Criminal subcultures no longer owned the streets in the immediate vicinity of drug-selling areas, and drug killings dropped precipitously. New York City appeared to have won its war on drug crime without winning its war on drugs.

As a public relations matter, also, the New York version of harm reduction worked wonderfully. The targets of special effort—public markets

and drug killings—were also the visible manifestation of the drug problem that scared citizens the most (at least if they didn't have children).
Removing the public face of the drug phenomenon made the average citizen feel safe, and not without reason. Emergency room physicians and
nurses may be seeing the same number of heroin and cocaine users, but
the drug killings on nightly news and the street environments visibly
dominated by drug commerce are gone.

There is ample evidence that the harm-reduction priorities and limited
ambitions of the police were the deliberate choices of One Police Plaza.
The priorities of eradicating public drug markets and going after guns
were obvious. But that starting point for priorities wouldn't signal harm
reduction if the police then committed the same resources and priorities
to apprehending drug sellers who moved indoors and arresting drug
users. But that isn't what happened in New York City. Marijuana arrests
shot up and stayed high, but that, as we saw in Chapter 5, was a pretext to
remove young men of color who looked suspicious from the streets and
get their fingerprints. The better measure of police priorities are the statistics on the rise and fall of the narcotics units. No segment of the NYPD
rose faster than narcotics during the 1990s, and no segment of the police
force fell faster after the turn of the century. The 137% increase in manpower took place in the years when the attack on public markets was
launched and carried to success. After that success, while drug sales and
consumption were pretty stable, the narcotics units fell by more than 60%
to fewer officers than had been on the narcotics staff of a much smaller
police force 18 years before. The natural inference is that police leadership
believed that the narcotic division's surge campaign has done its job, but
if that is true, then that job was far more limited and more specific than an
all-out war on drugs in New York City.

This clear evidence that New York's police were practicing harm reduction is dissonant with the ideological reputation of the New York force. In
any competition between "wets" and "dries" on the questions of drug control, the right wing is concentrated in the camp of the legalist supporters
of prohibition (except when libertarians embrace decriminalization).
Harm reduction is more often associated with public health perspectives
and a few policy analysts in the middle of the road like the late John Kaplan
(Kaplan 1982; MacCoun 2006). The hard-line reputation of policing generally and the William Bratton/Jack Maple brand of Compstat enforcement
would suggest a more unqualified embrace of anti-drug legalism since this
was supposed to be the era of zero tolerance law enforcement. As with

the "quality of life" story of expanded misdemeanor arrests, there appears to be a large gap between slogan and substance in the understanding of the police reforms in New York City.

If my interpretation of the drug enforcement data is correct, what happened in New York City was the most dramatic demonstration of policing strategy as an instrument of drug-related harm reduction in modern U.S. history.

The New Credibility of Police as Agents of Crime Prevention

The political appeal of investments in police as a crime policy has always been substantial across the political spectrum, with conservative publics regarding the police as the essence of law and order, and more liberal audiences, while concerned about abuse of police authority, preferring the investment in urban policing to the further expansion of incarceration. In addition to this lesser-of-evils appeal to liberals, one further advantage of fiscal support for police to liberals was the opportunity to financially reward cities rather than states. The obvious political appeal of augmenting the police—both as a reward for cities and an alternative to expansion of imprisonment—had driven the Clinton administration into the 100,000 extra cops proposals in the 1994 federal crime bill. Pushing for extra manpower was also a shift in focus from earlier federal adventures in police assistance when police seemed to be getting technology, tanks, and helicopters from the largess of the national government.

What the New York City experience has added to political appeal is empirical credentials for considering police investments as methods of reducing crime. There are, as Chapter 5 demonstrated, several gaps between the new image of policing and the reality of the police role in New York City. The police are the cause of less than half of the city's total crime decline. But the city's experience has generated persuasive evidence that police, in addition to apprehending criminals, have a major capacity to prevent crime.

In an ideal world, the particular aspects of policing that generate crime reductions would be known now or soon to be determined. This may not happen. The high reputation of New York policing has already created consultation with other departments, the hiring of senior New York veterans (including former Chief Bratton in Los Angeles), and now the hiring of Bratton disciples from his longer tour of duty in Los Angeles to senior positions in other police departments. So a good deal of technology transfer is already happening and will continue. If consistently good results are generated in these new cities, that will accelerate the process of imitation and emulation. If the results are uneven, the impact on the reputation of preventive policing is uncertain. The rigorous tests that haven't happened in New York City and Los Angeles are not likely to spring up in cities that hire executives from these leadership cities or emulate programs with Compstat-trained consultants. So when specific questions about cost and benefit get asked, answering them will continue to be anything but easy.

But specific questions may not get asked for quite a while. And the lack of precise data on program impact is no less a problem for incapacitation initiatives. The bulk of American crime control over the past generation has proceeded on an empirical foundation closer to faith healing than to science. So even the considerable limits of current knowledge about the impact of police programs does not put police at a comparative disadvantage when competing with prisons or supervisory prevention programs.

Police-based programs will be visible and attractive alternatives to court and punishment programs for a long time. And the New York story—both the reality and the legend—are important reasons for the revival in prospects for preventive policing.

The Revival in Prospects for Prevention and Supervision as Crime Prevention

A wide range of criminal justice and social service functions have not been implicated in explanations of the New York crime decline or mentioned as beneficiaries of any lessons that might be learned from the experience. Whatever people think the city's crime decline was about, it didn't seem to be about juvenile probation officers, or after-school recreation or educational counseling for high-risk/low-achieving students. And it certainly had nothing to do with 1994's notorious midnight basketball programs.

While programs like closing open air drug markets and intensive patrol of hot spots seem miles removed from after-school play, the objective of each kind of program is to make small changes in the environment in which criminal decisions get made. Proponents of long-term incarceration could scoff at police closing two or three square blocks of a city to public drug traffic because they argue that persistent offenders can always buy or sell drugs elsewhere. And there is evidence that drug purchase and sale and consumption continued at a pretty steady pace in New York. But not drug killings or public settings that local residents consider dangerous and inaccessible.

Even though the extra police presence is transient and the extra police numbers are not huge, most criminal offenders seem responsive to modest and even temporary alterations in the environment of the city. So the huge declines in crime are conclusive evidence that the criminal proclivities of most of the people who were committing most of the crime in New York City in 1990 were volatile and variable—small changes in their environments could produce big changes in the number of serious crimes they commit.

And the same susceptibility to modest changes that may be driving down crime when unemployment goes down or police close drug markets is also a necessary condition for the effectiveness of prevention, supervision, drug treatment, and defensible space in building and pathway design. The further removed the people at the margin of committing serious crime are from the "life-course persistent" person with a fixed propensity to continuing crimes for a long period, the better the prospects that any attempt at intervention based on changing behavior in the short run might make a large impact on crime.

The same type of modestly motivated but distractible potential offender who might back away from burglaries if the police presence is intense in his neighborhood is also a pretty good candidate to respond to greater supervision from a probation officer spending time and imposing a schedule of rewards and sanctions (see Kleiman 2009).

The broad lesson that emerges from the huge drop in New York is the variability of most crime to modest changes in circumstances. That doesn't guarantee that after-school tutoring will keep kids from failing in school or from being vandals. But it shows that much of the population at risk is malleable, their propensities prone to change with modest provocation. Anything that is prone to work at all can work well with a population not that difficult to change.

So the apparent susceptibility of potential offenders to modest environment modifications is an encouraging indication for a very wide spectrum of anti-crime interventions—for beat police, for probation officers, for tutors in after-school programs, for parents and mentors. The malleability that is a common characteristic of persons at risk to commit serious crime is potentially important good news for any credible program of help or supervision or diversion. The characteristics of offenders evident in New York's recent history might even be good news for midnight basketball.

Chapter 8

Crime and the City

MORE OFTEN THAN not, disagreements about the efficacy of crime pre-vention measures are grounded in different fundamental assumptions about the nature of crime and of criminals. One stunning demonstration of this was the widespread belief that police couldn't exert a major preventive influence on crime rates. The skeptics believed essentially in a model of persistent criminality that could outwait or outrun the urban police presence. Send two officers to 125th Street to discourage street robbery? That will only divert the robbery to 138th Street. After all, cops can't be everywhere. And a strong police presence that results in one fewer robbery on Tuesday will probably just mean one more robbery on Thursday or next week.

But if one of the main reasons why we distrusted the influence of police and all other temporary interventions in criminogenesis was the belief in the fixed and predictable behavior of high rate criminals, then one of the most important lessons of New York City's relentless march toward safety is that criminal offenders are more malleable and criminal events are easier to prevent than the conventional wisdom had recognized. Prevent an auto theft on 125th Street, and that is just as likely to result in one less auto theft in New York City rather than an auto theft 10 blocks away. Avoid a robbery on Tuesday night and it is likely that this year's robbery volume has been reduced by one. Temporary impacts generate permanent positive effects.

This chapter argues that the crime decline documented in this study requires a fundamental rethinking of the relationship between urban life and urban crime in the twenty-first century. Most of the high rate of life-threatening violence and predatory crime that observers have regarded as an inherent element of the structure and social content of polyglot big cities in the United States is not a necessary outgrowth of modern urban life.

The chapter is organized around four topics. The first section revisits the data presented in Chapter 1 to argue that the scope of New York's decline is singular because its variability undermines conventional assumptions about the link between urban populations and urban crime rates. The following section then contrasts previous assumptions about the malleability and variability of urban crime with the experience in New York City since 1990. The third section provides preliminary data on the impact of crime policies and crime rates on minority populations. The final section considers the implications of what we are learning about the malleability of urban crime for criminological theories about crime causation and distribution, and for social theories about modern urban life.

A. The Arithmetic of Criminological Surprise

Figure 8.1 shows variations in rates of criminal homicide in New York City and the average for the other of the ten largest U.S. cities in 1990. Both the nine-city average and New York homicide drop during the 1990s, and both rates vary substantially over time. By 2009, the New York total had dropped 82% from its high, while the nine-city average had dropped 56%. But why is the larger temporal variation in New York a major *substantive* surprise?

Figure 8.2 converts a graphic representation of 2009 New York City crime rates as a proportion of their 1990 levels for all seven traditional "index" felonies into a rhetorical statement about the variability of urban crime. The figure repeats data about the decline in crime from Chapter 1, but this time each one of the offenses has all of its 1990 rate divided into what turned out to be "variable" and "fixed" segments. The figure assumes for this exercise that 2009 levels are as low as crime will ever go, even though there is no foundation for this assumption. So the figure is a *minimum* estimate of the variability of crime in New York.

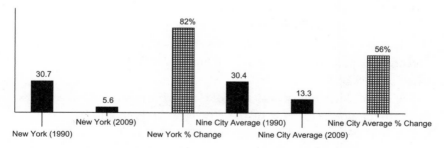

FIGURE 8.1. Homicide Declines from 1990–2009, New York and Mean Rate for the Other Nine of the Ten Largest Cities in 1990.
Source: FBI, Uniform Crime Reports 1990–2009.

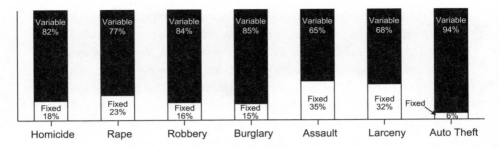

FIGURE 8.2. Percentage of 1990 Crime Volume that Varies in the Next 19 Years, Seven Index Offenses.
Source: FBI, Uniform Crime Reports.

Assuming that the 2009 value for each crime is as low as that rate can go, the important offenses in New York City's street crime portfolio were all subject to extensive downward variation in two decades. With no major changes in population, culture, or economy, more than four-fifths of homicides, robberies, burglaries, and auto thefts recorded in 1990 were not recorded in 2009. The variation for rape was 77%.

What this *must* mean is that most of the serious crime that happened in New York City in 1990 wasn't a necessary outgrowth of the people or the culture or the economy of the city. Very modest changes within the city could and did produce or at least witness huge changes in serious crime.

What sets off the arithmetic of New York crime from the other major polyglot cities of the United States is the huge variability demonstrated on the downside for crime. By 2009, using homicide as a measure, New York had come all the way back from the crime growth associated with the major population and crime changes of the 1960s and 1970s (only homicide totals were trustworthy and comparable to current data in the early 1960s). But this achievement is much greater than breaking even with 1961 because the changes over time in the population mix of the city should produce higher homicide rates. Figure 8.3 compares the proportion of the population in the two "high homicide rate" groups discussed in Part I in New York for 1960 and 2008.

Using the deterministic calculus of estimating crime volume and risks from the demographic mix of the city, New York should have a much higher homicide rate in 2009 than in 1961 just because of its population changes. But it doesn't.

In one important sense, this chapter is an attempt to change the focus of analysis from an incompletely understood aspect of New York's crime

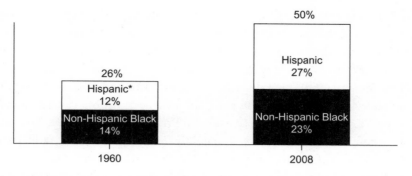

FIGURE 8.3. Proportion of New York City Population in High Homicide Victimization Groups (Black or Hispanic).
* No 1960 census estimate equivalent to the "Hispanic" aggregate used in 1970 and later years is available. We used the ratio of total Hispanic population reported as Puerto Rican by birth or parentage in 1970 (63.5%) to estimate a total Hispanic population for 1960 by multiplying the 612,574 in that category by their relation to total Hispanic in 1970 (1.575) to produce an estimate of 964,683 persons of Hispanic origin or 12.4% of the total. This estimate is probably high because the proportion of non-Puerto Rican Hispanics has been increasing over time and was probably greater than 63% in 1960.
Sources: 1960 Census; 2008 American Community Survey.

decline—the specific reasons why crime dropped—to the substantive implications of the scale of the decline. The central argument is that the scale of the New York decline is, by itself, a decisive indication that very substantial variations in individual and community crime rates are possible without major structural changes in the city. Never mind that so little is known about the why of New York's transition to safe streets, the scale of the change itself is important evidence that similar levels of change are achievable futures in other cities. This demonstration of what I call the "inessentiality" of high rates of safety crime in the next section is the single most important lesson from New York City about urban crime.

An Earlier Precedent?

The mention of changing demographics also invites consideration of the only other modern fluctuations in crime statistics that might compete with New York as a demonstration of the variability of crime in urban areas over time. Why wasn't the huge expansion of crime and violence in the decade after 1964 itself a clear case of essentially similar cities experiencing very different rates of crime?

This question is both interesting and important. Between 1964 and 1974, the national government of the United States commissioned a series of blue ribbon investigations of crime (The President's Commission on Law Enforcement and Administration of Justice, *The Challenge of Crime in a Free Society*, 1967), civil disorder (U.S. Riot Commission, *Report of the National Advisory Commission on Civil Disorders*, 1968), violence (U.S. National Commission on the Causes and Prevention of Violence, *To Establish Justice, To Insure Domestic Tranquility: Final Report*, 1969), and standards and goals for criminal justice (U.S. National Advisory Commission on Criminal Justice Standards and Goals, *Criminal Justice System*, 1973) (the dates in parentheses are the years of final reports from these efforts). The predominant assumptions of these efforts and the academic research they relied on was that the increases in crime and violence were linked to changes in the age distribution of the population, the mix of minorities living in big cities and their social and economic prospects, changes in criminal justice, and changes in youth culture. The assumption was that important structural changes were taking place.

There was in the late 1960s and 1970s a readiness to link problematic increases in crime and violence to structural features of urban life, and to further assume that increases which were caused by fundamental changes could only be substantially reduced by equally fundamental changes. There were the standard divisions between liberals and conservatives on the nature of urban problems and the most hopeful path to solutions, but there was evident agreement across ideological categories that the increases in crime and violence reflected fundamental changes in American urban life. It was almost as if questioning the link between the crime wave and the deep structures of urban life would deprive the crime problem of the dignity it deserved.

So serious observers of crime and violence in the 1970s (including this one) assumed that changing rates of homicide, robbery, and burglary reflected fundamental shifts in urban American life. Whether in fact this was true of the decade after 1964 is not known now and may be unknowable in retrospect.

But there are two related features of the post-1990 experience of New York City that require a new look at how very much crime rates can vary *without* major structural changes in urban life. The first is the size and breadth of the city's crime decline: more than four-fifths of the 1990 peak rates, and more than two-thirds of the average rates of the 1980s for robbery, burglary, and auto theft, with a close to two-thirds drop in long-standing homicide levels. This major drop happens in all four of the city's major boroughs with the interborough comparisons much more remarkable for the underlying similarities of pattern they display than for any discovered differences (see Part I). So the crime drop was large, long, and broad. By most statistical measures, the New York crime decline was as big or bigger than the explosive growth of crime after 1964 (and the crime statistics after 1990 were much more reliable than in the earlier era).

Yet a search for major structural or social changes that might match the geography and the timing of the crime drop has not produced plausible candidates. There were shifts in Manhattan's population composition that were consistent with lower crime, but not in the other three major boroughs. Housing conditions improved in public housing after the mid-1980s (Barker 2010), but there is no strong evidence that better housing reduces the criminality of residents (Harcourt and Ludwig 2006). The acute phase of the crack cocaine emergency ended in the mid-1990s in New York as well as other cities, but the size, breadth, and length of the decline far overshot even the most extreme imaginings of crimes and violence attributable to the crack phenomenon, and cocaine use remained high. Rather than the two-decade crime decline being the result of fundamental changes in the culture or composition of the city, the decline in crime was itself the major citywide change that most observers noticed.

Just a Matter of Degree?

In one sense, the fact that crime volumes can vary over time in urban environments that don't change much is old news. The great American crime decline of the 1990s was a nationwide demonstration project that major crime declines did not require or in that case involve basic substantive change. What, after all then, is the difference between a decline of 40% (the national norm) and one of 80%?

One approach to this issue is provided by the actual death rate differences between homicide in New York in 1990 and 2009. The 1990 rate was 30.6 per 100,000 per year, and the 40% drop from that total which was the average for a big city would produce a homicide rate of 18.4 per 100,000 in the city. (This hypothetical New York total is inserted in Figure 8.4 for comparison.) The 82% that New York City recorded by 2009 produced a homicide rate of 5.6 per 100,000. The 18.4 rate per 100,000 would place New York City in a middle position among major-city homicide rates in recent years, as shown in Figure 8.4.

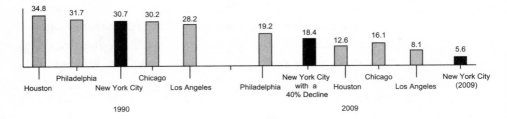

FIGURE 8.4. Homicide Rates in Five Largest U.S. Cities, 1990 and 2009, and Homicide if New York's 2009 Rate Was a 40% Decline.
Source: U.S. Department of Justice, FBI Uniform Crime Reports. (The 40% rate added for New York City in 2009 is hypothetical and not based on crime data.)

But an 18.4 homicide rate would still be over three times as high as the actual homicide experience in New York in 2009, and that huge additional difference underscores the singular importance of the New York City decline. An average decline of 40% would leave New York with a 2009 rate three times as high as it had in the early 1960s. The actual decline was to a level lower than that in the early 1960s. It is not that crime rates dropped in a city that didn't change fundamentally, it is that crime rates dropped by a much larger margin than seemed possible without the city itself changing its fundamental characteristics. What we now know is not merely that crime rates can change in big cities without basic change, but that crime rates can change by 80% and more in big cities without basic structural changes.

The rest of this chapter explores three related questions that are generated by the size of the New York decline. The following section addresses what the New York story teaches about the relationship between urban populations and social structures and crime. The short lesson is that the same populations and structures can produce a very wide variety of different crime levels. The third section examines the impact of the crime decline on the segments of the population that are most affected by both crime and crime control—racial and ethnic minorities in lower income neighborhoods. The final section then considers whether the New York experience challenges major theories about the causation and distribution of crime.

B. The *Inessentiality* of Urban Crime

The central demonstration from New York City is that the great majority of the high rates of crime and violence that American cities experienced in the 1970s and 1980s is not a necessary or natural outgrowth of the people who live in big cities, the economic structure of urban life, or the institutions and government of urban America. The lesson is not that *much* of the high crime of our recent bad old days is unnecessary, or even that *most* of the high crime was unessential, but rather that the *great majority* of street crimes are not a necessary part of modern big cities in the United States.

The critical comparison here is between the total variance of crime in New York and the modest changes in the city—between the 80% or so that safety crime has dropped and the 10% or so that Chapter 3 suggested the city itself has changed in other respects over two decades. There is one obvious limit to our current knowledge about this 80% crime decline—we don't know the particular causes for slightly over half of the changes in burglary, robbery, and auto theft and an even larger proportion of the declines in homicides and rape. So the finding that 80% of the city's crime is not closely linked to its populations and cultures does not translate into a cookbook with specific recipes for 80% crime reductions. I wish it did.

If the full measure of New York's decline can't be explicated with current knowledge of its circumstances, what is the importance of knowing that variation on this scale is possible? Plenty. It is of theoretical importance for understanding the nature of American crime and of great practical importance for designing and implementing measures to control crime.

We now know that most of the crime associated with New York in the 1970s and 1980s was not an organic outgrowth of the people who lived in the city or the way they lived. Single-parent families, chronic illegal drug commerce and use, economic inequality, problematic urban educational systems, and cultural values that emphasize male aggression and machismo can produce a city with homicide rates of 5.6 as well as producing a city with a homicide rate of 30.7. And it seems likely that variability of that general magnitude is no less possible in St. Louis, Chicago, Oakland, and Houston.

This is not to deny that there are important links between many cultural and social features and rates of crime and violence. New York City will never achieve rates of street crime and violence in the range of Hong Kong and Tokyo. And violent crime in New York City remains intensely concentrated among minority males in socially isolated environments.

From the standpoint, however, of both social theory and public health, I would argue that the variable part of New York's recent crime experience—the difference between a homicide rate of 30 and of six—is more important than whatever fraction of current rates of crime and violence turns out to be a fixed cost of current urban populations and structures—the difference between homicide rates of six or less and of one or less per 100,000.

The importance of the extraordinary variability of crime rates for crime prevention was explored in Chapter 7. Crime prevention strategies that depend on fixed and predictable individual propensities to offend—the chief example being incapacitation—are disadvantaged by unpredictable variability in crime commission rates. But plausible methods of reducing criminal opportunities or incentives are all beneficiaries of conditions in which potential offenders respond to changes in circumstances.

The combination of consistent populations and sharply lower rates of serious crime that New York experienced *must* result because criminal propensities are situational and contingent. The same person can commit many more or many fewer serious offenses, depending on modest changes in street environments in his immediate neighborhood, in where and how drugs are purchased, and in whether the particular locations where robberies and assaults have taken place frequently are now under special police surveillance. That sort of variability suggests that other modest situational shifts such as requiring more frequent supervision or urine testing as a condition of probation or parole, may also have significant impact. We don't have to change the world to substantially reduce safety crime.

The practical problem is that many of the specific mechanisms at work in New York City in the 1990s and since are unknown. Chapter 5 identified four or five policing elements that are proven or probable successes. But for the most part, the known susceptibility of New York City crime to situational change can't yet be translated into a detailed program plan. It is only a hunting license for criminal justice actors in New York and elsewhere to innovate and evaluate.

We do know what *doesn't* have to happen for crime and violence to drop to comfortably tolerable levels in America's big cities. Basic changes are not necessary because New York City didn't need them. And massive further investment in incarceration was at no time in the 19 years after 1990 part of the New York portfolio.

Robert Merton reminded us that "whatever is, is possible" (quoted in Siberman 1978). For that reason, New York is proof that most of the crime and violence that we had come to fear was hard-wired into the culture and organization of the modern American city is not a necessary part of life in any American city. The magnitude of decline from peak rates that New York City has experienced is possible in most cities from the near historic highs that most major cities experienced around 1990. The specific mix of tactics that generate crime prevention will change from place to place, and the careful calculation of costs and benefits in many different settings is both necessary and difficult. But as the next section will show, both the costs and most important benefits of declining crime are concentrated among the poor and marginal segments of the urban landscape.

C. The Poor Pay More and Get More

The risks and burdens associated with urban life fall most heavily on poor and minority populations, but nowhere else with the special force of urban violence and crime. African American and Hispanic minorities are the overwhelming majority of the victims of any big city's most dangerous forms of criminal violence. The same communities of color also dominate the statistics on criminal offenders, and this creates a second major cost to the communities and the families where crime and violence is concentrated. The blunt ends of urban crime control—stops, arrests, jailing and imprisonment—remove young men of color from the same streets and neighborhoods where they are the predominant crime victims. Not without reason has urban violence been called the most regressive tax in modern American life.

If there is any bright side to the intense concentration of criminal offending and victimization among the urban poor in New York City, it is that real progress in crime control becomes one benefit where New York's poor get more value than more advantaged populations that have already moved out of high-risk neighborhoods and live in buildings with doormen. But just as poor neighborhoods benefit from lower crime, the sons and brothers of families of color are also disproportionately at the receiving end of aggressive policing and "quality of life" law enforcement. So the political economy of crime control in its New York City style is complicated—the poor both pay more for aggressive street policing and benefit more to the extent that crime control efforts succeed. The size of the New York crime decline and the scale of some of the city's expanded police efforts make the period since 1990 into a case study of extreme variations in crime, in punishment, and in policing. This section will produce some basic data on how these extreme variations affect the young men from communities of color who are at special risk from both crime and the agencies of crime control.

Homicide is both the most serious criminal threat in the modern city and the violent crime most concentrated in urban racial and ethnic minorities. Figure 8.5 provides comparisons over time for three groups of New Yorkers: the total homicide rate, which is actually an average of all ages, genders, and racial and ethnic groups; the homicide rate for Black males between ages 15–44; and the homicide rate for non-Black Hispanic males ages 15–44.

The percentage of decline in homicide rate is fairly evenly spread across the aggregate totals and the two high risk subgroups, but this is importantly misleading. The two high risk groups were 11.5% of New York City's population in 1990 but 62% of all homicides then. These two high-risk male groups were 63% of the lives saved between 1990 and 2009: 1,005 of a total decline of 1,591 in killings.

For younger minority males in New York City, the concentration of homicide risks was even higher in 1990: 227 per 100,000 for Black males 15–24 and 153 per 100,000 for non-Black Hispanic young men. For this age group, criminal homicide was by far the leading killer of young men in 1990—accounting for 62% of all deaths, just under two-thirds of the death rate from all causes. The silver lining to this devastating 1990 concentration is that the drop in homicides over the next 19 years reduced the total death rate for young men under 24 in New York City by more than half all by itself!

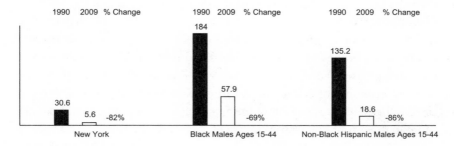

FIGURE 8.5. Homicide Rates per 100,000 in Two Years for New York City, Black Males Ages 15–44, and Non-Black Hispanic Males Ages 15–44.
Source: New York Police Department (homicides); Bureau of Census and American Community Survey (population).

Careful and detailed statistics on city-level crime victimization are only available for homicides, but it is almost certainly true that life-threatening assaults—New York City's shootings and stabbings—were clustered in the same population groups that dominate the homicide statistics. Offenses like rape and robbery are also frequently close-to-home events where the social and residential distribution of crime victims overrepresent those urban minorities as victims where rates of offending are high. So the first major benefit from a crime decline in the minority communities where crime is concentrated is less crime, less violence, and less fear of crime. The concentration of benefits to high-risk populations does *not* come from a more even spread in the risk of violence over time—the concentration of all homicides among minority males 15–44 fell only slightly in 20 years from 61% to 58%.

The Imprisonment Decline

In New York City, a second major benefit to communities of color was a big drop in the most extreme criminal punishments—an abatement of what liberal critics have come to call the "school to prison pipeline." During a period of sharply expanding imprisonment in the United States (see Appendix B), the prison and jail populations from New York City never rose by much (+11% at peak in 1997) and then dropped substantially. Like the homicide scorecard, poor minority males were the leading beneficiaries of lower rates of incarceration and for the same reason—because they were the group at highest risk of prison and jail in 1990.

Chapter 4 discussed aggregate trends in incarceration in New York City and other places and mentioned some of the different ways available to measure the net effect of the divergence between the city's trends and those of the rest of the country.

Figure 8.6 continues this type of analysis with specific data on young minority males. The data in Figure 8.6 are from court commitments to prison from New York City. Missing are parole returns and the shorter commitments to the city's jails and police lock-ups. So these are the longer term commitments to the deepest end of the range of criminal sanctions in New York.

The rate of prison commitments from the city is down by almost half over the 19-year span, and the drop in commitment rates for the youngest minority males is down even more, by 62% from over 6,500 to 2,500 per year. Just these raw numbers show an impressive distinction—the drop

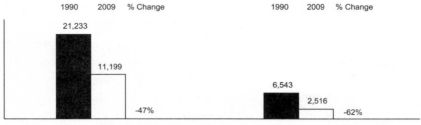

FIGURE 8.6. Court Commitments to Prison from New York City for Black and Non-Black Hispanic Males Ages 15–24.
Source: New York State Department of Correctional Services.

in prison commitments from 1990 to 2009 represents diverting more minority youth who used to go to New York prisons (6,500–2,500 = 4,000) than the number still committed to prison in 2009 (2,513).

And there are good reasons to regard those raw number differences as an understatement of the changes in risk in New York City. The number of Black and Hispanic males 15–24 expanded by 29% in the city during the years after 1990, so the rate per 100,000 minority males of prison commitment dropped by 70% in New York City over 19 years. That is a major decline, and it is *not* solely a function of the concentration of young minorities in the prison pipeline in 1990.

And the 70% decline took place in a nation where the general rate of imprisonment went up 65% between 1990 and 2008. The number of Black and Hispanic males expected to go to prison from applying the 1990 per capita rate to the 2008 population would have been 8,377, more than three times the commitment rate that happened. And if that rate had increased to keep pace with the national 65% increase in rate per 100,000, a total of 13,822 Black and Hispanic males between 14 and 24 would have been committed to prison in 2009.

Figure 8.7 illustrates this new mathematics of imprisonment in simple graphic form. The imprisonment cohort in column D (following national trends) is more than five times as many Black and Hispanic young men as the actual commitment total from the city in 2009. And that is a *one year* rate difference. In a decade's time, there would be more than 100,000 additional commitments to prison in the column D future than if the New York pattern in 2009 holds constant. And that is more than 100,000 such extra commitments for a base population of 384,889 males in 2009. So

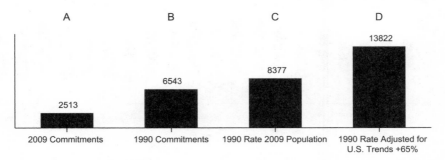

FIGURE 8.7. Incarceration Volume of Non-Black Hispanic and Black Males Ages 14–24 from New York under Three Policy Frameworks.
Sources: New York State Department of Correctional Services for 2009 and 1990 commitment rates; American Community Survey and Bureau of the Census for 1990 and 2009 population data; U.S. Department of Justice, Bureau of Justice Statistics for imprisonment rates in 1990 and 2008.

the difference in 10-year prison commitment expectancies for 14-to-24-year-old Black and Hispanic males is more than 25% of the total population. Because single individuals can and do experience multiple prison commitments in the same decade, this does not quite equal a difference in prevalence rate of 25% of the population of young males in 10 years. But the very big difference between the incarcerative trajectories of New York City and most other American cities is not a small matter for the incarceration risks of minority males. About 80% of the young men who would have gone to prison if New York had followed the national trends did not go to prison in 2009.

Policing and Arrests

So much for the good news. While the aggregate impact of imprisonment on minorities in New York City is substantially diminished over time, the pattern of exposure to arrest and short-term incarceration is mixed. And some of the news for young men of color is not happy. Figure 8.8 contrasts the yearly volume of felony and misdemeanor arrests in New York City over the years after 1990.

Felony arrests drop substantially over the period of the crime decline, and that pattern of decline is more pronounced for the most serious offenses. Violent felonies drop by half in 19 years, with violent felonies other than assault down by 54%. Drug felonies decline by 46% while the

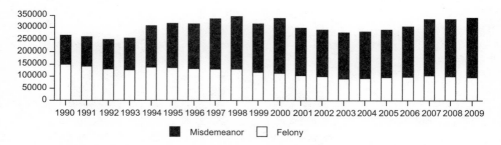

FIGURE 8.8. New York City Felony and Misdemeanor Adult Arrests, 1990–2009. *Source*: New York State Division of Criminal Justice Services, Computerized Criminal History System (as of 4/2010).

heterogeneous assortment of "other" felony arrests drop only 7% from 45,000 to 42,000. Even with all of this decline at the deep end of New York criminal justice, the net number of total arrests in the city goes up over time and goes up more than the expansion of city population. While total felony arrests dropped by more than 50,000 over 1990–2009, the volume of misdemeanor arrests more than doubled from 118,634 in 1990 to 245,131 in 2009. That meant that the arrest volume in New York City for all offenses increased 48% while the population increased only 12% and the crime rate set world records for decline. The consequences of misdemeanor arrests are usually of shorter duration than for felony arrests but can be both punitive and long lasting. Detention prior to arraignment is very common. Permanent records of both the arrest and any resulting adjudication are quite common as well.

The concentration of misdemeanor arrests on minority males is almost as extreme as for more serious charges, and there is no evidence that this racial concentration is diminishing over time. The misdemeanor arrest pool was 83% male in 1990 and 82% male in 2009, while the concentration of misdemeanor arrests among Black and Hispanic defendants was 84% in 1990, compared to 83% in 2009. These very similar percentages of concentration in 1990 and 2009 do not mean that the prejudicial impact of misdemeanor arrests has not changed in New York. It *has* changed because the incidence of the disadvantage has *doubled*.

And the statistics on formal arrest are far from the broadest impact of New York City policing on minority males. Using the 2009 statistics reported in Chapter 5, no fewer than 581,000 persons were stopped and frisked in New York in 2009, and the overwhelming majority of the targets of these stops were minority males. The prejudicial impact of being the subject of a stop include the force used and the loss of liberty of the encounter, the risk of arrest if marijuana, weapons, or "other contraband" is found, and the record of the subject's identity and the stop used to be kept by police. (State legislation prohibits keeping this information for non-arrest stops as of 2010. See § 140.50 of the Criminal Procedure Law, effective July 16, 2010.) With almost 600,000 of these events each year and 86% minority male targeting, it would seem difficult to grow up as a Black or Hispanic male under current policing circumstances without some experience of "stop and frisk." The official statistics published by the New York Police Department show a huge increase in officially reported incidents of stop and frisk after 2003, but this seems late in the game for the huge expansion in the tactic—years after police manpower explosions and aggressive patrol were at full force. So the timing of the great expansion is an open question. But there can be little doubt that the incidence of stopping and frisking grew substantially with the policing changes of the 1990s and that this is a new tax on a large number of minority males. We just don't know its precise timing.

Over time, then, the significant benefits to minority males of lower death and injury from crime and sharply reduced rates of imprisonment have to be balanced against the increased burden of expanded misdemeanor arrests and police street stops when coming to a judgment about the net effect of changes in crime and law enforcement in the city. The large declines in catastrophic outcomes—violent death and imprisonment—are probably more important than the broader prejudice of misdemeanor arrests and promiscuous targeting of minority youth for stop and frisk screenings.

A Real or Counterfeit Trade-Off?

But there is in fact no firm basis for assuming that the benefits to New York's minority populations are the result of the extra burdens imposed by pretextual arrest and preemptive stop and frisk tactics. A rigorous test of the effectiveness of Compstat and hot spot emphasis with and without the aggressive street interventions has not yet been done in New York or anywhere else. And it is not on the horizon. So there is no scientific foundation for regarding the burdens of aggressive policing as a necessary trade-off for lower crime and reductions in incarceration. If the value added by stop and frisk policing to crime prevention proves to be significant, the trade-off in minority communities will be a real one and not an easy choice. As long as serious crime is concentrated in communities of color, the predominant targets of aggressive policing will have to be the young men of color who walk neighborhood streets. Some of the prejudice of police stops can be removed (such as making an administrative record of the subjects of frisks with no indication of law violation), and using summons for misdemeanors can reduce the burdens now imposed by arrest, but preventive street policing cannot be made much more colorblind than the demographic patterns of violent crime. So if these tactics are necessary to prevention, they will themselves be administered as a special tax on minority males—all the more reason that a definitive evaluation of aggressive tactics becomes a moral imperative.

D. A New Perspective for Urban Sociology

The opening section of this chapter called the crime drop in New York City a "criminological surprise," and that description has to be accurate—social scientists would not have expected that a major American city could reduce its rate of safety crime and lethal violence by four-fifths without major population or institutional change. And that's what happened. But *why* was this such a surprise, and how much of the sociology of crime and violence in the United States has been undermined by the results of New York City's natural experiment?

What I have been calling the tenets of "supply-side criminology" have been completely rebutted by a stable population showing major crime declines without surging incapacitation, and the proponents of supply-side doctrines in the 1990s insisted they were relying on criminological and demographic findings. If that was correct, then much of modern criminological understanding would also seem ripe for reexamination. But were they correct in their reading of mainstream work?

Probably not. In fact, supply-side advocates pushed the empirical results of cohort studies well beyond their actual findings. What Wolfgang, Figlio, and Sellin had found was that most juvenile police contacts are concentrated in a small fraction of boys studied—that two-thirds of the serious contacts were accounted for by 6% of the boys who were studied (Wolfgang, Figlio, and Sellin 1972). This was a finding on the *distribution* of juvenile arrests. James Q. Wilson then assumed in a 1995 analysis that an expansion of the youth population would necessarily lead to more serious crime. Since 500,000 more male adolescents would produce 6% or 30,000 more males at high risk, that meant "30,000 more young muggers, killers and thieves" (Wilson 1995 at p. 507). His argument was that more kids equals more serious crime. John DiIulio then took the process one step further by assuming that the 6% (again, five or more police contacts in seven years in the study) of any expansion in the young population would be "juvenile super-predators." We know that Wilson and DiIulio were very wrong about this in 1995 and 1996, and that supply-side determinism was also a demonstrable error of high magnitude throughout the 1990s. But were Wolfgang, Figlio, and Sellin also dead wrong? Was Terrie Moffitt off course with her "life course" persistent offenders versus "adolescence limited" patterns? As a strict logical matter, the answer is no.

What the cohort studies were predicting was the distribution of crime in populations, not the volume of crimes or the kind of crimes that can be expected. Moffitt, Farrington, Wolfgang, Figlio, Sellin, and Thornberg never predicted the number of "muggers, killers and thieves" in any population and never predicted the number of robberies, murders, and thefts in any era. And this is not a small distinction. We saw in Chapter 4 that the number of young men in the New York City population actually increased from 1990 to 2009. Despite the large drop in the crime rate, might it still be the case that a small fraction of the youth population is responsible for most of the serious arrests among youth? Probably the answer is yes, but that hasn't stopped a larger youth population from committing 80% fewer serious crimes.

James Q. Wilson, writing eight years after his supply-side argument for 30,000 extra muggers puts the critical distinction he had learned in the interim very powerfully:

> There are two great questions about crime: why do people differ in the rate at which they commit crimes, and why do crime rates in a society rise and fall? You might suppose that the answer to these two questions would be the same. If we can explain whey people differ in their criminality, then all we need to do is add up their individual differences in order to know how much crime there is in their society. But in fact, the answers to these questions are not at all the same. The forces that put people at risk for committing crimes overlap only in part with the factors that influence how much crime a nation will experience. (Wilson 2003 at p. 537)

Two factors save traditional studies of the distribution of criminality and the crime causation theories they tested from being directly contradicted by the variability of serious crime levels noted in New York City. First off, the cohort studies and crime causation theories were concerned with the distribution of crime, not with those features that "influence how much crime a nation [or a city] will experience." Second, the focus of criminological explanation in cohort studies is usually pretty general even in the study of its distribution. Wolfgang, Figlio, and Sellin simply summed up the number of police contacts as their measurement of delinquency in the 10,000 boys they studied (Wolfgang, Figlio, and Sellin 1972). And Terri Moffit and David Farrington were studying the persistence of total criminal behavior through similar contacts. To comprehend the difference that this kind of measure might make in assessing the level of a crime problem, the reader is invited to consult the New York trends in Figure 8.8 again—in 2009, when homicide, robbery, burglary, and auto theft had dropped by more than four-fifths since 1990, the rate per 100,000 population of arrests had actually increased. So by the conventional measures in use in cohort studies, delinquency and criminality in New York City had actually increased.

Yet the distributive focus of empirical criminology did encourage the kinds of assumptions that led to the folly of supply-side predictions. The major defects of conventional criminological method for understanding the situational and contingent fluctuation of serious crime rates were most often sins of omission rather than sins of commission. The problem was not that that criminological theory falsely assumed fixed criminal proclivities, but rather that too many criminologists failed to investigate the causes of changes in serious crime rates over time. Further, the focus on life courses and criminal careers and language such as "life course persistent" may also have encouraged erroneous assumptions. To some extent, also, the focus on *criminals* rather than on *crime* did foster assumptions of relatively fixed proclivities. The omissions of criminological theory were the failure to appreciate and to study the situational and contingent influences on the rate and type of crime being committed. There was too much attention to the study of criminals and too little to crime as a changing phenomenon.

There were, of course, important exceptions to the failure to examine dynamic and situational features of serious urban crime. Public health approaches to urban violence were both centered on rates and costs and pragmatic in assessing the potential impact of countermeasures. Routine activity theory embraced the situational and contingent character of criminal behaviors and maintained a primary focus on crime as a situational decision and activity rather than a moral career (Cohen and Felson 1979; Felson and Clarke 1993).

Social Theories of Crime Causation

There are, however, explicit social theories of crime causation that are not limited to the distribution of crime and violence but expressly address causation of high rates of crime and life-threatening violence.

In the long history of such accounts, the most powerful and persuasive is that of William Julius Wilson in his 1987 masterpiece *The Truly Disadvantaged,* which details the social isolation that generates and fosters high rates of crime and violence.

> The communities of the underclass are plagued by massive joblessness, flagrant and open lawlessness, and low achieving schools, and therefore tend to be avoided by outsiders. Consequently, the residents of these areas, whether women or children of welfare families or aggressive street criminals, have become increasingly socially isolated from mainstream patterns of behavior. (Wilson 1987 at p. 58)

There are some aspects of the demographics of New York City in 2009 that fit well with a continued emphasis on social isolation—rates of homicide for African American males are high into the double-digits per 100,000 (see Figure 8.5). So there are huge rate differences that remain that may be enough to accommodate theories of the influence of social isolation. But much of the changes in New York crime involved the same population of "truly disadvantaged" youth and young adults—declines of two-thirds and more in rates of killing, robbery, burglary, and rape, without any indicators of significant declines in social isolation. Why this variability? And how does this fit with the theory of social isolation of crime causation?

There is some tension between regarding the cultural and time allocation features of social isolation as a direct cause of crime and the wide fluctuations in rate experienced in New York City. Social isolation does not, apparently, produce fixed proclivities to commit homicide, or robbery, or burglary, so there is a substantial amount of variation in crime rates that can occur within the context of stable and pathological levels of social isolation. How can profound changes in problematic behavior in the face of this continued isolation be explained?

The easiest explanation is that high rates of criminal behaviors are frequent results when young men exist in conditions of social isolation but that there is only a loose linkage between such social circumstances and particular criminal outcomes. Young men can take crack or smoke marijuana blunts, they can participate with others in street robbery or simply congregate and listen to music. In the language of public health, the circumstances of social isolation are a "risk factor" for rates of safety crime, but there is no linear relationship between levels of social isolation and rates of offending. If so, the New York story is a dramatic example of how loose the linkage can be between social circumstances and levels and types of criminality.

Many of the precursors to crime that we have long recognized turn out to be necessary but not sufficient conditions for the high rates of offending that have been chronic conditions in the American metropolis.

Yet, even if the New York story emphasizes the shortcomings of traditional criminological theory, understanding the social roots and distribution of serious crime remain important elements in understanding and controlling crime. The structural features of a culture of violence may not have prevented the total homicide reduction central to New York's relative safety, but African American homicide rates per 100,000 in 2011 remain in double digits in New York City—still a substantial public health and civic problem and an order of magnitude greater than homicide victimization of non-Hispanic whites and Asians. The fixed propensities of criminal offenders and criminal careers were vastly overstated in the 1980s and 1990s, but persistent offenders remain an important challenge for crime control policy in New York City and every other American metropolis. And the concentrations that remain in New York's crime and justice statistics may soon impose a limit to declines in rates of the most serious crimes.

What we need from criminology and urban sociology is not a total reorientation to the situational and the contingent, but a rebalancing to accommodate the variable as well as the fixed. What the natural experiment in New York City tells us will be of greatest promise is the careful study of the interaction of structural and situational features.

But what's the big deal? With so much not known about urban crime—including the mix of forces that drove down rates in New York, the elements of policing required for street success, and the limits of crime reduction that can be produced by situational and area specific tactics—why regard the 20-year history of New York City as such a watershed? For one reason. Finding as we have that the operating forces that produce epidemic levels of serious crime in the city are relatively superficial, that they are not essential elements of urban life, provides a decisive response to one of the deepest fears generated in the last third of the twentieth century. We now know that life-threatening crime is not an incurable urban disease in the United States.

Staten Island: Crime, Policing, and Population in New York's Fifth Borough

The main analysis of this study included crime and population data from Staten Island in the citywide analyses reported throughout the book but did not provide detail on Staten Island trends individually, as I did with the other four boroughs. Chapters 1 and 2 not only compare trends among the four major boroughs but also compare each of these to the other major cities, which is justified given their population, density, and demographic diversity.

Staten Island is by far the city's smallest borough in population (one-third the next largest in 1990), the least dense, the least citified, and the least demographically diverse. So it would be inappropriate to compare it as I do with the other four with top ten U.S. cities. But it would be equally inappropriate to ignore Staten Island, where many changes, including the police changes discussed in Chapter 5, took place. Hence this appendix.

Table A.1 shows the population of Staten Island and its racial and ethnic composition for 1990 and 2009.

Over the 19 years after 1990, Staten Island grew over twice as fast as the city as a whole (30% versus 12%) and diversified from four-fifths to two-thirds non-Hispanic whites. The highest growth rates were for Hispanic (154%) and Asians (118%). Still, three-quarters of the Staten Island population is composed of usually low crime groups.

Figure A.1 shows aggregate 1990 crime rates for New York City and Staten Island. With the exception of auto theft, where Staten Island had a 1990 rate equal to the city level, this borough had about half the burglary and robbery rates of the rest

Table A.1. Staten Island Population and Population Composition, 1990 and 2009.

	1990 Population	Percentage	2009 Population	Percentage
White Non-Hispanic	303,081	80%	326,017	66%
Black	30,630	8%	54,090	11%
Hispanic	30,239	8%	76,710	16%
Asian	16,941	4%	36,880	8%
Total	378,977		491,730	

Source: U.S. Bureau of the Census.

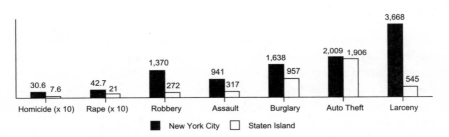

FIGURE A.1. 1990 Offense Rates, New York City and Staten Island.
Source: New York City Police Department; see Appendix D.

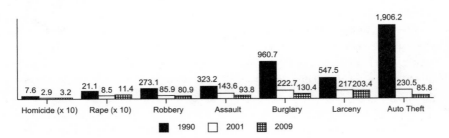

FIGURE A.2. Annual Rates per 100,000 for Seven Index Crimes, Staten Island; 1990, 2001, and 2009.
Source: New York City Police Department; see Appendix D.

of the city, one-third the assault rate, and only a quarter of the homicide and robbery rates recorded citywide.

Figure A.2 shows changes in Staten Island crime over the 19 years after 1990. There are two aspects of the crime pattern over time in Staten Island that corroborate the pattern for the rest of the city. First, there is much more crime reduction in the "street" offenses of burglary, robbery, and auto theft than in other crimes. Since Staten Island shared the rest of the city's increase in police and changes in policing, the concentration of decline in street-sensitive categories is some confirmation of police effects. Two of the street crimes, auto theft and burglary, decline as much as in the citywide totals, with robbery declining "only" 70% being the only exception. This may be an indication of slightly more resistance to further decline when robbery rates begin much lower.

The second pattern worth note is that crime on Staten Island declines in the post-2000 period, except for homicide and rape. While there is no comparison area to contrast to Staten Island, the significant post-2000 drops for assault, burglary, and auto theft are again consistent with the contribution of police to the crime reduction.

The Invisible Economics of New York City Incarceration

Chapter 4's discussion of demographic changes in New York City mentions the relatively substantial declines in incarceration rates of New York City residents as a development that has not received much attention in New York City, New York State, or elsewhere. The chapter mentions some factors that help to explain the absence of newspaper headlines about correctional cost savings in New York.

But this kind of attention deficit disorder carries substantial costs. Not paying close attention to what doesn't explain, predict, or prevent crime effectively can leave governments ready to repeat their previous mistakes when the next crime panic crosses the radar screen. As important, the identification of unnecessary or ineffectual strategies of crime control can identify where resources might profitably be diverted to more effective methods. One example of this type of comparison—missing to date from discussion of New York City—is comparing the costs of the city's famous police expansion with its never-mentioned savings from incarceration.

Figure B.1 provides information on three different incarceration policies. Column B in the figure estimates the number of persons who would have been locked up from New York City by 2007 if the 1990 rate per 100,000 population in the city had held constant. The 12% increase would have expanded the total city population in jail and prison by 6,700 to just under 63,000. This constant incarceration assumption produces more than 17,000 additional persons in jail and prison than were actually confined in 2007 (Column B minus Column C).

But this assumption is far too modest, because the 15 years after 1990 were a period of growing rates of imprisonment in the United States. Column D provides an estimate of incarceration from New York City that multiplies the city's actual 2007 population by an expansion of the 1990 incarceration rate to match the extent which the aggregate prison and jail rate of incarceration grew in the rest of the United

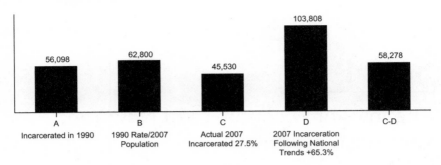

FIGURE B.I. Incarcerated Persons in New York City under Different Policies. *Source:* Bureau of Justice Statistics, *Annual Survey of Jails* (jail); State of New York Department of Correctional Services (prison).

States between 1990 and 2007 (65.3%). On those assumptions, the city's prison and jail population would have grown to 103,808, almost twice the 1990 prisoners and more than 58,000 extra prisoners from the actual 2007 New York City total.

Estimating Dollar Cost Savings

There are a variety of different ways to estimate the monetary cost of a period of incarceration and therefore the cost savings when one less commitment is made. The most conservative cost estimate would simply calculate total public expenditures and thus represent public expenditures avoided. For small numbers of prisoners added or subtracted, the marginal public cost may be a pro rata share of the operating budget of the prison and jail systems. For a high cost system like New York, a $25,000 per person estimate would be modest, particularly when the need for a large prison system expansion might impose capital costs on top of operating costs. Using a $25,000 unit cost and the 58,778 total produces a cost avoidance estimate of $1.47 billion per year. If the marginal cost of an additional police officer is $100,000, the estimated prison savings have already more than paid for the maximum expansion of the police force and have saved twice the annual expense of the net expansion of the police in the city as of 2010.

Why aren't cost savings even of this magnitude readily apparent, or even noticed? One reason is that different levels of government support different sectors of the system. The state government pays for prisons while the city pays for policing, so that the expenditures made and those saved don't come out of the same public purse. Even more important than this, unless there are sharp actual declines in public expenditures, even the agencies that are saving the money might not notice it. All but 11,000 of New York City's more than 58,000 persons not behind bars in 2007 in Figure B.1 were expansions avoided rather than the more visible reduction of people in cells that used to be full and are now empty. It is only when the state of New York is compared to the other metropolitan states in 2011 that the full prison population impact of different policy trends over 20 years become visible.

So negative lessons are important to a rational political economy of crime control. And the poor children of single parents growing up in New York City who were supposed to necessitate thousands of new prison cells (but didn't) are one of the happier lessons of the American present. But only if we notice.

The bad news about the failure to notice the cost consequences at the state level of government of city level expenditures is that the same problems—different levels of government paying for services and failure of non-impacted state governments to calculate the cost savings from avoiding changes that other jurisdictions experience—are not isolated phenomena in New York but are a chronic part of the political economy of criminal justice in the United States.

When state-level governments avoid cost increases that other states experience, they may not notice. And when city-level expenditures reduce the economic burden on state-level programs, there is again no obvious way that this good fortune can get sufficiently noticed at the state level of government to create incentives for the cost saving tactics to be continued.

The complicated political economy of police versus incarceration cost accounting thus requires attention from external sources—the federal government or institutions devoted to the study of intergovernmental economic impacts.

Studies of New York Police Factors

The first problem encountered when reviewing the empirical literature on police effects in New York City is that there isn't much empirical literature on this critical topic. And one reason that there are not many attempts to measure specific features of the police changes is the enormous difficulty of any plausible analysis. Only the brave would try to allocate causal credit when a kitchen sink full of changes happen together.

The first published attempt to study the nature of presumed policing effects was Steven Levitt in 2004. Discussing his doubts that changes in management and tactics enhanced the effectiveness of police work, Levitt instead attributed the entire marginal difference between New York City and other places to the increased New York manpower:

> By my estimate, the unusually large expansion of the police force would be expected to reduce crime there by 18 percent more than the national average, even without any change in policing strategy. If one adds 18 percent to New York City's crime homicide experience . . . (changing the decline from 73.6 percent to 55.6 percent), New York City is about average among large cities. (Levitt 2004 at p. 173)

This analysis claims that the known effects of marginal additions to policing when applied to the New York City policing experience during the 1990s leave no additional crime reduction to attribute to management and information changes, hot spot emphasis, or anything else in policing or other aspects of the city's experience. The data presented in this argument is limited in several respects. The 18% crime reduction claim is not based on New York experience but one estimated elasticity of police effects from a regression analysis published by Levitt. But that is not the only elasticity of police manpower estimate that Levitt has published (see

Levitt 1997), and a very large number of regression exercises have attempted to estimate the observed effects of police manpower variations on crime rates, with no consistent findings. Two authorities on policing surveyed 41 regression studies on the issue, eliminating all but 9 studies for failure to plausibly deal with identification problems. "[W]e were left with nine studies containing twenty seven dependent variables, presumably crime rates that police manpower might influence" (Eck and Maguire 2000 at p. 217). And the result in these regressions?

> Police strength has no effect on crime in fifteen equations (55%), a positive effect in four equations (15%) and a negative effect in eight equations (30%). Thus, even when we examined only the most rigorous studies, we could not find consistent evidence that increases in police strength produce decreases in violent crime. (Eck and Maguire 2000 at p. 217)

The problem with the lack of any consensus on the size and nature of general manpower impacts on crime is that there is no plausible single estimate to plug into to determine what New York would have experienced if new police had been added to a department not changed in any other respects.

There are other limits as well to the Levitt argument. He mentioned only homicide, excluding many other offenses, several of which had much larger New York differences. Further, his assertion that a 55.6% homicide drop was "average among large cities" stretches the actual data—the mean homicide rate decrease for the other nine of the ten largest U.S. cities was 46% during the 1990s, a full 10% less than the adjusted decline Levitt derives for New York City.

But from the perspective of 2011, another critical limit of the Levitt argument is its stopping point in year 2000 at the all-time high point of manpower in the NYPD. Extending Levitt's mechanical manpower effects argument forward from 2000 to 2009 would predict substantial increases in New York City crime because of the many thousand fewer police officers. And this should also mean that New York City should experience a substantial negative change in its crime performance when compared to other cities. Neither happened (as shown in Chapter 5). So recent history has not been kind to the Levitt analysis.

Much of the structure of Steven Levitt's analysis can also be found in the article on New York City published by Richard Rosenfeld and his associates. The strategy they use to search for the causes of the New York City crime decline is to build a model to explain New York homicide experience over time and to make one element of that model the variations in manpower of the department. The manpower effects they found in the 1990s were significant, but there was some additional decline left unexplained that other police features might have caused, and the effect on homicide was "only marginally significant" (Rosenfeld, Fornango, and Baumer 2005 at p. 10).

Unlike Levitt, this study used variations over time in New York homicide and police manpower to test for the magnitude and direction of a manpower effect. Like

Levitt, they only discuss homicide, which is critical given their findings because homicide rates are less than one-twentieth those of a crime like robbery, and thus a robbery analysis is much more likely to provide statistically significant effects. Here again, an additional critical problem is the failure to test past 2000. The study looks at only half the period of New York decline and misses the entire period when declining police manpower and declining crime co-occurred.

Kelling and Sousa (2001) report a study involving precinct-level measures of misdemeanor arrests and felony crimes in New York during two years. There is a negative correlation between misdemeanor arrest rates and felony crime levels, which the authors conclude demonstrate that "broken windows" police strategies reduce felony crime. One problem with this analysis is that the study doesn't control for any other police or criminal justice variable, such as the number of police per 100,000 in a precinct, or the rate of felony crime arrests per 100 felonies reported, or the aggressiveness of the police in street patrol. If manpower or felony arrest risk or aggressiveness is also positively associated with misdemeanor arrest risk, these omitted variables might be the cause for the decline in felonies. This is a sufficiently devastating problem so that other limits—such as the assumption that variations in misdemeanor arrest are a good measure of a "broken windows" emphasis and the inclusion of only the years up to 2000—are of minor additional importance.

The correlation of the one measure of police effort that is included in this study with lower felony crime rates is circumstantial evidence that some aspect of policing is associated with lower crime, but there is no indication of what aspect of policing—of several possibilities—is the likely cause of reductions in reported crime.

Corman and Mocan (2005) do a study of monthly crime fluctuations for New York City from 1974 to 1999. These authors construct a model of crime causation in New York that includes a variety of economic and social factors, as well as a large number of police and criminal justice variables. Among the policing variables that they separately introduce are measures of arrest risk for felony crimes, measures of police strength, and a measure of police misdemeanor arrests as a proxy for "broken windows" emphasis in policing. Their justification for misdemeanor arrests as a reliable measure of "broken windows" emphasis is rather brief:

> In this paper we measure the extent of the "broken windows" policing by using misdemeanor arrests as a measure of police signaling, in a model that controls for the number of police as well as felony arrests. (Corman and Mocan 2005)

This does control for police strength (unlike Kelling and Sousa) but again assumes that the extra efforts devoted to misdemeanor arrests are part of "quality of life" signaling. Their only measure is aggregate misdemeanor arrests, so they never confronted the wild variations in misdemeanor arrest trends documented in Figures

5.10 and 5.12, or the alternative hypothesis that these were instrumental arrests of persons that patrol regarded as high risk for street crime.

For the period 1974–1999, Corman and Mocan find a rather mixed picture of crime prevention for both extra police manpower and for misdemeanor arrests—their measure of "broken windows" crime prevention. For the independent effect of the number of police on felony crime, Corman and Mocan find significant effects limited only to auto theft, but this could be an artifact of the order in which they introduce variables: "Controlling for other measures of deterrence, the size of the police force has an impact on motor vehicle thefts only" (Corman and Mocan at p. 14).

But one of their "deterrence variables" is the rate of felony arrests, so that only the impact of more police that doesn't increase felony arrests is left to exert an independent impact in their regression. These findings thus do not directly contradict the large estimates of police strength effects in Levitt (2002).

The rate of misdemeanor arrests has a significant impact on two offenses, auto theft, and robbery. The authors assume this is a distinctive signaling effect, although why it should be limited to those two crimes and not the other five index felonies is not specified. The only alternative preventive effect that the authors discuss is incapacitation due to misdemeanor punishment, which they do not consider substantial. But whether the "signals" that instrumental stops and arrests send to high-rate offenders and the extra incapacitation that might come from finding persons with felony warrants outstanding through misdemeanor arrests and fingerprinting is not discussed. So here again, there is reason to believe that some police effects related to misdemeanor arrests reduce two crimes in the 1990s, when the rate of felony arrests and the size of the police force are controlled for. But the residual effect is modest, limited to two crimes, and certainly not specific to "broken windows" signaling.

A final limit of the Corman/Mocan study is that it covers only the first half of the New York crime decline era and includes no other method to control for or remove the nationwide downward trend of the 1990s (Zimring 2006). The first half of New York's crime decline era had expanding incarceration (until 1997) and additional police. The second half didn't have either. So it would be interesting to see how the same model Corman and Mocan use would work in the period 2000–2009.

Bernard Harcourt and Jens Ludwig reanalyze the Kelling and Sousa data and argue that:

> the crime patterns across New York precincts that Kelling/Sousa attributes to the effects of broken windows policing can be explained by mean reversion: broken windows policing (as measured by misdemeanor arrests) was conducted most intensively in New York within the city's most violent neighborhoods, which are the areas that experienced the largest increases in violent crime during the 1980s and the largest declines during the 1990s. (Harcourt and Ludwig 2006 at p. 291)

Steven Messner and his associates test for the relationship between cocaine over-dose death rates and misdemeanor arrest rates over the 74 precincts and the precinct level homicide rate, but separately test for gun and non-gun homicide. They find a significant negative correlation between misdemeanor arrest rates and gun homicide but not for non-gun homicide. Richard Rosenfeld, Robert Fornango, and Andres Rengifo produce another precinct-level analysis of homicide and robbery rates. Their analysis produces statistically significant but moderate relationships between their measure of order maintenance policing and homicide and robbery: "Growth in OMP accounts for roughly 1–5% of the robbery decline and 7–12% of the homicide decline" (Rosenfeld et al. 2007 at p. 377). For both of these precinct level analyses, the "mean reversion" issue identified by Harcourt and Ludwig may also be generating misleading indication of policy effects because effort has been concentrated in places of previous high crime increase.

In two unpublished papers, Dennis Smith and Robert Purtell explore the relationship between variations in policing in areas of New York City and trends over time in crime at the precinct level. The first study (Smith and Purtell 2007) argues that those areas implementing the department's "operation impact" had more extensive crime declines over time than non-impact areas, and Smith and Purtell regard this as evidence that the intensity of police response caused larger crime reductions. The problem with this inference is again what Harcourt and Ludwig call mean reversion, that the "impact" policy was selectively applied by the police in higher crime areas, and regression from higher rates may well be mixed with the effectiveness of the special programs. Without less-biased selection of treatment zones, programmatic impact can't be isolated.

In their second analysis (Smith and Purtell 2008), the authors test the contribution of rates of reported stop-and-frisk incidents per 1,000 citizens on trends in seven index crimes in 73 of the city's 76 police precincts. They report a significant negative relationship between stop-and-frisk rates and trends one month later in three index offenses—robbery, burglary, and auto theft—as well as close to significant effects for homicide. The study provides no measurement of other police behavior (such as misdemeanor arrests [see Kelling and Sousa], patrol intensity, or hot spot efforts) that might be related to the incidence of stop-and-frisks. So other police effects may be the true cause of part of any crime reduction. And, again, the police are selecting areas for more intensive stops on criteria that may include recent history of high crime levels and thus provide larger than average propensity for regression to more normal crime levels. So regression may be masquerading as crime prevention. Or other aggressive tactics may be influencing crime levels but stop-and-frisk falsely gets the credit. The moral here is that once policies are self-selected by police managers, the problems of sorting out program effects are insoluble.

The portfolio of regression exercises that attempt to sort out the contributing causes of New York City's crime drop in the 1990s are not persuasive evidence on policing effects either individually or cumulatively. One problem is that the published studies cover only half the crime-decline period (ending between 1998 and 2000). A second pervasive problem is that the studies use different aggregates of misdemeanor arrests as their measures of "broken windows" or "order maintenance" policing, when the detailed data presented in Chapter 5 demonstrate that aggressive street-level policing in New York in the 1990s did not follow a broken windows or order maintenance pattern. What the measures used are really testing is some combination of aggressive street interdiction of suspicious persons and police effort more generally.

But did effort and aggression prevent crime? The problem here is that the various analyses come to very different conclusions about the magnitude of measured effects.

A final concern with drawing any conclusions about police effects by only studying the 1990s is that this was the decade when crime declined everywhere in the United States. With so little known about the causes of this nationwide decline, the estimates that analysis covering this period might generate for any particular causes may be artificially enhanced by the mysterious national downdraft.

While there are inherent limits on the potential for this type of regression exercise, there are also two improvements that will make future studies more persuasive: (1) expanding empirical soundings to encompass the period from 1990 to 2009, and (2) using comparisons with other cities as an explicit control for cyclical trends not fully understood (Zimring 2006, Chap. 8). Not only would the period of decline be twice as long as that examined in previous studies, but it also involves much more variation in police and criminal justice variables. A period of adding new police has been followed by a period of substantial reductions in the police force, making the period from 1990 to 2009 a natural experiment with variations in both directions to test against crime trends. The second period in the decline was also distinctive because it happened while other cities and regions of the country were not in a general decline and when trends in jail and prison incarceration in New York City went down as against a continued national upward movement until at least 2005.

Are the New York Declines Real?

There is a second debate in criminological literature and media about systematic pressure to downgrade or ignore citizen crime reports to produce the illusion of crime reductions that are not real. The principal document in the New York debate is a survey of retired New York City police captains who report pressure from headquarters to ignore citizen offense reports or to "downgrade" them from more serious crimes to minor ones (e.g., robberies get reported as "theft" or "lost property"). Since this kind of underreporting looks like crime reduction, it will exaggerate the extent of the crime reduction, making the police department look good. The retired captains reported that the pressure was extensive and produced undercounts and downgrading although the extent couldn't be quantified (Eterno and Silverman 2009; Eterno and Silverman, Letter, *New York Times,* February 17, 2010; Rivera and Baker, *New York Times,* November 1, 2010). A second report was published in *The Village Voice* in two installments with selections of officer conversations secretly recorded in the 81st Precinct that contain frequent complaints about arrest and activity quotas and statistical reporting (Rayman 2010). While the impact of downgrades on the distortion of crime trends was aggressively disputed by ex-commissioner Bratton (Bratton, op-ed, *New York Times*, February 17, 2010), Commissioner Kelly appointed a panel to review crime-reporting procedures and quality control in early 2011.[1]

Behind this New York City squabble is a serious problem that is inherent when police are responsible for collecting and auditing crime statistics because they are also interested parties in the outcome. Outside scrutiny in such circumstances is absolutely essential, and may not be enough. A better system would separate data reporting and accounting into independent agencies or use independent measures of crime trends. But the police still must collect each citizen's crime report and classify it, so police involvement in crime reporting will be with us for the foreseeable future.

Did Compstat make New York look good by increasing distortion and underreporting over time and by distorting more than in other big cities? The data from this study show that for three important crimes the answer is no. Then why are the 81st Precinct gossips and retired police captains so angry? The discussion in Chapter 5 provides a good explanation for this as well.

The best way to test the validity of police crime statistics as a measure of actual crime trends is to find data on crime trends over time that are completely independent of police-reporting influence, and Chapter 1 did that for the most serious crime (homicide), for the crime with the biggest decline (auto theft), and for the crime with the most extensive reputation for distortion by downgrading (robbery). In all three cases, the independent tests confirm the magnitude and the timing of the drops. That doesn't mean that crime reporting in New York City is without distortions and pressure. But it is conclusive evidence that the size of the drop and the New York difference relative to other cities has not been magnified by increases in underreporting and downgrading.

Then why are the retired captains and precinct kibitzers so angry at Compstat? Because it was deliberately used as a method of taking away the discretionary powers of precinct and local officers and replacing it with central police headquarters power. "Compstat was not merely a method of gaining control over crime in New York City, but also a strategy for the equally difficult task of getting control of the NYPD." The captains, particularly those who chose or were pushed to retire into Eterno and Silverman's sample, were losers in a power struggle with the architects and managers of Compstat. And the Precinct 81 complainers were having their work lives ruled by downtown statistical categories and managers. They too had lost a power struggle to central control.

Sources for Data on New York City Crime, Arrests and Police Staffing

Data on a wide variety of crime, arrest and police staffing were acquired for the study and reported in the text. Annual roles of "Part I" crimes were obtained from the Uniform Crime Reports. Data on index crime by borough depended on New York Police Department statistics, now collected and reported for the period after January 1, 2000, and available at: <http://www.fbi.gov/about-us/cjis/ucr/ucr>.

Data on arrests by year were reported by the Department to the uniform crime reporting program for both Part I (index) arrests and Part II (non-index arrests) through 2002. For all those years, I have used the FBI statistics. After 2002, however, the New York department classified non-index arrests on the basis of New York law and did not send any "Part II" arrest data to the FBI. I used the NYPD data for all years after 2002. That data is available for 2000-2010 at <http://www.nyc.gov/html/nypd/html/crime_prevention/crime_statistics.shtml>. There are non-trivial differences between the categories discussed in the text (see Farrell 2010, p. 1, in note 1 to Chapter 4).

The information on police staffing by year by function and by borough were provided by the New York Police Department and are not available on the department's website or any other public source. It is now posted on the Oxford University Press website, available at <www.oup.com/us/companion.websites/9780199844425>.

References

Anti-Drug Abuse Act of 1988, co-sponsored by New York Senator Alfonse D'Amato, enacted as Pub. L.100-690, November 18, 1988, 102 Stat. 4181 and codified at 21 U.S.C. 848(e)(1)(A)-(B).

Anti-Terrorism and Effective Death Penalty Act. 1996. Pub. L. No. 104-132, 110 Stat. 1214.

Asian American Federation. 2004. *Neighborhood Profile: Manhattan's Chinatown*. Asian American Federation of New York Census Information Center.

Baker, Al. 2007, November 21. "City Police Stop Whites Equally but Frisk Them Less, a Study Finds," *New York Times* (NYPD Documented UF-250 Stops, 2002). Available at: http:// www.nytimes. com/2007/11/21/nyregion/21rand.html.

Baker, Al. 2011, February 3. "'Cheerful News' on Crime Data and the Integrity Thereof," *The New York Times*. Available at: <http://cityroom.blogs.nytimes.com/2011/02/03/cheerful-news-on-crime-data-and-the-integrity-thereof/?scp=1&sq=al%20baker%20zimring&st=cse>.

Barker, Vanessa. 2010. "Explaining the Great American Crime Decline: A Review of Blumstein and Wallman, Goldberger and Rosenfeld, and Zimring." *Law & Social Inquiry*, 35(2), 489–516.

Barnett, Arnold, Daniel J. Klietman, and Richard C. Larson. 1975. "On Urban Homicide: A Statistical Analysis." *Journal of Criminal Justice* 3: 85–100.

Bennett, William J., John J. DiIulio, and John P. Walters. 1996. "Drugs, Crime and Character." Bennett, William J., John J. DiIulio, and John P. Walters, eds. In *Body Count: Moral Poverty . . . And How to Win America's War against Crime and Drugs*. New York: Simon & Schuster.

Bittner, Egon. 1970. *The Functions of the Police in Modern Society: A Review of Background Factors, Current Practices, and Possible Role Models*. Chevy Chase, MD: National Institute of Mental Health, Center for Studies of Crime and Delinquency.

Blumstein, Alfred, Jacqueline Cohen, Susan Martin, and Michael Tonry, eds. 1983. "Research on Sentencing: The Search for Reform." Washington, DC: National Academy Press.

Blumstein, Alfred, and Joel Wallman, eds. 2000. "The Recent Rise and Fall of American Violence." In *The Crime Drop in America*. Cambridge: Cambridge University Press, at p. 9.

Blumstein, Alfred, Jacqueline Cohen, Jeffrey A. Roth, and Christy A Vischer, eds. 1986. *Criminal Careers and "Career Criminals,"* Vol. 1. Washington, DC: National Research Council, National Academy Press.

Braga, Anthony, and David Weisburd. 2010. *Policing Problem Places: Crime Hot Spots and Effective Prevention.* New York: Oxford University Press.

Bratton, William, with Peter Knofler. 1998. *Turnaround-How America's Top Cop Reversed the Crime Epidemic.* New York: Random House.

Bucerius, Sandra M., "Fostering Academic Opportunities to Counteract Social Exclusion," in Natasha A. Frost, Joshua D. Freilich and Todd R. Clear, eds., *Contemporary Issues in Criminal Justice Policy: Policy Proposals from the American Society of Criminology Conference* (Belmont, CA: Wasdworth/Cenage Learning 2010) pp. 235–245.

Bureau of Vital Statistics, New York City Department of Health and Mental Hygiene. Various Years.

Center for Disease Control and Prevention. National Center for Health Statistics, Vital Statistics. 2007.

Center for Economic Opportunity. 1970–2008. New York City (poverty data). Available at the CEO website: <http://www.nyc.gov/html/ceo/html/home/home.shtml>.

Center on Race, Crime and Justice, John Jay College of Criminal Justice. 2010. "Primer on Stop, Question & Frisk Policing Practices in NYC." (NYPD Documented UF-250 Stops, 2003-2008). Available at: http://www.jjay.cuny.edu/web_images/PRIMER_electronic_version.pdf.

Committee to Review Research on Police Policy and Practices, Wesley Skogan and Kathleen Frydl, eds., 2004. *Fairness and Effectiveness in Policing: The Evidence.* Washington, DC: The National Academies Press.

Corman, Hope, and Naci Mocan. 2005. "Carrots, Sticks and Broken Windows." *J. of L. & Econ.* 48: 235–266.

Dillon, David. 1997. "Street of Themes; New York's Once-Sleazy 42nd Street Is Now a Shiny Entertainment Complex." *The Dallas Morning News*, June 15.

Dilulio, John. 1995. "The Coming of the Super-Predators." *Weekly Standard*, November 27. (p. 1).

Dwyer, Jim. 2008. "On Arrests, Demographics, and Marijuana." *New York Times*, New York Metro, April 30, at B1.

Eck, John, and Richard Maguire. 2000. "Have Changes in Policing Reduced Violent Crime? An Assessment of the Evidence." In Alfred Blumstein and Joel Wallman, eds., *The Crime Drop in America* (pp. 207–265). New York: Cambridge University Press.

Eisenhower Commission, U.S. National Commission on the Causes and Prevention of Violence. 1969. *To Establish Justice, To Insure Domestic Tranquility: Final Report.* Washington, DC: U.S. Government Printing Office.

Farrell, Michael. 2010 at p. 1 (personal correspondence).

Felson, Marcus, Ronald V. Clarke. 1993 "Routine Activity and Rational Choice." In *Advances in Criminological Theory*, Vol. 5. New Brunswick, NJ: Transaction Press.

Figlio, Robert, Marvin E. Wolfgang, and Thorsten Sellin. 1972. *Delinquency in a Birth Cohort*. Chicago: The University of Chicago Press.

Fiscal Policy Institute. Social and Economic Conditions; Fiscalpolicy.org.

Fries, Arthur et al. 2008. *The Price and Purity of Illicit Drugs, 1981–2007*. Institute for Defense Analyses paper P-4369; available at: < http://www.whitehouse drugpolicy.gov/publications/price_purity/price_purity07.pdf>.

Goldstein, Herman. 1977. *Policing a Free Society*. Cambridge, MA: Ballanger.

Goldstein, Herman. 1990. *Problem Oriented Policing*. Philadelphia: Temple University Press.

Goldstein, Paul J., Henry H. Brownstein, Patrick J. Ryan, and Patricia A. Bellucci. 1989. "Crack and Homicide in New York City: A Conceptually Based Event Analysis." *Contemporary Drug Problems* 16(4): 651–687.

Greenwood, Peter W., with Allan Abrahamse. 1982. *Selective Incapacitation: Report Prepared for the National Institute of Justice*. Santa Monica, CA: Rand Corporation.

Greenwood, Peter and Susan Turner. 1987. *Selective Incapacitation Revisited: Why the High Rate Offenders Are Hard to Predict*. Santa Monica, CA: Rand Corporation.

Harcourt, Bernard, and Jens Ludwig. 2006. "Broken Windows: New Evidence from New York City and a Five-City Social Experiment." *The University of Chicago Law Review* 73: 271–320.

Johnson, Bruce, Andrew Golub, and Eloise Dunlap. 2000. "The Rise and Decline of Hard Drugs, Drug Markets, and Violence in Inner-City New York." In Blumstein and Wallman, eds., *The Crime Drop in America* (pp. 164–206). New York Cambridge University Press.

Johnson, David. 2006. "The Vanishing Killer: Japan's Post-War Homicide Decline." *Social Science Japan Journal* 9: 73–90.

Kaplan, John (1983). *The Hardest Drug: Heroin and Public Policy*. Chicago, IL: The University of Chicago Press.

Kelling George, Anthony Pate, et al. 1981. *The Newark Foot Patrol Experiment*. Washington, DC: Police Foundation.

Kelling, George, and William Sousa. 2001. *Do Police Matter? An Analysis of the Impact of New York City's Police Reforms*. New York: Manhattan Institute.

Kleimanm, Mark. 2009. *When Brute Force Fails: How to Have Less Crime and Less Punishment*. Princeton, NJ: Princeton University Press.

Lauritsen, Janet L., Brian E. Oliver, Robin J. Schaum, and Richard Rosenfeld. 2008. *Crime Victimization in the New York Metropolitan Area, 1980–2003: Comparing Victims' Reports of Crime to Police Estimates*. Available at: <www.crimetrends.com>.

Levitt, Steven. 1997. "Using Electoral Cycles in Police Hiring to Estimate the Effect of Police on Crime." *American Economic Review* 87(3): 270–290.

Levitt, Steven. 2002. "Using Electoral Cycles in Police Hiring to Estimate the Effect of Police on Crime: A Reply." *American Economic Review* 92(4): 1244–1250.

Levitt, Steven. 2004. "Understanding Why Crime Fell in the 1990s: Four Factors That Explain the Decline and Six That Do Not." *Journal of Economic Perspectives* 18(1): 163–190.

Maple, Jack, with Chris Mitchell. 1999. *The Crime Fighter: How You Can Make Your Community Crime Free.* New York: Doubleday.

Maxwell, Christopher, Joel Gardner, and Jeffrey Fagan. 2002. "The Preventive Effect of Arrest on Intimate Partner Violence." *Criminology and Public Policy* 7: 51–80.

McGarrell, Edmund F., Steven Chermak, and Alexander Weiss. 2002. *Reducing Gun Violence: Evaluation of the Indianapolis Police Department's Directed Patrol Project.* Hudson Institute: Crime Control Policy Center. Indianapolis, Indiana.

McKinley, James C. 1990. "Council and Dinkins Offer Competing Plans on Police." *New York Times,* New York Metro, August 2, at B1.

Messner, Steven F., Sandro Galea, Kenneth J. Tardiff, Melissa Tracy, Angela Bucciarelli, Tinka Markham Piper, Victoria Frye, and David Vlahov. 2007. "Policing, Drugs, and the Homicide Decline in the 1990s." *Criminology* 45(2): 385–414.

Metropolitan Police Crime Mapping: Data tables. (Crime patterns in London, 2007). Available at: http://maps.met.police.uk/tables.htm.

Moffitt, Terrie E. 1993. "Adolescence-Limited and Life-Course-Persistent Antisocial Behavior: A Developmental Taxonomy." *Psychological Review* 100(4): 674–701.

Morris, Norval. 1951. *The Habitual Criminal.* Cambridge, MA: Harvard University Press.

National Center for Health Statistics, *Vital Statistics in the United States.* Various Years.

National Crime Insurance Bureau. Available at the web site of the National Crime Insurance Bureau: https://www.nicb.org//

National Police Academy Public Policy Research Center. 2007. Crimes in Japan in 2007. (Crime patterns in Tokyo, 2007; Table 5, p. 68). Available at: http://www.npa.go.jp/english/seisaku5/20081008.pdf.

National Surveys on Drug Use and Health (from SAMSA).

New South Wales Bureau of Crime Statistics and Research. (Crime patterns in Sydney, 2007). Available at: http://www.bocsar.nsw.gov.au/Lawlink/bocsar/ll_bocsar.nsf/pages/bocsar_lga_Sydney.

New York City Department of Education Report. 2000–2004. Available at: <http://schools.nyc.gov/Accountability/Reports/Data/Graduation/Class_of_2000_Final_Longitudinal_Report.pdf>.

<http://schools.nyc.gov/Accountability/Reports/Data/Graduation/Class_of_2001_Final_Longitudinal_Report.pdf>.

<http://schools.nyc.gov/Accountability/Reports/Data/Graduation/Class_of_2002_Final_Longitudinal_Report.pdf>.

<http://schools.nyc.gov/Accountability/Reports/Data/Graduation/Class_of_2003_Final_Longitudinal_Report.pdf>.

<http://schools.nyc.gov/Accountability/Reports/Data/Graduation/Class_of_2004_ Final_Longitudinal_Report_shortversion.pdf >.

New York City Department of Health and Mental Hygiene. Vital Statistics (homicide by race and ethnicity 1990).

New York City Department of Health Statewide Planning System (SPARCS). New York.

New York City Police Department, New York; also NYPD web site: <http://www.nyc .gov/html/nypd/html/home/home.shtml>.

New York City Police Department, Memorandum from Director Central Records Division to Executive Director Support Services Bureau, April 5, 1999, p. 1.

New York City Police Department. 2010. *Crime and Enforcement Activity in New York City, January 1–June 30 2010.*

New York Civil Liberties Union. "Stop-and-Frisk Campaign: Stop And Frisk Fact Sheet." (UF-250 Stops, 2002). Available at: http://www.nyclu.org/node/1598.

New York Police Department Comstat Unit. Provided by NYPD; see Appendix D.

New York State Criminal Justice Agency.

New York State Department of Correctional Services. Data provided to Hannah Laqueur. Various Years. HUB System Profiles: Profile of Inmate Population Under Custody. Albany, NY.

New York State Division of Criminal Justice Services, Computerized Criminal History System (June 2009; April 2010).

Office of National Drug Control Policy, Executive Office of the President. 1989. *National Drug Control Strategy.* Washington, DC: U.S. Government Printing Office.

Pace, Eric. 1990. "Police Proposal Prompts a Call for More Jails." *New York Times,* September 18.

Paone, D., Heller, D., Olson, C., and Kerker, B. 2010. Illicit Drug Use in New York City. *NYC Vital Signs* 9(1); 1–4. New York: New York City Department of Health and Mental Hygiene.

Papachristos, Andrew, Tracey Meares, and Jeffrey Fagan. 2007. "Attention Felons: Evaluating Project Safe Neighborhoods in Chicago." *Journal of Empirical Legal Studies* 4: 223–272.

Reiss, Albert J. 1971. *The Police and the Public.* New Haven, CT: Yale University Press.

Rosenfeld, Richard, Robert Fornango, and Eric Baumer. 2005. "Did Ceasefire, COMPSTAT and Exile Reduce Homicide?" *Criminology and Public Policy* 4(3): 419–450.

Rosenfeld, Richard, Robert Fornango, and Andres Rengifo. 2007. "The Impact of Order-Maintenance Policing on New York City Homicide and Robbery Rates: 1988–2001." *Criminology* 45: 355–384.

Sampson, Robert J. 2006. "Open Doors Don't Invite Criminals." *New York Times.* Op-ed, March 11, at A15.

Sampson, Robert J., and John H. Laub. 1993. *Crime in the Making: Pathways and Turning Points Through Life.* Cambridge, MA: Harvard University Press.

Sherman, Lawrence W., and Dennis P. Rogan. 1995. "Effects of Gun Seizures on Gun Violence: 'Hot Spots' Patrol in Kansas City." *Justice Quarterly* 12(4): 673.

Sherman, Lawrence W., and Richard A. Berk. 1984. "The Specific Deterrent Effects of Arrest for Domestic Violence." *American Sociological Review* 49: 261–272.

Sherman, Lawrence W., Janell D. Schmidt, Dennis P. Rogan, Patrick R. Gartin, Ellen G. Cohn, Dean J. Collins, and Anthony R. Bacich. 1992. "The Variable Effects of Arrest on Criminal Careers: The Milwaukee Domestic Violence Experiment." *Journal of Criminal Law and Criminology* 83: 137–169.

Silberman, Charles E. 1978. *Criminal Violence, Criminal Justice.* New York: Random House.

Silverman, Eli. 1999. *NYPD Battles Crime-Innovative Strategies in Policing.* Boston: Northeastern University Press.

Skogan, Wesley. 2006. *Police and Community in Chicago: A Tale of Three Cities.* New York: Oxford University Press.

Skogan, Wesley, and Susan Hartnett. 1997. *Community Policing Chicago Style.* New York: Oxford University Press.

Skolnick, Jerome H. 1966. *Justice without Trial: Law Enforcement in a Democratic Society.* New York: John Wiley.

Statistics Canada. Integrated Meta Data Based (IMDC). Ottawa. 2010

Steinberg, Jacques. 1999. "Storm Warning: The Coming Crime Wave is Washed Up." *New York Times,* January 3 ("Week in Review").

Stern, William J. 1999. "The Unexpected Lessons of Times Square's Comeback." *City Journal.* Autumn.

Substance Abuse and Mental Services Administration. 2008. *Results from the 2007 National Survey on Drug Use and Health: National Findings.* Rockville, MD.

The President's Commission on Law Enforcement and Administration of Justice. 1967. *The Challenge of Crime in a Free Society.* Washington, DC: Government Printing Office.

U.S. Commission on Civil Rights. "Stop, Question, and Frisk" in Police Practices and Civil Rights in New York City. (NYPD Documented UF-250 Stops 1990–1997, Footnote 63). Available at: http://www.usccr.gov/pubs/nypolice/ch5.htm#_ftn6.

U.S. Department of Commerce, Bureau of the Census. (Various Years). Annual Survey of Public Employment.

U.S. Department of Commerce, Bureau of the Census. (Various Years), Public Use Micro-Sample.

U.S. Department of Commerce, Bureau of the Census. (Various Years). *American Community Survey Reports.* Washington, DC: U.S. Government Printing Office. Retrieved from http://www.census.gov/acs.

U.S. Department of Commerce, U.S. Census Bureau, Bureau of Justice Statistics. Various Years. *Annual Survey of Jails.* Washington, DC: U.S. Government Printing Office.

U.S. Department of Justice, Federal Bureau of Investigation. Uniform Crime Reports. Washington, DC: Prepared by the National Archive of Criminal Justice Data and Bureau of Justice Statistics. Available at the web site of the Federal Bureau of Investigation: <http://www.fbi.gov/about-us/cjis/ucr/ucr>.

U.S. Department of Justice. Federal Bureau of Investigation. 2007. Criminal Justice Information Services Division, *Supplementary Homicide Report.*

U.S. Department of Justice. National Institute of Justice. 1998. *Arrestee Drug Abuse Monitoring (ADAM) 1997.*

U.S. Department of Labor, Bureau of the Census for the Bureau of Labor Statistics (unemployment data); available at: http://www.bls.gov/cps/lfcharacteristics. htm#unemp.

U.S. National Advisory Commission on Criminal Justice Standards and Goals. 1973. *Criminal Justice System.* Washington, DC: Government Printing Office.

U.S. Riot Commission (Kerner Commission). 1968. *Report of the National Advisory Commission on Civil Disorders.* Washington, DC: Government Printing Office.

Weiss, Alexander, and Sally Freels. 1996. "The Effects of Aggressive Policing: The Dayton Traffic Enforcement Experiment." *American Journal of Police* 15(3): 45–64.

Wilson, James Q. 1975. *Thinking about Crime.* New York: Basic Books, 1975.

Wilson, James Q. 1995. "Crime and Public Policy" (pp. 488–507). In James Q. Wilson and Joan Petersilia, eds., *Crime* Oakland, CA: Institute for Contemporary Studies.

Wilson, James Q. 2002. "Crime and Public Policy." In James Q. Wilson and Joan Petersilia, eds., *Crime: Public Policies for Crime Control.* San Francisco, CA: Institute for Contemporary Studies.

Wilson, James Q., and Barbara Boland. 1978. "The Effect of the Police on Crime." *Law and Society Review* 12: 367.

Wilson, James Q. and George Kelling. 1982. "Broken Windows, the Police and Neighborhood Safety," *Atlantic Monthly.* March.

Wilson, William Julius. 1987. *The Truly Disadvantaged: The Inner City, The Underclass and Public Policy.* Chicago: The University of Chicago Press.

Windlesham, Lord David. 1998. *Politics, Punishment, and Populism.* New York: Oxford University Press.

Wolfgang, Marvin E., Robert M. Figlio, and Johan Thorsten Sellin. 1972. *Delinquency in a Birth Cohort.* Chicago: University of Chicago Press.

Zedlewski, Edwin W. 1987. *Making Confinement Decisions.* Washington DC: National Institute of Justice.

Zimring, Franklin E. 1978. *Confronting Youth Crime: Report of the Twentieth Century Fund Task Force on Sentencing Policy toward Young Offenders,* New York: Holmes and Meier.

Zimring, Franklin E. 1981. "Kids, Groups, and Crime: Some Implications of a Well-Known Secret." *Journal of Criminal Law and Criminology* 72: 867.

Zimring, Franklin E. 1982. *The Changing Legal World of Adolescence*. New York: The Free Press.

Zimring, Franklin E. 1988. "Drug Death Penalty: A Federal Tantrum." *New York Times*, September 16, p. 19.

Zimring, Franklin E. 1998. *American Youth Violence*. New York: Oxford University Press. Chap. 3.

Zimring, Franklin E. 2003. *The Contradictions of American Capital Punishment*. New York: Oxford University Press.

Zimring, Franklin E. 2004. *An American Travesty: Legal Responses to Adolescent Sexual Offending*. Chicago: University of Chicago Press.

Zimring, Franklin E. 2005. *American Juvenile Justice*. New York: Oxford University Press.

Zimring, Franklin E. 2006. *The Great American Crime Decline*. New York: Oxford University Press.

Zimring, Franklin E. 2010. "The Scale of Imprisonment in the United States: Twentieth Century Patterns and Twenty-First Century Prospects." *The Journal of Criminal Law and Criminology*. 3: 1225-1245.

Zimring, Franklin E., and Bernard Harcourt. 2007. *Criminal Law and the Regulation of Vice*, American Casebook Series. St. Paul: Thompson/West Publishers.

Zimring, Franklin E., and Gordon Hawkins. 1973. *Deterrence: The Legal Threat in Crime Control*. Chicago: University of Chicago Press.

Zimring, Franklin E., and Gordon Hawkins. 1987. *Capital Punishment and the American Agenda*. New York: Cambridge University Press.

Zimring, Franklin E., and Gordon Hawkins. 1991. *The Scale of Imprisonment*. Chicago: University Of Chicago Press, Chap. 3.

Zimring, Franklin E., and Gordon Hawkins. 1992. *Prison Population and Criminal Justice Policy in California*. Berkeley, CA: Institute for Governmental Studies.

Zimring, Franklin E., and Gordon Hawkins. 1995. *Incapacitation: Penal Confinement and the Restraint of Crime*. New York: Oxford University Press.

Zimring, Franklin E., and Gordon Hawkins. 1997. *Crime Is Not the Problem: Lethal Violence in America*. New York: Oxford University Press.

Zimring, Franklin E., Gordon Hawkins, and Sam Kamin. 2001. *Punishment and Democracy: Three Strikes and You're Out in California*. New York: Oxford University Press.

Zimring, Franklin, Jeffrey Fagan, and David Johnson. 2010. "Executions, Deterrence, and Homicide: A Tale of Two Cities." *Journal of Empirical Legal Studies* 7: 1–29.

Index